# Reading Strategies of First- and Second-Language Learners: See How They Read

# Reading Strategies of First- and Second-Language Learners: See How They Read

**Edited by**

**Kouider Mokhtari**
*Miami University, Ohio*

**Ravi Sheorey**
*Oklahoma State University*

*Christopher-Gordon Publishers, Inc.*
*Norwood, Massachusetts*

*In loving memory of Kouider's father, Boulenouar Mokhtari, and for Ravi's sisters, Usha and Sudha, for their unflinching love and support*

# Credits

Every effort has been made to contact copyright holders for permission to reproduce borrowed material where necessary. We apologize for any oversights and would be happy to rectify them in future printings.

Material p. 59-60, "Appendix A: Metacognitive Awareness of Reading Strategies Inventory (MARSI)," from the Journal of Educational Psychology, 94(2), 249-259, © 2002, reprinted with permission from the American Psychological Association.

Material p. 63-64, "Appendix B: Survey of Reading Strategies (SORS)," from the Journal of Developmental Education, 25(3), 2-10, © 2002, reprinted with permission from the National Center for Developmental Education, Appalachian State University, Boone, NC.

Material included in chapter 9 from System: Journal of Applied Linguistics and Educational Technology, Vol. 29, R. Sheorey and K. Mokhtari, "Differences in the Metacognitive Awareness of Reading Strategies Between Native and Non-Native Readers," 431-449, © 2001, reprinted with permission from Elsevier.

**Christopher~Gordon Publishers, Inc.**
*Bridging Theory and Practice*

Copyright © 2008 Christopher-Gordon Publishers, Inc.

Christopher-Gordon Publishers, Inc.
1420 Providence Highway, Suite #120
Norwood, MA 02062
800-934-8322 (United States)
781-762-5577 (International)

Printed in the United States of America

10 9 8 7 6 5 4 3 2 1                    11 10 09 08

Library of Congress Catalog Card Number: 2007932749
ISBN–13:978-1-933760-18-6

# Table of Contents

# Contributors

**Peter Afflerbach,** *University of Maryland*

**Linda Baker,** *University of Maryland, Baltimore County*

**Helen Fisher,** *Illinois State University*

**Mark R. Freiermuth,** *Gunma Prefectural Women's University, Japan*

**Lara J. Handsfield,** *Illinois State University*

**Robert T. Jiménez,** *Vanderbilt University*

**Yumi Kamimura,** *Ibaraki Christian University, Japan*

**Angel Kymes,** *Oklahoma State University*

**Kouider Mokhtari,** *Miami University, Ohio*

**Scott Paris,** *University of Michigan*

**P. David Pearson,** *University of California at Berkeley*

**Bruce Perry,** *Miami University, Ohio*

**Alex Poole,** *Western Kentucky University*

**Carla Reichard,** *Miami University, Ohio*

**Ravi Sheorey,** *Oklahoma State University*

**Edit Szoke Baboczky,** *Pecs University, Hungary*

# Abbreviations/Acronyms Used

ANOVA    (analysis of variance)

C-EM      (compensatory-encoding model)

CSI       (cognitive strategy instruction)

EFL       (English as a foreign language)

ELL       (English language learner)

ESL       (English as a second language)

GLOB      (Global [reading strategies])

L1/NL     (first language/native language)

L2/SL     (second language)

MARSI     (Metacognitive Awareness of Reading Strategies Inventory)

NAEP      (National Assessment of Educational Progress)

PROB      (Problem-solving [reading strategies])

SORS      (Survey of Reading Strategies)

SUP       (Support [reading strategies])

TOEFL     (Test of English as a Foreign Language)

# Acknowledgments

Back in the early 1990s when we first met on the campus of Oklahoma State, where Ravi had been teaching for a while in the Department of English and Kouider had just then joined the Department of Curriculum and Instruction, we figured out pretty quickly that we had at least one research interest in common: reading. Pretty soon we came to realize that our interest in reading complemented our respective specialties: Kouider's primary interest was in teaching and researching reading in the first language, while Ravi was more interested in second-language reading, and both of us were interested in reading comprehension strategy research. And so began our adventures in reading research involving first- and second-language readers.

Soon thereafter, as we began to publish papers together, we found out, to our surprise and joy, that we worked very well together, whether it was brainstorming new ideas over Friday afternoon coffees, reading and editing each other's drafts, or producing final versions of papers for publication. In the late 1990s, Kouider got interested in the role of metacognition in reading and, in particular, the crucial importance of metacognitive awareness of reading strategies. Not satisfied with the existing instruments to measure metacognitive awareness of reading strategies, he took upon himself (with the assistance of Carla Reichard) the ambitious task of developing an inventory of his own. It wasn't long before he pulled in Ravi as well in the discussions, as the latter was interested in adapting the instrument to measure the reading strategies of second-language readers. Thus were born the Metacognitive Awareness of Reading Strategies Inventory (MARSI), and its ESL adapted version, the Survey of Reading Strategies (SORS); the former was published by Kouider and Carla, and Kouider and Ravi soon followed it up with the publication of the latter. Since their publication in 2002, the two surveys have been used for research and teaching purposes by a variety of scholars all around the world and have been translated (in original or modified forms) in one-half dozen languages.

This book is the result of our continuing interest in metacognition and reading comprehension strategies research. From the start, we aimed at bringing together a set of papers that together would provide theoretical perspectives on the various aspects of first- and second-language readers' strategies and suggest techniques for improving the reading skills of first- and second-language readers. A majority of the papers included in this book were written specifically for this volume, while the few that were previously published have been updated. Our rationale for examining the reading strategies of both first- and second-language readers is simply that the global spread of English in the current age of the Internet means that not including readers of English as a second language would be tantamount to ignoring a large population of non-native readers.

We would like to thank a number of people without whose support, cooperation, and encouragement we would not have been able to complete this book. First of all, we are extremely grateful to our contributors, who unfailingly met all the deadlines. Our thanks also go to our anonymous reviewers for their feedback and helpful suggestions on earlier drafts of all the chapters. We are deeply indebted, too, to our graduate research assistants and to the many thousands of students and their teachers for permitting us to come into their classrooms to develop and evaluate their ideas about metacognition and reading comprehension strategies that eventually led to this book. Additionally, we are grateful to Mr. P.S. Dhotrekar, formerly of the Centre for Policy Research, India, and Mrs. Leela Dhotrekar, for their meticulous checking of the references in the manuscript, and for helping us make sure that in-text references matched the list of references.

Kouider would like to thank members of his family in Morocco as well as in the United States. He is deeply grateful to his many graduate students, and especially Cory Kapelski, Anne Gardner, and William Rogers, who were extremely helpful in shaping some of the reading strategies research presented in this book. Ravi's thanks go to his many students in graduate seminars who gave valuable feedback on second-language reading and reading strategies. He is also grateful to his former colleagues at Pannon University (formerly Veszprém University), in Veszprém, Hungary, for their help in data collection. He would like to thank, with special affection, his former students, Kelsie Baab and Gabriella Kiss, for their help in data entry, and Jon Smythe, for his invaluable and timely research assistance.

Our respective wives and children (Kouider's wife Carla and sons Adam and Ben; Ravi's wife Surekha, son Neal, and daughter-in-law Deb) gave us their quiet support throughout this project.

Last, but certainly not the least, we thank Sue Canavan at Christopher-Gordon, our publisher, for her interest and support. She always responded to all our inquiries promptly, got the manuscripts reviewed in a timely manner, and made many helpful suggestions during the development of this book. She set reasonable timelines for us and gently encouraged us to meet our deadlines. Publishers of her ilk make the writing of a book a pleasure.

If, in spite of all the assistance and encouragement we got from all these people, there are shortcomings in the book, the culprits are just the two of us.

**Kouider Mokhtari**
*Oxford, Ohio*

**Ravi Sheorey**
*Stillwater, Oklahoma*

# Foreword

It is an honor and a privilege to write the foreword to Reading Strategies of First- and Second-Language Learners: See How They Read. Thank you, Kouider and Ravi, for the invitation. I would like to situate the book within a larger context and show the readers why this volume is an important contribution to research on the reading strategies of first- (L1) and second-language (L2) readers.

The book brings together two often separate bodies of research: reading in English as a second language and "just plain" reading as it is studied by native speakers of English. This latter type of reading is, of course, L1 reading, but it is never called that unless it is contrasted to L2 reading. Chapters in this volume address strategies of reading in one's native language, reading in one's second language, and within-student comparisons of reading in L1 and L2. Researchers of L2 reading are far more likely to be conversant with the L1 literature than are researchers who focus on L1 only to know the L2 literature. This book represents a welcome opportunity for those in the latter category, including myself, to learn more about the L2 research.

The research questions about reading strategies that are addressed in this volume have a long and productive history. The perspective that effective readers must have some awareness and control of the cognitive activities they engage in as they read that framed the nascent research on metacognition in the late 1970s and early 1980s was not new (e.g., Baker & Brown, 1984). Researchers since at least the turn of the 20th century were aware that reading involves the planning, checking, and evaluating activities now regarded as metacognitive strategies (Thorndike, 1917).

The empirical research reported in this volume by the editors and their coauthors focuses on adolescents and young adults. The review chapters contributed by nonaffiliated authors provide a context for understanding the development of reading strategies and metacognition at earlier ages as well. As the chapters make clear, reading strategy use, even of mature readers, is frequently less than optimal, whether in print or (in the new and brave world of) online contexts. The chapters also illustrate that the reading strategies of L1 and L2 readers bear many similarities, suggesting universalities in strategy use, but they also show some distinctive differences, especially when proficiency in L2 is not strong.

In a paper prepared for the 1995 Buros-Nebraska Symposium on Measurement and Testing: Metacognitive Assessment (Baker & Cerro,

2000), my coauthor and I reviewed the literature on the assessment of metacognition in children and adults, with particular attention to the domain of reading. We critically examined instruments and approaches used in research, as well as those that were recommended for teachers, and concluded that few good instruments were available. We called for the development and validation of strong, theoretically based instruments. Several years later, in 2002, the Metacognitive Awareness of Reading Strategies Inventory (MARSI) was introduced by Kouider Mokhtari and Carla Reichard (2002) in the Journal of Educational Psychology. I subsequently described the new instrument as one that promised to be valuable to researchers and educators alike (Baker, 2004).

The MARSI is a 30-item questionnaire for students in Grades 6 and above. Students rate on a 5-point scale how frequently they engage in each of the 30 strategies included in the instrument. They receive a total score and subscores for three different types of strategies: global reading strategies (e.g., "I have a purpose in mind when I read"), problem-solving strategies (e.g., "I try to get back on track when I lose concentration"), and support reading strategies (e.g., "When text becomes difficult, I read aloud to help me understand what I read"). Many of the empirical studies reported in this volume use the MARSI to provide new insights about the reading strategies of adolescents and adults. I was particularly impressed to learn that further validation and refinement of the MARSI is ongoing in order to enhance its usefulness both as a research and diagnostic tool.

Shortly after the MARSI was developed, Kouider teamed up with coeditor Ravi Sheorey to create the Survey of Reading Strategies (SORS; Mokhtari & Sheorey, 2002). This instrument is closely modeled on the MARSI but tailored for use by English as a second language (ESL) adolescents and adults. I had not been familiar with the SORS prior to my involvement with this book project, but I have now learned that the SORS, too, fills a critical niche. Like MARSI, it is a tool that can be used by researchers and teachers alike. Several of the studies reported in this volume use the SORS, including two that were conducted outside of the United States with college students who were studying English or using English for their disciplinary studies.

My first reading of the subtitle of this volume, "See how they read," immediately made me think of the nursery rhyme about three blind mice and its exhortation to "see how they run."

Running, unlike reading, is objective and easily observable; its measurement does not require access to internal processes that are difficult to define operationally. Now, thanks to books like this and the instruments developed by the editors and their colleagues, we are much better able to "see how they read" than we once were. I trust you will find this volume as interesting, informative, and thought provoking as I did.

Linda Baker
*University of Maryland, Baltimore County*

# References

Baker, L. (2004). Reading comprehension and science inquiry: Metacognitive connections. In W. Saul (Ed.), Crossing borders in literacy and science instruction: Perspectives on theory and practice (pp. 239–257). Newark, DE: International Reading Association.

Baker, L., & Brown, A. L. (1984). Metacognitive skills and reading. In P. D. Pearson, M. Kamil, R. Barr, & P. Mosenthal (Eds.), Handbook of research in reading (Vol. 1, pp. 353–395). New York: Longman.

Baker, L., & Cerro, L. (2000). Assessing metacognition in children and adults. In G. Schraw & J. Impara (Eds.), Issues in the measurement of metacognition (pp. 99–145). Lincoln, NE: Buros Institute of Mental Measurements, University of Nebraska.

Mokhtari, K., & Reichard, C. A. (2002). Assessing students' metacognitive awareness of reading strategies. Journal of Educational Psychology, 94, 249–259.

Mokhtari, K., & Sheorey, R. (2002). Measuring ESL students' awareness of reading strategies. Journal of Developmental Education, 25(3), 2–10.

Thorndike, E. (1917). The psychology of thinking in the case of reading. Psychological Review, 24, 220–234.

# 1 | Introduction

**Ravi Sheorey**
*Oklahoma State University*

**Kouider Mokhtari**
*Miami University, Ohio*

The ability to read fluently and efficiently remains the hallmark of a literate person in a world where written language, especially reading an international language such as English, is deeply embedded in today's literate environment. Reading effectively, with appropriate speed and comprehension, is particularly important for students at all levels of education for both native and non-native speakers because so much of the information that students need is in the multiple texts they read. According to Carrell (1998), it is through reading that native speakers of a language acquire not just new information, but also new vocabulary, while Krashen (1993) has suggested that for non-native speakers, reading in the target language "is a powerful means of developing literacy, of developing reading comprehension ability, writing style, vocabulary, grammar, and spelling" (p. 22). Indeed, it is difficult to imagine how, without a solid proficiency in reading, students can accomplish their academic objectives. And, as we begin the new millennium, the English language has clearly become the dominant language of global commerce and communication and of science and technology—to say nothing of English being the primary language of the rapidly spreading Internet commerce and communication. Consequently, for increasing numbers of non-native speakers, the ability to read in English, especially reading informational texts written in English, has become a prerequisite for accessing new information; in other words, we dare say, knowledge of English has become a new standard of what may be termed "international literacy."

Reading researchers have long understood the crucial importance of reading in modern life and have devoted considerable time and effort in conducting extensive research on different aspects of reading in a first (L1) as well as a second language (L2), beginning with the research to understand the complex processes involved in reading comprehension in an effort to find ways to facilitate and enhance reading proficiency (e.g., Goodman, 1967). This research led to models of reading that typically conceptualized reading as an active process of text comprehension made possible by readers' utilizing their background knowledge and using appropriate strategies or techniques (e.g., previewing the text, using contextual clues, or figuring out the meaning of unfamiliar words). More recent models have conceived of reading as a psycholinguistic process, in which readers interact with the text by using their prior knowledge (Carrell, 1985; Carrell & Eisterhold, 1983) and cultural background (Pritchard, 1990; Steffenson & Joag-Dev, 1984). In addition to model making, reading researchers have given considerable attention to understanding what proficient, skilled readers typically do while reading, including identifying the strategies they use and how, and under what conditions, they use those strategies. This line of research has been useful in instructing struggling L1 and L2 readers to increase their awareness and use of reading strategies to improve comprehension (see, e.g., Block, 1992; Devine, 1993; Garner, 1987; Jiménez, Garcia, & Pearson, 1996; Kern, 1989; Kletzien, 1991; Mokhtari & Reichard, 2002; Paris, Lipson, & Wixon, 1983; Pressley, 2002; Pressley & Afflerbach, 1995; Sheorey & Mokhtari, 2001; Song, 1998; Zhicheng, 1992).

In this book, we deal with one aspect of reading that, in our opinion (supported by plenty of research cited throughout this volume), is critical to ensuring high levels of reading comprehension in both the first and second language, namely, the awareness and use of *reading strategies* among student readers in academic contexts. In other words, good readers—that is, those who comprehend well what they read—do not, as Pressley (2002) says, "just dive into the text, proceeding from the beginning to end" (p. 294); rather, they use a variety of reading strategies when they encounter a text. Our focus on this aspect of reading is consistent with what has come to be known in recent years, in both L1 and L2 literacy research and instruction, as a learner-centered approach wherein the primary goal is to empower learners and allow them to take control and responsibility for their own learning. In the chapters that follow, we aim to inform, stimulate, influence, and contribute to the research on one crucial aspect of reading, namely, the development of L1 and L2 readers' metacognitive awareness and use of reading strategies when reading academic materials. The language of reading we focus on here is English, both as a native language and as a second or foreign language.

Our rationale for examining the reading strategies of L1 and L2 readers is both inter- and intranational. Internationally speaking, the learning and teaching of English has now become a global enterprise, with the learning and teaching of reading in English one of the major objectives of English language teaching curricula. As Grabe and Stoller (2002) pointed out: "L2 reading ability, particularly with English as the L2, is already in great demand as English continues to spread, not only as a global language but also as the language of science, technology, and advanced research" (p. 2). Given the rapid spread of English around the world, it would be safe to assume that the English-reading population of non-native speakers of English is comparable, if not larger, than the native-English-reading population. Therefore, neglecting the reading strategies of the L2 reading population would have resulted in our having ignored a large population of readers. In the United States, the English-speaking country where we reside and teach, a high proficiency in the reading comprehension of multiple texts in L1 has always been considered one of the defining characteristics of a literate person. Yet, one of the most significant problems identified by the annual reports issued by the National Assessment of Educational Progress (NAEP) is that when reading grade-appropriate materials, many secondary students in the United States find it difficult to understand the main idea of the text, make simple inferences based on what is read, or evaluate the information presented. Simply stated, they can read, but they cannot always understand what they read. The fact that significant numbers of students across all grade levels are unable to comprehend what they read highlights the pressing need for (i) increasing our understanding of the underlying causes of comprehension difficulties encountered by these students and (ii) developing instructional strategies aimed at improving these students' ability to comprehend the texts they read. Not surprisingly, a number of research studies (cited throughout this volume) have dealt with what successful readers do when they engage in extracting meaning from a written text. One major characteristic of these readers (whether they read in L1 or L2) is that they are aware of, and use a variety of, strategies to decode the texts they read. Indeed, Pressley and Afflerbach (1995) reported, after examining 38 studies, that proficient readers are *strategic* and *constructively responsive* and take *conscious steps* to comprehend what they are reading.

We should mention one more reason for our focus on the reading strategies of both L1 and L2 readers. The growth of a large number of immigrant students (typically referred to as English language learners [ELLs]) in the ethnically diverse American schools and the non-native, overseas students in American colleges has resulted in considerable interest and research in L2 reading. For these groups of students, the ability to read and comprehend multiple texts in English is a key to academic success. In our opinion, for both native and non-native-English-speaking students, one of the means of successfully comprehending reading materials is for them to be aware of, and use, appropriate reading strategies. We do not suggest, of course, that the processes involved in reading in L1 and L2 are similar nor that L1 and L2 readers are likely to use the same reading strategies; rather, our purpose here is to present research studies that deal with the reading strategies of both native and non-native students when they read academic texts, and to suggest implications for reading instruction in a first and second language.

## Theoretical Background

As we have suggested previously (Sheorey & Mokhtari, 2001), we consider the activity or process of reading, following Flavell (1979), whether in L1 or L2, as a "cognitive enterprise" in which there is an interaction among three related elements, namely, the reader, the text, and the context in which reading occurs. In order for a reader to accomplish the task of comprehending the text successfully, the reader must be aware of, and use, conscious and deliberate strategies. Indeed, the consensus view is that strategic awareness *and* monitoring of the comprehension

process are critically important aspects of skilled reading. Such awareness and monitoring is often referred to in the literature as "metacognition," which can be thought of as readers' knowledge about themselves
as readers, their knowledge about the reading process, their understanding of a given reading task, and the strategies they use to monitor and enhance comprehension. It is, according to Grabe and Stoller (2002), "Our
knowledge of what we know. ... [which] permits us to reflect on our planning, goal setting, processing of tasks, monitoring of progress, and repair
of problems. Metacognitive knowledge represents a basic way to understand...our explicit and conscious use of reading strategies" (p. 46). Such
metacognition, according to Auerbach and Paxton (1997), "entails knowledge of strategies for processing texts, the ability to monitor comprehension, and the ability to adjust strategies as needed" (pp. 240–241). In fact,
the degree of metacognitive knowledge and the frequency, type, and use
of reading strategies are important clues to the reading abilities of novice
and expert readers. According to Paris and Jacobs (1984), "Skilled readers
often engage in deliberate activities that require planful thinking, flexible
strategies, and periodic self-monitoring...[while] novice readers often
seem oblivious to these strategies and the need to use them" (p. 2083). A
similar view is expressed by Pressley and Afflerbach (1995), who, after
examining 38 research studies on native-English-speakers' reading, theorized that proficient readers are strategic and "constructively responsive"
and take conscious steps to comprehend what they are reading. "There
is ample evidence," said Devine (1993), "that the ability to monitor cognitive activities clearly differentiates good learners from poor learners"
and that, similarly, poorer readers typically lack "metacognitive experiences—those flashes of awareness" (pp. 108–109) that render them unable to detect comprehension breakdowns during reading and, therefore,
they are unlikely to use appropriate strategies to repair the problem and
regain control of the reading act. In our view, the reader's metacognitive
knowledge about reading includes an awareness of a variety of reading
strategies and that the transactional enterprise of reading is influenced
by this metacognitive awareness of reading strategies.

The importance of metacognitive awareness in strategic behavior and
reading comprehension in both L1 and L2 reading is amply demonstrated
by a considerable body of research in reading strategies (e.g., Baker &
Brown, 1984; Block, 1992; Carrell, 1998; Garner, 1987; Paris & Jacobs, 1984;
Sheorey, 2006; Sheorey & Mokhtari, 2001). As Carrell, Pharis, and Liberto (1989) pointed out: "Metacognitive control, in which the reader consciously directs the reasoning process, is a particularly important aspect of
strategic reading. When readers are conscious of the reasoning involved,
they can access and apply that reasoning to similar reading in future situations" (p. 650). The research literature on metacognitive awareness of
reading strategies indicates the need to increase our understanding of
readers' metacognitive knowledge about reading and reading strategies
in order to develop them into active, constructively responsive readers.
This work has been very important in prompting reading researchers to

examine readers' awareness of the reading process, monitor reading comprehension, and examine how readers use strategies before, during, and after reading. In addition, such research has provided teacher educators and practicing teachers with practical suggestions for helping readers increase their awareness and use of reading strategies.

## Definition

The terms *skills* and *strategies* appear frequently in the literature on reading, but the two terms are not, and cannot be, used interchangeably (see Afflerbach, Pearson, & Paris, this volume, chapter 2, for a detailed discussion of the differences and relationship between skills and strategies). Our concern here is with strategies, and we concur with Paris, Wasik, and Turner (1991) that:

> Skills refer to information-processing techniques that are automatic…
> [and] are applied to a text unconsciously.…In contrast, strategies are actions selected deliberately to achieve particular goals. An emerging skill can become a strategy when it is used *intentionally*. Likewise, a strategy can "go underground"…and become a skill. (italics added; p. 611)

Indeed, an essential element of strategic behavior, whether it is reading a book or navigating a car in heavy traffic, is *intentionality* or, in the case of reading, deliberate or conscious procedures used by readers to enhance text comprehension. Pritchard (1990) defined a reading strategy as "a deliberate action that readers take voluntarily to develop an understanding of what they read" (p. 275). Seen in this light, the strategies that the reader uses to develop textual comprehension are not merely a by-product of the reader's interaction with the text; rather, they are crucial to that interaction because of those steps or mental activities that readers *deliberately* undertake to comprehend written texts.

To illustrate what they are, Grabe (1991) identified some of the reading strategies as follows: "adjusting the reading speed, skimming ahead, considering titles, headings, pictures and text information, anticipating information to come, and so on" (p. 379). Carrell et al. (1989) also provide a specific, contextualized explanation of reading strategies:

> Imagine that you have been assigned to read [a] passage about nutrients in food. What would you do to ensure that you understood the material? How would you choose to process the information?…What happens when you ask a reader to skim or scan, to take notes on, underline or reread the passage, to guess unknown words from context, or skip them and tolerate the vagueness and ambiguity? These are all questions about *reading strategies*. (italics added; pp. 648–649)

The preceding discussion would indicate that reading strategies are basically comprehension strategies, and they reveal, as Block (1986) pointed out, "how readers conceive a task, what contextual cues they attend to, how they make sense of what they read, and what they do when they do not understand" (p. 465). Thus, readers use strategies in order to facilitate their comprehension of the text; or, to put it differently, strategies give students a plan of attack as they attempt to comprehend the text in front of them, and using these strategies gives them a sense of control over the reading process. To sum up, because this book deals with reading in the educational context, we conceive of reading strategies as *intentional* or *deliberate* mental plans, techniques, and actions that readers undertake while reading academic or school-related materials. Seen in this light, reading strategies are not merely a by-product of the reader's interaction with the text; they are crucial to that interaction and the reader makes a *conscious* choice in implementing them.

## Scope and Plan of this Book

As we have mentioned above, this book contains a set of papers that deal with one major aspect of reading in English as a first and as a second language, namely, reading strategies, including the theoretical, empirical, and pedagogical issues associated with this aspect of reading. Within the pages of this book, readers will find reading strategy studies dealing with not only native speakers of English, but also those dealing with the students who use English [as a second language] to study at American university campuses (who typically speak a multitude of languages and hail from all over the world) as well as studies on the reading strategies of specific non-native student groups (i.e., Arabic, French, Hungarian, and Japanese) who study English in environments where English is used as a *foreign* language. A majority of the papers deal primarily with reading strategy usage when reading traditional printed or paper-based textual materials. However, given the explosive spread of the Internet since the latter part of the 20th century and the consequent increase in online reading of school-related materials, we also include two papers that examine reading strategies in the online format as well. The discussion of reading strategies when reading in L1 and L2 and of reading off- and online under one roof, so to speak, is not intended to suggest or imply that reading in L1 and L2 or on- and offline are the same; nor do we suggest that strategy usage is similar in L1 and L2 or when reading online and printed texts. As Bernhardt (2003) convincingly (at least to both of us multilinguals) pointed out: "The mere existence of a *first*-language...renders the *second*-language reading process considerably different from the first-language reading process" (p. 112); similarly, Kymes (chapter 13, this volume), after reviewing recent literature on the topic, argued for the reconceptualizing of strategy usage in online environments. Our primary motivation for including papers on these related subjects was intended to explore and stimulate a discussion of reading strategies in various contexts of L1 and L2 learners. While theorizing, reporting of individual studies, or scholarly discussions are important in themselves, equally important are the pedagogical or practical applications of theoretical issues and empirical studies. To that end, we provide specific instruments to identify and categorize the metacognitive awareness of reading strategies among L1 and L2 readers, explain how to use these instruments, report on the studies conducted with these instruments, discuss the various implications and applications of our findings, and suggest future directions for further research.

After the foreword by Linda Baker and this introductory chapter, the second and third chapters in this collection deal with some of the theoretical issues associated with reading strategies. Peter Afflerbach, P. David Pearson, and Scott Paris clarify the distinction between skills and strategies and the relationship between the two concepts, a distinction that matters because both skills and strategies play an important role in reading instruction and because, the authors argue, reading instruction would suffer if the two constructs are not clear in the minds of researchers and practitioners. According to the authors, skills are automatic actions, while strategies are intentional efforts on the part of readers to make sense of the text. Linda Baker reviews the literature and discusses the role of metacognitive skills of reading, lists contributors to, and consequences of, metacognitive development, and examines experimental studies that evaluate the effects of enhancing metacognitive knowledge and strategies on reading comprehension. The paper also addresses how instructional practices are changing to incorporate a stronger metacognitive focus, but the author cautions that the ultimate goal of teaching conscious (i.e., metacognitive) comprehension monitoring is to help students turn it into internalized self-regulation.

The next two chapters in this collection deal, respectively, with measuring L1 and L2 readers' perceived use of reading strategies and a method of analyzing the data on reading strategies. Kouider Mokhtari, Ravi Sheorey, and Carla Reichard provide details about the development and psychometric characteristics of two instruments to identify the metacognitive awareness and reading strategy use of L1 and L2 readers, respectively: the Metacognitive Awareness of Reading Strategies Inventory (MARSI), and its ESL adapted version, the Survey of Reading Strategies (SORS). In addition to providing the complete surveys in the appendices to their paper, the authors also provide information on how to administer and interpret the results of the survey for classroom instructional purposes. A number of studies included in this volume have used one of these instruments for data collection on the metacognitive awareness and use of reading strategies. In the next chapter, Kouider Mokhtari and Bruce Perry explore, in an attempt to reevaluate MARSI, the use of Rasch analysis, which is based on the premise that data are represented on a single unitary construct or latent trait (in this case, awareness of reading strategies) in accordance with a particular theory of reading (e.g., metacognition and reading), which supports that construct. The authors suggest that this reevaluation constitutes an important preliminary step in revising and updating MARSI, if available data so warrant, as a measure of students' metacognitive awareness of reading strategies when applied to academic or school-related readings.

The next few chapters report studies carried out on various populations of native and non-native readers which examine the perceived and/or actual use of reading strategies, along with a chapter (chapter 8) that takes a critical look at cognitive strategy instruction for bilingual and biliterate students. Kouider Mokhtari's and Carla Reichard's study, reported in chapter 6, was designed to find out whether the type and frequency of reading strategies perceived to be used by students are impacted by two different purposes, namely, reading for school and reading for enjoyment. The results of the study revealed that students do, indeed, modify their reading strategy use, depending on whether they were reading texts for academic purposes or for entertainment; that when reading for study purposes, the (eleventh-grade high school) students reported that they were likely to use reading strategies more frequently than when reading for enjoyment. Moreover, neither gender nor reading ability made any significant difference in their findings. In chapter 7, Kouider Mokhtari, Carla Reichard, and Ravi Sheorey describe the results of a study that sought to examine if there were any differences between the strategies readers (51 high school native English speakers) *say* they use versus the ones they *actually* do *use*. The authors found that students did not report actually using as many reading strategies when reading two specific textbook chapters as they professed to use when thinking about reading for academic purposes in general. These findings, according to the authors, were not entirely surprising, as the use of specific strategies is likely to depend on a variety of ancillary factors, such as the circumstances under which the reading task occurs, the type of texts read (e.g., textbook chapter vs. lab report), the reader's reading ability (skilled vs. less skilled), the purpose for reading (studying for a test vs. researching a topic), and the impact of classroom instruction.

In chapter 8, Robert T. Jiménez, Lara J. Handsfield, and Helen Fisher take a critical look at theory, research, and cognitive strategy instruction in an effort to understand the comprehension processes of *bilingual* and *biliterate* readers. The authors critically examine how cognitive strategies have been taught in the classroom with multilingual students, exemplifying their discussion with two strategies geared toward both mono- and multilingual readers, namely, accessing prior knowledge and generating questions. According to the authors, these strategies, although recognized to be effective, are often taught in restrictive ways that, inadvertently, prove to be detrimental to multilingual English language learners. They argue that rather than viewing bilingual and biliterate students through the prism of mainstream monolinguality, reading teachers should try to utilize the potentially different ways of interacting with text when the reader is literate in more than one language.

In the next chapter, Ravi Sheorey and Kouider Mokhtari compare the metacognitive awareness or perceptions of the reading strategies of English as a second language (ESL) college students studying in the United States with those of native-English-speaking American college students; the paper also examines whether there are any differences by gender and self-rated reading ability. The authors report a number interesting findings, namely, that both groups showed a clear preference for problem-solving strategies; that non-native students reported using support mechanisms (e.g., using a dictionary or taking notes) significantly more than native-English-speaking students; that ESL students, whether they self-rated themselves as having high or low reading ability, reported using support strategies significantly more than native readers; and that in the U.S. group, females show greater awareness of reading strategies (i.e., reported a higher frequency of usage). In chapter 10, Kouider Mokhtari presents a case study of the perceived or professed reading strategies of three triliterate readers versus their actual or real-time use to explore the potential impact of multiple literacies in languages (in the present study, Arabic, English, and French) that differ from one another. The three multiliterate readers reported using (or perceived to be using) a wide range of strategies while reading academic materials, leading the author to conclude that strategy transfer can occur even when reading in another language, such as Arabic, which is quite different from English or French in terms of direction, orthography, lexicon, and syntax. On the other hand, there was a discrepancy between reported (or perceived) strategy use and real-time or actual strategy use among all three participants, in that several of the strategies were either not used at all or were used quite infrequently. The results suggest that once readers become aware of a set of strategies and their usefulness in one language, they are likely to use these strategies when comprehending texts in another language.

In the two papers that follow, the authors examine the reading strategies of two specific groups of students, studying in an environment where English is a *foreign* language, an environment which is different from other studies in this volume. Ravi Sheorey and Edit Szoke Baboczky explore the awareness and perceived use of reading strategies of Hungarian college-level students majoring in English, while Ravi Sheorey's and his colleagues' study deals with the reading strategies of Japanese computer science students. Although both these groups study English in an English as a foreign language (EFL) environment, they are different in one respect and alike in another: For obvious reasons, Hungarian English majors need to have a much higher level of proficiency in English than Japanese students, for whom the medium of instruction is Japanese, and English is simply a "library language" to enable them to read technical texts in English. Both of these groups of students have one common characteristic, namely, that they can be considered "academically superior" because they are selected for admission to a university and a technical institution, respectively, in a competitive process that rewards high academic accomplishment in admission decisions. Results of the Hungarian study revealed that Hungarian English majors appear to prefer strategies similar to those used by skilled readers, and female participants reported using strategies with significantly higher frequency than male participants; but unlike the results of some other studies, this study did not find a linear relationship between the reported use of reading strategies and English proficiency (perhaps because of a lack of variation in the English proficiency among the students, who were all English majors). However, the results did show a significant linear relationship between the time spent on reading (approximately 8 or more hours per week) and the perceived use of reading strategies. In the case of Japanese computer science students, the authors found that, like the Hungarian students, the Japanese students also displayed a "moderate" frequency of (perceived) strategy use; but unlike the results of the Hungarian study, a significant linear relationship was found between reported reading strategies and (self-rated) English proficiency. In neither group were there any significant differences between (self-rated) high- and low-reading-ability participants. Finally, Hungarians preferred problem-solving and support strategies, while the Japanese students favored problem-solving strategies.

Chapters 13 and 14 touch upon the new and exciting research field of online reading. Angel Kymes argues that there are significant differences between print and electronic or online texts and that, therefore, we need to reconceptualize [print] reading strategies to fit the very different reading experience of online texts. After reviewing literature on online reading and exploring the differences between on- and offline reading, Kymes suggests that practitioners should not lose sight of the fact that the goals of comprehension and understanding apply to both types of reading, and that perhaps some of the print-based strategies may be applicable to online reading as well—at least during the current ever-changing online environment. To that end, Kymes offers specific suggestions to promote and increase students' awareness of reading strategies online. It is important to note that extensive research on online reading has been completed and reported by a handful of research teams in the US with the goal of better understanding reading comprehension processes online, and eventually expanding the theory of new literacies emerging from the Internet and other information communication technologies. For a sampling of such exciting work, visit the web site [www.newliteracies.uconn.edu], which is the home of the New Literacies Research Team, headed by Don Leu [University of Connecticut] and David Reinking [Clemson University]. In chapter 14, which compares the strategy usage of ESL students when reading texts online and in print, Alex Poole and Kouider Mokhtari report that the 7 student participants in their qualitative study relied on a certain set of reading strategies regardless of whether they read the text in an online or print format; at the same time, each participant also had a preferred suite of reading strategies when reading texts in both formats. The students also employed several reading strategies simultaneously when encountering a reading problem while reading texts in a print as well as an online format. One of the strategies used prominently in online reading was that of participants' reliance on an online bilingual dictionary, obviously, say the authors, because of the availability and relative ease of access to such dictionaries in an online environment.

In the final chapter, we summarize the research presented in this volume and dwell on the various applications of research not only in identifying the reading strategies of L1 and L2 readers, but also offer suggestions on how to teach reading strategies that are typically displayed by constructively responsive or expert readers. In addition, we offer a few suggestions for continuing research in the reading strategies of L1 and L2 readers.

# 2 | Skills and Strategies: Their Differences, their Relationships, and Why it Matters

**Peter Afflerbach**
*University of Maryland*

**P. David Pearson**
*University of California at Berkeley*

**Scott Paris**
*University of Michigan*

## Introduction

In the literature on reading, two words, *skill* and *strategy*, are widely used, yet inconsistently defined. This is unfortunate, as skills and strategies are central to all students' reading success. Helping English language learner (ELL) students develop to their potential presents a series of challenges that demand our full effort and attention, and consistent conceptualization of skill and strategy can help us in these efforts. In this chapter, we propose that detailed definitions of these words and agreement in the use of these words are of utmost importance as we conceptualize and describe reading. Just as important is the consistent use of skill and strategy when we develop and use reading curriculum.

## Current Uses of "Skill" and "Strategy" in Professional Discourse

In this section, we describe what we believe to be a state of confusion in the use of the words skill and strategy. The genesis of this chapter was prompted, in part, by the fact that the terms skill and strategy represent practically and theoretically important concepts, but appear to have different meanings for different people. Because skills and strategies are the focus of important reading instruction and because they characterize successful readers, we must strive to use these terms in predictable, regular ways.

Our experience is shaped by the observation of, and participation in, our profession's discourse, and this suggests that it is important to distinguish skill from strategy, while acknowledging their developmental relationships. To set about investigating our hypothesis that skill and strategy are used inconsistently, we sampled from the professional discourse, including our colleagues' ideas, state education department documents, school district documents, commercial instructional materials, and federal government publications. Our first query was to colleagues (i.e., professors, teachers, and graduate as well as undergraduate students), as we asked them to define or characterize skill and strategy. The responses we received varied and included the following:

- Strategies are the hallmark of skillful reading.
- We learn skills and apply strategies.
- Skills make up strategies.
- Strategies lead to skills.
- Skill is the destination, strategy is the journey.
- We learn strategies to do a skill.
- Skills are automatic, strategies are effortful and mediated.
- We use strategies as tools.
- Strategies that work require a skill set.
- We have to pay attention in learning skills, but eventually we use them automatically.
- You don't think about skills, and you do think about strategies.

Our interpretation of this sample suggests that people are ready and willing to define or characterize skills and strategies. We note also that there is considerable variation in how professionals define the two terms, as well as how the two terms are related. Following our questions to colleagues, we turned to the use of skill and strategy in state department of education and school district official documents. Consider how skill and strategy are used by the State of Washington in describing grade-level expectations for reading:

- In the first grade, students apply concepts of print, phonological and phonemic awareness, oral language skills, and phonics. They continue to expand their reading vocabulary and demonstrate comprehension by participating in a variety of responses. Students choose and read a variety of books for pleasure.

- In the second grade, students become fluent as readers and apply comprehension and vocabulary strategies to a wide variety of literary and informational text. They demonstrate comprehension by participating in discussions, writing responses, and using evidence from text to support their thinking. Reading for pleasure continues to be an enjoyable habit.

- In the third grade, students select and combine skills to read fluently with meaning and purpose. They apply comprehension and vocabulary strategies to a wider variety of literary genres and informational text. Students demonstrate comprehension by participating in discussions, writing responses, and using evidence from text to support their thinking. They read for pleasure and choose books based on personal preference, topic, or author (State of Washington, Grade-Level Expectations for Reading. Retrieved from: http://www.k12.wa.us/CurriculumInstruct/default.aspx on November 15, 2006).

In the above example, skills are first mentioned in relation to oral language in kindergarten and then again in the first grade. It is not until the second grade that strategies are expected, in this case as they relate to comprehension and vocabulary. In the third grade, students are described as again using vocabulary and comprehension strategies. Note also that third graders are expected to "combine skills to read fluently with meaning and purpose." Skills are portrayed as important early in the career of developing readers, with skills followed by strategies. There is a clear affiliation of skills with the mechanics of reading, such as phonics. In contrast, strategies appear affiliated with the meaning-making aspects of reading. There is no account of how skills and strategies might be related to one another, mutually exclusive of one another, or developmental in nature.

We next consulted the information on teaching ELL students contained on the Metropolitan Nashville Public Schools Web site. We were interested in the courses that are offered to ELL students in reading and language development. The course ELL III is described as follows:

> A course of study for non-native speakers of English whose proficiency level is below adopted standards as established by oral and written tests. The course provides for a sequential development of English skills in listening, speaking, reading, and writing. Instruction is based on adopted texts and supplementary materials for each skill level.

Students enrolled in the ELL III course in the Metropolitan Nashville Public Schools are expected to perform in Standard Conventions of English/Grammar, demonstrating that they are "...able to use and understand all skills covered in ELL II," as well as:

- parts of speech
- types of sentences
- subject/verb agreement
- types of pronouns and their usage
- adjectives and adverbs: comparative and superlative forms

The above learning goals suggest that skills are related to identifying parts of speech and being efficient in grammar. Students are also expected to be capable of knowing and using "ELL reading strategies...for performing the following tasks":

- interpreting and analyzing outlines, summaries, and discussions
- reading aloud and presenting orally prepared readings
- reading independently student- and teacher-selected reading texts
- making inferences and drawing conclusions
- recognizing propaganda techniques
- identifying various types of points of view
- identifying resource material for application to real-life situations
- identifying literary elements and figurative language

(Retrieved February 2, 2007, from: http://www.mnps.org/Page 10743.aspx)

We note that, in contrast to skills, strategies here appear to be related to more complex mental operations that, more often than not, involve the construction of meaning, or efforts to create such meaning. Thus, a consideration of a state board of education's grade-level expectations for Grades 1–3 and a school district's designated course content for ELL learners suggests that a common conceptualization of reading skills is that they include the (relatively) more simple and mechanistic tasks related to reading. Reading strategies, on the other hand, appear to be most closely associated with more complex mental routines and the construction of meaning.

Up to this point, we could not detect a solid theme for the skill and strategy information that we gathered from various sources. We next consulted an authoritative reading research source, the National Reading Panel Report (2000), and found the following account:

> The rationale for the explicit teaching of comprehension skills is that comprehension can be improved by teaching students to use specific cognitive strategies or to reason strategically when they encounter barriers to understanding what they are reading. (pp. 3–4)

The above account continued our experience of finding skill and strategy featured in consequential discourse of our profession, but here reading skills and reading strategies appear to be used interchangeably.

## The Consequences of Inconsistent Use of "Skill" and "Strategy"

Before going further, we want to pose the following question: Is it really necessary to dwell on how different people use "skill" and "strategy" in different situations? We believe that it is and that the distinction between skills and strategies is extremely important, for both theoretical and practical reasons. The research evidence is clear: Skills and strategies are different (Paris, Lipson, & Wixson, 1983; Pressley & Afflerbach, 1995). Additionally, how teachers think about skill and strategy is of utmost importance because we cannot possibly teach well those things that we don't carefully define and fully understand. Definitions are important because they are the foundation for how we think about the constructs related to reading success. They provide a common language for practitioners and theorists, and they provide the touchstone for discussions of whether ideas, as expressed by an individual or a group, have a connection to the reality that research findings represent. The body of research demonstrates that skill and strategy are different, and this has important implications for our conceptualization of them and for how we might introduce them and help students learn them. Theory-driven instruction and teachers who are reflective practitioners are agents of positive change in schools. Both rely on precise definitions and clarity of conceptualization to realize their promise.

Despite the current inconsistency in the use of reading skill and reading strategy, there is a rich history of research and instruction associated with the two terms. A century of research has contributed to our understanding of the nature of developing and accomplished reading (Davis, 1944; Huey, 1908; Snow, 2002; Thorndike, 1917). Successful readers possess abilities and knowledge that allow them to construct meaning from text. These readers work within the constraints of human memory systems (Atkinson & Shiffrin, 1968), manage their goal-oriented approaches to reading (Brown, 1975; Flavell & Wellman, 1977), identify and remember important information in text, and monitor and evaluate their reading (Pressley & Afflerbach, 1995). They do so in increasingly diverse types of texts, from the printed page to the electronic page (Afflerbach & Cho, in press). Implicated, if not described in considerable detail, reading skill and strategy are requisite components for successful reading.

The findings from a century of reading research sometimes find their way into reading instruction (Pearson & Fielding, 1991; Pressley, 2000; Smith, 1965). This reading instruction is marked by its own set of terms. These terms, including "skill and drill," "whole language," and "balanced approach," also appear to defy consistent definition (Goodman, 1975; Pearson, 2004). Because reading instruction marks a major intersection of theory and practice, clarity in the use of such terms would appear to be of critical importance, as this helps connect what is taught in reading with what is known about reading.

## Definitions and Characterizations of Skill and Strategy: A Modest Proposal

In this section, we consider the commonalities and distinctiveness of "skills" and "strategies." *Reading skills* are *automatic actions* that result in the decoding and comprehending of texts with speed, efficiency, and fluency, usually without the reader's awareness of the components or controls involved. Reading skills operate without the reader's deliberate control or conscious awareness. They are used out of habit, and are practiced and mastered to the point where they function automatically. As such, they usually are deployed much faster than strategies because they do not require the reader's conscious decision making. This has important, positive consequences for each reader, as all reading work is conducted within the boundaries of our limited working memory systems. That is, the more reading work we can do automatically and without the allocation of memory resources, the more of these resources we have to take on complex reading demands and remembering and applying what we learn from reading.

*Reading strategies* are *deliberate, goal-directed attempts to control and modify* the reader's efforts to decode text, understand words, and construct meanings out of text. The reader's deliberate control of work, the goal-directedness of the work, and the reader's awareness of work define a strategy. Control and working toward a goal characterize the strategic reader who selects a specific path to a reading goal (i.e., the means to a desired end). For example, the reader who deliberately pauses after each paragraph to evaluate his/her understanding while reading with the goal of summarizing the text is using strategies. Awareness helps the reader select an intended path, the means to the goal, and the processes used to achieve the goal. The reader can examine the strategy, monitor its effectiveness, and revise the goal or means to the goal (or both), if necessary. If the evaluation of reading at the end of each paragraph signals a lack of understanding, the reader may reread, slow the rate of reading, or consult an authoritative source to determine word meaning. Indeed, the hallmark of strategic readers is the flexibility and adaptability of their actions as they read. Thus, whether a reader's actions are under automatic or deliberate control is a key difference between skill and strategy.

It is important to note that reading strategies, however mindful and effortful, are not always successful. Thus, the determination of a reader as strategic and a definition of reading strategies do not necessarily imply only positive and useful actions. A reader may choose an inappropriate goal, such as reading at a fast pace because a text is deemed familiar, and then fail to comprehend the text in its entirety. Or, a reader may make several predictions about the contents of a text and the author's purpose, without sufficient prior knowledge to justify the predictions. In these cases, strategies are selected and employed, but they are faulty. The actions are strategic, connecting specific means to specific goals, but they are inappropriate and ineffective for reading. It is important that readers have strategic stances toward reading text, but being strategic does not guarantee success. It is the appropriateness of the goal, the means, and the path to connect them that must be negotiated in every situation to be strategic and successful. This is fundamentally different from a skill that is well practiced and executed in the same manner across situations.

Consider a further example that will clarify the distinction between skill and strategy, as well as demonstrate their relationship. Suppose a student determines he or she has only a vague understanding of a paragraph as he or she reaches the end of it. The student wants to do something that will increase his or her comprehension so he or she slows down and asks, "Does that make sense?" regularly as the student reads at the completion of each sentence and paragraph. This is a reading strategy— a deliberate, conscious, metacognitive act. The strategy is prompted by the student's knowing that the act of constructing meaning is not going well, and the strategy is characterized by a slower rate of reading and a deliberate act of self-questioning that serves the goal of monitoring and building better comprehension. If this strategy is successful, the student may continue to use it throughout the school year. With months of practice, the strategy requires less effort and attention, and the student uses it with increasing speed and efficiency. When the strategy becomes effortless and automatic (i.e., the question "Does that make sense?" is asked automatically, almost subconsciously, at the end of reading sentences and paragraphs), the reading strategy has become a reading skill. In this developmental example, skill and strategy differ in their intentionality and their automatic/nonautomatic status. Yet, they are clearly related as practiced and successful strategies evolve into skills.

For all readers, the progression from effortful and deliberate strategies to an automatic use of skills while reading occurs at many levels—decoding, fluency, comprehension, and critical reading. Novice readers need to associate visual patterns of letters with their phonemic pronunciations, and a hoped-for consequence of our instruction is that their decoding progresses from deliberate to fluent actions. Indeed, we expect developing readers to learn, practice, and master such work to the point of automaticity. Students, especially where reading instruction focuses on constructing meaning, learn to find or construct main ideas, skim text, and reread first as deliberate actions and, with practice, later accomplish the same actions with less effort and awareness. In this view of learning, deliberate reading strategies can transition into fluent reading skills. We note that reading skills and strategies may serve the same goals and may result in the same behaviors. For example, readers may decode words, read a text fluently, or find a main idea using either skills or strategies (or both). The distinction may not be important to the student or teacher at a single point in time, but across time, the movement from deliberate and effortful reading to more fluent and automatic reading is a good thing, representing expected student reading development.

Practice alone may not be sufficient for some students to make progress from deliberate, resource-consuming strategy to facile skill use. Instruction about how and why to use strategies can be quite effective; for example, providing students with information about how to summarize and predict text while showing the rationale for using these strategies (National Reading Panel, 2000). As we focus on metacognition in skill use, scaffolded and guided practice that helps developing readers move toward accomplished reading may also be required. Some readers may need to be persuaded that effective reading is one result of strategy use, and teachers may need to provide more explicit motivation to use and practice the strategies. In this view, fluent reading skills are more "advanced" actions than reading strategies because they are faster, more efficient, and require less thinking and social guidance. However, it is important to promote both skilled and strategic reading because students need to know how to read strategically. Paris and his colleagues (Paris, Lipson, & Wixson, 1983; Paris, Wasik, & Turner, 1991) described reading strategies as "skills under consideration" to denote that the same actions could be either a skill or strategy, depending on the readers' awareness, control, intention, and the specific reading situation.

There are two specific situations in which it is useful to be a strategic reader. The first occasion to use appropriate strategies is during initial learning. Effective strategy instruction involves teachers modeling specific strategies. These comprehension strategies include predicting, inferencing, summarizing, deriving vocabulary, determining claims and evidence in argumentative texts, deriving subtexts, and reading critically, and they can be embedded in dialogic reading with teachers. The strategies represent a range of relative difficulty (as always, relative to the situation in which readers use the strategies) and some may seem basic and elementary. Yet these strategies, described, modeled, and supported by teachers and classmates, help students direct their attention, choose actions, and successfully carry them out. It is here that we encounter a seeming paradox: While we hope for increasing automatic skill use for our students, we introduce and teach strategies in a manner that is comprehensive, sometimes slow, and always about the detail of successful strategy use. We hope that these strategies are learned well and that they evolve into skills. A crucial part of reading development is the shifting control for using strategies, first in response to others and later as self-initiated strategies. Fluent reading begins with strategies that integrate intentions, actions, and goals, and fluency increases with repeated practice. From here, developing readers can undertake increasingly complex tasks in relation to the increasingly difficult texts they read.

Careful reading and troubleshooting, prompted by a reader's metacognition, is a second occasion when strategic reading is required. Practice may help readers develop fluent decoding, word recognition, and understanding, but when reading does not go smoothly, however, strategic intervention may be required. For example, if a text includes unfamiliar content, many difficult words and convoluted syntax, or if a reading-related task is too challenging (e.g., summarize and then synthesize these essays on the Civil War into a single coherent review), readers' usual skills may not work, and deriving word meaning and comprehension may suffer. Strategic readers who are metacognitively aware of the specific difficulties can generate alternative actions. For example, as difficulties are encountered, readers may slow their reading rate, reread, focus on words perceived to be important, or ask for help with new words. Strategic readers are problem solvers as they detect problems, determine when their goals are not accomplished, and generate alternative means to reach the goals. Thus, troubleshooting, or cognitive monitoring and repair, are essential aspects of strategic metacognitive routines, including reading. In this sense, strategies can compensate when usual skills fail.

## Implications for Instruction and Assessment

We note that there is a third instructional counterpart to the above situations: being metacognitive with explicit teaching, when teachers can explain, model, and use reading strategies. Teachers need to be able to break down successful reading into different parts so students become aware of the parts, understand how they work together, and practice combining the parts into the skilled performance that is reading. This cognitive disassembly or "defossilizing" a skilled action into smaller teachable, learnable parts (Vygotsky, 1978) is often challenging for teachers. It is not always easy for teachers to identify the components of accomplished reading and determining the possible sources of difficulty that readers may encounter, but it is possible, as demonstrated by reciprocal teaching (Palincsar & Brown, 1984). For example, breaking apart complex cognitive activity requires thorough, precise task analysis. A task analysis helps us focus on what exactly we are asking students to do. When we request students to make predictions about text contents or author motives, we can analyze the task and determine that students must have prior knowledge for the text content and why authors write, respectively, to make such predictions. They must have a strategic means for combining their applicable prior knowledge with information in text to generate an accurate, useful predication. In addition, the reader must have a means of monitoring the accuracy and usefulness of the prediction as reading begins and progresses.

Professional development activities can help teachers learn how to conduct such task analyses by which they will best understand the procedural knowledge underlying a skilled action. By analogy, it is like the perceptive coach who observes and diagnoses subtle components of a complex performance and then offers advice about what the athlete needs to improve, how to do so, and how to coordinate the new actions. This involves demonstrating strategies and accompanying these strategies with detailed explanation of how to implement the strategy, along with a rationale for why one would choose to be so strategic.

Classroom interventions that help students become strategic readers include this metacognitive layer of discussion (e.g., Palincsar & Brown, 1984; Paris, Cross, & Lipson, 1984; Pressley, Almasi, Schuder, Bergman, & Kurita, 1994). It is clear that students who learn about reading strategies can use the knowledge to become fluent and skilled and to monitor and make efficient their own reading. This thoughtful, deliberate use of the strategies may also provide a motivational advantage for students. Reading skills are motivated by goals of fluency, effortlessness, and accuracy; they give rise to the student reader's pride in ability, not effort. In contrast, reading strategies are motivated by control, good decision making, and adaptability; they reinforce a student's belief in self-efficacy based on both ability and effort. Strategic readers feel confident that they can monitor and improve their own reading so they have both knowledge and motivation to succeed. This is especially important when we work with student readers who, by dint of their past school reading experiences, especially need encouragement and the experience of success.

Based on our conceptualization of skill and strategy, we believe that there are several further implications for instruction. Teachers need to provide explicit instruction to develop both skills and strategies. As students are learning these, frequent practice in applying them while reading accessible texts (i.e., texts that are at the student's current level of competency) may be sufficient to help many students practice basic strategies and then shape them into increasingly fluent, and perhaps automatic, skills. However, our challenged readers, including ELL students, may need more than the modeling and explanation that mark successful strategy instruction. These students need to know how and why reading strategies are valuable, two crucial features of learning that may escape students who are asked to practice strategies without the benefit of cognitive explanations. Thus, even "basic" skills can benefit from being taught initially as strategies, but the goal is a fluent, proficient, and increasingly automatic use of skills.

We want students to easily recount, summarize, and critique texts without always having to use slow, deliberate strategies, such as searching back in text and rereading. How can that be accomplished? Teachers need to explain how to think to their students. That is, teachers need to model, describe, explain, and scaffold appropriate reading strategies for students. For example, teachers can search for a main idea in a text and use thinking aloud to demonstrate how they reason about each sentence and idea. They can describe the differences between a topic sentence and a main idea, differences between an explicit and implicit main idea, and differences between a main idea and supporting details in their discussion. The details of our instructional focus and discourse of explanation encourage strategy use. The sooner the strategy is grasped, used, and practiced, the higher the probability of the strategy changing to skill use.

This may pose challenges as we devise our paths to successful teaching. As we teach, we may not understand our students' misconceptions about reading and may assume that an explanation given is an explanation understood. We may be challenged in diagnosing difficulties and "defossilizing" automatic skills. Our thoughtful task analysis and carefully planned explication of how to do things may not always reach our students. We may not be adept at making our thinking public (thinking aloud about strategies as we use the strategies), or our verbalizations may be difficult for ELL students to understand. And with diverse student needs, we may not have the instructional time to add the layer of strategy instruction and metacognitive explanations that some readers need. These barriers notwithstanding, we know it can be done. On a more positive note, we know that teachers who provide their students with strategies for taking responsibility for classroom roles (why we should be good and cooperative classroom citizens) are usually also very good at explaining strategies for constructing meaning and determining vocabulary measures, because they know the value of explicitly teaching different ways to accomplish a goal. Strategic teachers also set a precedent for intentional, self-regulated learning that spills over into reading instruction. Intentional strategies require that students take responsibility for their learning, and they also insure that students attribute success to their efforts and strategies.

We recommend reading instruction that follows a regular cycle of modeling, explaining, and guiding—all features of learning strategies that encourage students and lead them to increasingly independent practice and fluency. If practice does not lead to fluency, then more diagnostic and strategic teaching is warranted. Assessment must help us determine if a strategy has become so practiced that it has "gone underground" in the form of quick skill, or if it is missing. However, once the strategy has been learned and transformed into a fluent skill, teachers should introduce more challenging strategies and texts. This allows our students to successfully apply the mix of skills and strategies with increasingly difficult texts and tasks, reflecting school curriculum that does the same.

It also helps students develop flexibility in their reading, moving from skill to strategy and strategy to skill as the text and reading situation demand. Teachers also should consider reteaching so that important strategies, such as making inferences, finding main ideas, and summarizing, are taught several times each year and, perhaps, across different school years. The scope and complexity of these strategies are enormous, and there is ample variety of text difficulty and genre variety to practice so that the skills become automatic. The general rule is to teach students many strategies, teach them early, reteach them often, and connect assessment with reteaching.

We should point out that the skill or strategy designation applies to a repertoire of actions or processes more than it does to readers. Developing readers certainly become more "skilled" as they learn and practice, just as athletes, artists, and cabinetmakers become more skilled. However, the progression from effortful and deliberate strategy use to fluent skill use is contingent on factors other than a reader's increasing proficiency. There is always a text or a task lurking just beyond the horizon, waiting to humble any reader, even the most talented one. In other words, readers should not be surprised (and should be prepared) when they encounter what we call "Waterloo" texts (after the downfall of Napoleon)—texts that push us to our skillful and strategic limits. These texts force the reader, however experienced, to revert to a highly strategic (i.e., deliberate, intentional, and step-by-step) journey through its pages. Consider the following text, taken from a study that examined think-aloud protocol data of expert readers' strategies (Afflerbach, 1990). As you read, try to keep track of the strategies you use to try to construct meaning:

> It is legitimate to further characterize the broadpoint appearance as a major archeological horizon marker for the eastern seaboard. In the terms of Willey and Phillips, a horizon is "a primarily spatial continuity represented by cultural traits and assemblages whose nature and mode of occurrence permit the assumption of a broad and rapid spread." That a quick expansion of the broadpoint-using peoples took place is indicated by the narrow range of available radiocarbon dates, along with a correspondingly wide area distribution of components. Once established, the broadpoint horizon developed as a "whole cultural pattern or tradition" in its own right by persisting and evolving over an expansive region for 500 to 1000 years. (p. 37)

Most readers find this text challenging, and report that they use an impressive array of strategies to try to begin to construct meaning for the text. If you noted that the text led you to slow your rate of reading, reread portions of the text, focus on particular words (e.g., broadpoint), parse sentences into smaller (hopefully more comprehensible) parts, but that you failed to comprehend the text anyway, then you have had a "Waterloo text experience." This experience can serve many purposes, including a reminder of what an extraordinary task it is to comprehend unfamiliar text, how resourceful we are at choosing and employing strategies when our metacognitive awareness signals to us the need to do so, and how skill and strategy use may be related to the particular characteristics of the reading demand. Thus, readers never outgrow the need to consult their strategy repertoire. Proficient readers monitor their work, deploying the appropriate mix of skill and strategy as guided by the exigencies of the particular reading task.

One key to effective strategy instruction is assessment, so that teachers can introduce strategies that are on the leading edge of each student's reading proficiency. Teachers need to assess processes in both skilled and strategic modes. Measures of fluent reading (such as words correct per minute) and question answering are typically used to assess reading skills, but teachers may be unsure what to do if a student scores poorly when these skills are measured. We find it difficult to make inferences about students' growth and needs from such assessment. In this situation, an appropriate procedure is to assess the strategies. If a student cannot recount the contents of an expository text, the teacher should ask the student to try to identify the topic of the text. If a student cannot retell a narrative text, the student should be asked to identify the order of key events or use a graphic organizer to query if the student understands narrative elements and their relations. If students cannot answer multiple-choice questions quickly, the teacher should ask them to think aloud as they read the stem and response options and ask them to show how they search for confirming or disconfirming evidence in the text. Experienced teachers know how to diagnose disfluency and the lack of proficiency by checking the strategies that students should be using. The main reason for assessing strategies is to find clues about what is being done or is being done incorrectly so that teachers can identify and reteach needed strategies. Strategy assessments are formative; when done well, they provide diagnostic information that helps shape our understanding of students and plan instruction. In contrast, skill assessments are summative. Too often, teachers try to use skill assessments for diagnostic teaching or fail to assess strategy use so students are given repeated cycles of the same instruction and inappropriate, unhelpful assessments. We should not be surprised that students find this frustrating and unhelpful, or that the mismatch of assessment to skill or strategy results in wasted effort. Teachers may not be trained to assess students' reading in a strategic mode, even though this is a critical ability. There are limited commercial resources for assessing strategies. That is why most strategy assessments are informal and embedded in instruction, and why asking students to explain their thinking during or after reading provides such important insights for both teachers and students.

## Conclusions

In this chapter, we argued for the importance of clearly conceptualizing and defining skill and strategy, as well as noting their differences and relationships. We have identified a need to distinguish between reading skills and strategies, provided definitions and examples of the distinctions between reading skill and strategy, and discussed implications for instruction and assessment. We conclude by revisiting our major points and providing additional commentary. In our opinion, it is important that "skill" and "strategy" are used to distinguish automatic processes from deliberately controlled processes, respectively. At the heart of accomplished reading is a balance of both—automatic application and use of reading skills, and intentional, effortful employment of reading strategies—accompanied and coordinated by the ability to shift seamlessly between the two when the situation calls for it. The difficulty of the reading task, influenced by text, task, reader, and contextual variables, will determine this shifting balance. When students possess content-domain knowledge, read accessible texts, and work toward attainable goals, we will observe students applying their usual skills. In contrast, when knowledge for the text content is sketchy, texts are challenging, and reading tasks are complex, the reader's skill and strategy mix will tilt toward the more strategic reading that is required. The distinction between reading skill and strategy is important for understanding how readers continue to learn, how they repair difficulties while reading, and how they read fluently or puzzle and problem solve. While the automatic and fluid application of reading skills is a goal of instruction, we must remember that a particular reading skill is often preceded by a period in which the developing reader must be strategic. Developing readers must learn comprehension and vocabulary strategies before they can be expected to apply them accurately, quickly, and with increasing automaticity. Developing readers must learn to be metacognitive, and it is at the stage of conscious application of strategies that readers come to understand how reading works and how to identify and fix problems. Strategies represent a window on the intricate workings of the reader's mind. Metacognition also works to inform the reader of the optimal mix of skills and strategies, providing regular updates on the suitability and success of ongoing reading work.

Skillful readers are motivated because skill affords high levels of performance with little effort, whereas strategic readers are motivated to demonstrate control over reading processes with both ability and effort. Skill and strategy complement one another, and when they do, they can provide student readers with motivation and self-efficacy from both sources. In other words, students can complete a reading task efficiently and thoroughly, while thinking, appropriately, "I am good at this *and* I can work through the tough spots." Effective use of skills and strategies also encourages students' appreciation of the value of reading. In the final analysis, when we examine the broader goals of reading and examine reading holistically, we want readers to be both skilled and strategic. To characterize students as "skilled" readers is to recognize that they can orchestrate a wide array of processes to make reading "work," optimally or even automatically. To characterize students as "strategic" readers is to recognize that they are flexible and adaptable to particular circumstances—and when the situation calls for it, they can select just the right strategy to overcome any temporary roadblock they might encounter.

When teachers are teaching strategically, they help students to analyze reading tasks, to consider various approaches to performing the tasks, and to choose the most appropriate actions and strategies to reach the goal. Teaching skills involve practice and feedback to improve speed and efficiency (which, taken together, amount to what we call "fluency"). One challenge for teachers of reading is fully investigating the strategy-skill connection and determining how an effortful strategy can become an automatic skill. A related challenge is designing instruction that makes clear the steps of strategies while providing practice so that strategies, when appropriate, may transform themselves into skills.

We are convinced that the current lack of consistency in the use of "skill" and "strategy" reflects an underlying confusion about how the two are conceptualized. Such inconsistency can render our instruction less effective, even confusing, to both our students and us. Consistent conceptualization and use of "skill" and "strategy" will have several benefits. First, a clearer conceptualization provides a common language with which to discuss and reflect on the considerable information that is available from the research, practice, and theory related to skill and strategy. Second, clear conceptualization contributes to instructional clarity, where our teaching materials and procedures are referenced to a consistent set of understandings of reading and reading development. Third, we can achieve a certain curricular economy if we regard skills and strategies as two sides of any given process or task; this perspective of commonality could limit the proliferation of "standards" to teach and measure that often results when we add more independent elements to any curriculum. Fourth, this clarity situates our understanding of skill and strategy in a historical context, one marked by the dynamic of new knowledge generated by research, and one that is subject to ongoing discussion and revision.

# 3 | Metacognitive Development in Reading: Contributors and Consequences

**Linda Baker**
*University of Maryland, Baltimore County*

## Introduction

Recent years have seen a resurgence of scholarly interest in metacognition, with the publication of several edited volumes devoted exclusively to the topic (e.g., Chambers, Izaute, & Marescaux, 2002; Israel, Block, Bauserman, & Kinnucan-Welsch, 2005; Hacker, Dunlosky, & Graesser, 1998; Schraw & Impara, 2000), as well as the launching of a new journal in 2006, *Metacognition and Learning.* Despite the three decades that have passed since the publication of seminal papers on age-related changes in metacognition (e.g., Kreutzer et al., 1975; Markman, 1977; Myers & Paris, 1978), we still lack a significant understanding of factors influencing developmental change (Baker, 2002, 2005; Bauserman, 2005; Pressley & Block, 2002). The purpose of this chapter is to review developmental differences in students' reading-related metacognitive skills, to examine contributors to metacognitive development, and to consider the consequences of metacognitive development on reading development itself. Metacognition, as defined in this chapter, encompasses both knowledge about, as well as the regulation of, cognition. Metacognitive control in reading is often referred to as "comprehension monitoring," which involves deciding whether or not we understand (evaluation) and taking appropriate steps to correct comprehension problems that are detected (regulation).

I begin this chapter with a brief historical review of the early and continuing approaches to the study of metacognitive skills of reading and what we have learned from these approaches. Recent evidence is also presented that shows continuing growth in our knowledge base about developmental and individual differences in metacognition. The chapter then focuses on contributors to metacognitive growth, including the development of fluency in word recognition, increases in working memory capacity, motivation and other self-system factors, and, most fundamentally, changes in brain structure and function. The next portion of the chapter focuses on consequences of metacognitive development—specifically, the role of metacognition in reading comprehension. Correlational studies examine the relative contributions of metacognition and other factors in the prediction of reading comprehension ability, and experimental studies evaluate the effects of enhancing metaocogni-tive knowledge and strategies on reading comprehension. The final sec-tion of the chapter addresses how instructional practices are changing to incorporate a stronger metacognitive focus.

## Developmental Differences in Metacognition

*A Brief Historical Overview*

Baker and Brown (1984) and Garner (1987) synthesized a body of early research that showed that older students had more knowledge and control of their reading processes than younger students. One source of evidence of metacognitive knowledge comes from interview studies of children's conceptions of reading. The consistent pattern is that younger readers have little awareness that they must attempt to make sense of text; they focus on reading as a decoding process, rather than as a mean-ing-getting process. For example, Myers and Paris (1978) asked children in the second and sixth grades a series of questions assessing their knowl-edge of person, task, and strategy variables involved in reading. Older students understood that the purpose of skimming was to pick out the informative words, whereas younger readers said they would skim by reading the easy words. In addition, the older students were more aware of strategies for dealing with words or sentences they did not understand. They were more likely to say they would use a dictionary, ask someone for help, or reread a paragraph to try to figure out the meaning from context. Developmental differences in metacognitive knowledge about reading have been documented in countless studies since then, including those that have also used questionnaires to tap students' knowledge. Stu-dents' metacognitive knowledge remains an active and important area of inquiry (e.g., Annevirta & Vauras, 2001; Mokhtari & Reichard, 2002; Sperling, Howard, Miller, & Murphy, 2002; see also this volume).

A parallel line of inquiry that grew up alongside the developmental work focuses on *individual* differences in metacognition, typically involv-ing comparisons of better and poorer readers. Again, the pattern has been quite consistent, with better readers demonstrating more knowledge and control of reading than poorer readers (Baker & Brown, 1984; Baker, 2005). Recent research has gone beyond demonstrations of a correlation between reading ability and metacognition to examine issues related to the directionality of influence. In subsequent sections of the chapter, I consider these issues.

Research conducted in the 1960s and 1970s revealed the value of studying self-correction during reading as a window into the reading process, which Baker and Brown (1984) interpreted as evidence of com-prehension monitoring. If good readers make an error that does not fit in with the previous context, they stop and correct themselves. If the error is semantically acceptable, however, good readers may not self-correct because their comprehension still seems to be proceeding smoothly. Poor and average readers, on the other hand, are more likely to make oral reading errors (or miscues) that distort the meaning, and they are less likely to self-correct. These differential patterns have been found regardless of whether the readers are first graders or adults.

Rather than using tasks that required waiting for readers to make and correct their own oral reading errors, researchers in the early 1980s adapted the error-detection paradigm, originally used in studies of comprehension monitoring while listening (Markman, 1977). In this paradigm, errors or problems are introduced into texts, and various indices are used to determine whether readers notice the problems and attempt to resolve them (Baker & Anderson, 1982). Although caution is needed in interpreting the results of these studies, because of students' propensity to believe texts are true and well-structured (Baker & Cerro, 2000), the conclusion that remains valid today is that older, more skilled readers demonstrate better comprehension monitoring on these tasks.

Another approach used in early research and continuing through the present is to ask readers to reflect on their reading processes, either immediately after reading or during the process itself. For example, self-reports collected by Smith (1967) revealed that good readers adjusted their reading behaviors depending on whether they were reading for details or general impressions; in contrast, poor readers did not vary their behaviors and were less able to report the procedures they used. Collins et al. (1980) presented adult readers with short, difficult-to-understand passages and asked them to describe how they had processed the text. The protocol analyses revealed the complex processes involved in attempting to construct an interpretation of a passage, such as evaluating it for plausibility, completeness, and interconnectedness. More recently, Pressley and Afflerbach (1995) used verbal protocol analyses to develop a characterization of the skilled adult reader as one who engages in "constructively responsive reading." This construct was elaborated recently by Pressley and Gaskins (2006) as "metacognitively competent reading":

> Throughout the reading of the text, good readers do much monitoring, are very aware of characteristics of the text (e.g., its difficulty; relevance to their reading goals; when the text is ambiguous; when the author is attempting to bias the reader; and how the ideas in text relate to prior knowledge, for example, recognizing the ideas in the text as familiar to ones encountered before). The readers also monitor when they are having problems reading, for example, losing concentration or failing to understand terms in the text or get the meaning of the text. Such awareness of difficulties (or lack of them) can cause the reader to adjust reading, either speeding up or slowing down, or perhaps even seek other text to provide some background. (p. 101)

## Early Evidence of Metacognitive Skills: Implications for Early Instruction

Controversy exists as to how early-age children would benefit from receiving instruction designed to foster metacognition (Baker, 2002). Efforts to teach metacognitively oriented comprehension strategies to prereaders are rare, but there is evidence that such instruction can be successful as early as kindergarten (Glaubman, Glaubman, & Ofir, 1997). Several studies suggest that children would be receptive to such instruction long before they become fluent decoders.

One line of evidence comes from research showing successful comprehension monitoring during listening. Much of this research has involved preschool and kindergarten children (see Baker & Brown, 1984, for a review of early seminal studies). A recent study by Skarakis-Doyle (2002) provided a compelling demonstration of comprehension-monitoring abilities in children as young as 2½ years old. Children ranging in age from 2½ to 4 listened to highly scripted stories that they had previously been exposed to by their parents several times. The stories read to them by the researcher were modified to include different types of errors, as when an action was changed from singing to swimming in a context where swimming did not make sense. Children were videotaped as they listened, and tapes were coded for nonverbal as well as verbal evidence of problem detection. Nonverbal evidence appeared earlier in development than verbal, and older children were faster to show evidence of problem detection than younger children.

The Skarakis-Doyle (2002) study also provided further evidence that there may be an appropriate developmental sequence for teaching children to use different criteria or standards for evaluating their comprehension (Baker, 1985, 2005; Bauserman, 2005). Violations with respect to what the children knew were detected earlier and more easily than violations in story sequence.

Similarly, Baker & Brown (1984) found that kindergarten children were fairly successful in identifying information in simple stories that conflicted with what they already knew (e.g., that ice cream does not grow in gardens) but much less successful comparing ideas expressed within the text for consistency (e.g., a rabbit's fur is described as "snow white" in one part of the story and brown in another). In addition, the kindergarten children were more successful in detecting problems when they were given brief instruction as to the kinds of problems that might be present.

Such studies suggest that informal instruction in comprehension monitoring can begin using story read alouds in preschool and kindergarten classrooms (Smolkin & Donavan, 2002). The processes of monitoring for comprehension are similar in listening and reading, and children could be sensitized early on to the need to check their understanding. Parents, too, can play an important role. Borkowski et al. (2000) discussed the likely importance of metacognitively based instruction in the home, as did Baker (1994). That parents can foster young children's metacognitive knowledge and control of reading through shared book reading comes from a study by Brenna (1995), who examined the metacognitive reading strategies of 5 children, aged 4–6 years, who were reading fluently prior to formal instruction. She used semistructured interviews, role-playing (e.g., read a story to a puppet who was unable to read for itself), observations, and informal miscue analyses of oral reading, as well as interviews with the parents during several home visits. Results revealed connections between parent–child interactions and the development of particular metacognitive reading strategies. Parents stressed reading as problem solving, and they encouraged children to use different strategies to solve problems. Children were encouraged to correct the mistakes of others. In fact, one mother intentionally misread text to give her daughter a chance to detect and correct errors. "Such opportunities for error detection may have created a positive emotional climate for mistakes as well as helped children to be more able to detect their own reading errors" (Brenna, 1995, p. 59). The children used strategies characteristic of readers who are much older when they read aloud, including a variety of strategies for dealing with word identification problems. Of course, not all families engage routinely in shared book reading, and different families put more emphasis on talking about thinking and being reflective than others (Paris, 2002), so opportunities in the home are not universally available.

Research has also shown that children are capable of monitoring their comprehension while reading when they are beginning to learn how to read. For example, Juliebo, Malicky, and Norman (1998) studied a small sample of first graders participating in Reading Recovery. Metacognition was assessed by videotaping the intervention sessions and asking children to describe what they were doing through stimulated recall. Children's behaviors during the intervention session reflected self-regulation, and their responses in stimulated recall showed awareness of reading strategies. A similar type of study revealed self-monitoring in first- and second-grade classrooms (Van Leuvan & Wang, 1997). In a study using the error-detection paradigm, Finnish first graders were capable of monitoring their comprehension while reading. However, children who were struggling with decoding were less likely to recognize that there were inconsistencies in the texts they were reading than children who were better decoders (Kinnunen, Vauras, & Niemi, 1998). This may reflect a resource allocation problem that will be considered more fully in a subsequent section of the chapter. If children are struggling with decoding words, they do not have sufficient processing capacity available to focus on the meaning of the text. Alternatively, it may reflect the conception of reading as a decoding process rather than a meaning-getting process that has been documented in other studies of poor readers.

## Recent Longitudinal Evidence of Change in Metacognition

Most of the research on developmental changes in metacognition is cross-sectional, comparing children of different ages at the same point in time. Thus, we can conclude that older children are better at monitoring their understanding than younger children, for example, but we cannot determine what led to these differences. Longitudinal research provides more insight, revealing true growth within individual children, as well as stability in metacognition and its relations with other variables over time. For example, Annevirta and Vauras (2001) conducted a longitudinal investigation of Finnish children's metacognitive knowledge from preschool (equivalent to kindergarten in the United States) through the third grade. A metacognitive interview tapped knowledge about memory, learning, and comprehension. An example of a comprehension item is: How would you read a story to be able to understand it and tell it to the class afterward? For each question, the child had to explain the cognitive activities that he or she would use. Explanations were coded as "developing" and "nondeveloping" with respect to understanding of the cognitive processes. Metacognitive understanding of comprehension appeared to be developing last, with little evidence before the second or third grade. Understanding of memory processes was apparent even at the preschool level. Understanding of learning appeared next. For example, by the first grade, children recognized the active role of the self in learning, as opposed to relying on others. Examples of nondeveloping responses to the comprehension question were: "reading without any mistakes," "reading it slowly aloud," and "telling it quickly." A first-grade response that was coded as developing was: "I would read it many times and try to say it to myself." A second-grade developing response was: "reading a story and imagining it happening to me." It wasn't until the third grade that students described evaluating and monitoring their understanding. When children were younger, they showed the lack of understanding of reading as a meaning-getting process cited previously.

To what extent is there stability in metacognitive knowledge over time, and how consistent are relations between metacognition and reading comprehension over time? In one longitudinal analysis, Roeschl-Heils, Schneider, and van Kraayenoord (2003) followed up children who had participated in an earlier study (van Kraayenoord & Schneider, 1999). Children's metacognitive knowledge was first examined in Grades 3 or 4 in relation to reading motivation and reading comprehension and was reassessed in Grades 7 or 8. Patterns of intercorrelations among measures of the same constructs were stable over this time period. Students who scored higher on assessments of metacognitive knowledge in elementary school continued to do so in middle school. Similarly, relations among reading interest, self-concept, reading ability, and metacognition were statistically significant at both time points. Metacognitive knowledge was a significant predictor of reading comprehension in Grades 3 and 4 as well as in Grades 7 and 8.

A longitudinal study focused on similar questions was conducted by Bouchard (1998), beginning when children were in the fourth grade and following them into Grade 6. She examined interrelations between the self-system (e.g., children's beliefs about themselves as learners), metacognitive knowledge, and reading achievement. The self-system measures and reading measures were correlated at each time point, and they revealed similar patterns of relations over time. This evidence of stability in these two studies highlights the importance of intervention during the primary grades to address metacognitive as well as motivational dimensions of reading.

Longitudinal designs are also valuable for examining temporal relations involving the development of metacognitive knowledge and metacognitive control of reading. Relatively few studies have examined the relation between metacognitive knowledge and control. It is likely, however, that learners need to have a sufficient level of internalized metacognitive knowledge before they can use it effectively to guide their own learning (Brown, 1980). To address this issue, Annevirta and Vaurus (2006) examined the metacognitive skills of a subset of children in their larger longitudinal study described previously (Annevirta & Vaurus, 2001). Although the tasks did not involve reading per se, the issues addressed are sufficiently pertinent to warrant discussion here. Three groups of children, representing a subset of the sample, were selected for intensive study; some of them had initially low levels of metacognitive knowledge, some had intermediate levels, and some had high levels. The children were given developmentally appropriate problem-solving tasks each year, and they were videotaped while they performed the tasks. Videotapes were coded for verbalizations indicating comprehension monitoring, self-regulation, and help seeking (adaptive vs. dependent).

The results were consistent with the hypothesis that metacognitive knowledge was a precursor to control. Children whose metacognitive knowledge was initially low continued to show dependent help seeking each year, demonstrated less ability to guide behavior, and were weaker in directing and controlling their cognitive activities than children with more metacognitive knowledge at the outset. No comprehension monitoring was observed in either the average- or the low-metacognitive-knowledge groups at preschool, first grade, or second grade. A few children with high metacognitive knowledge evidenced comprehension monitoring in preschool and first grade, whereas more did in Grade 2. Children in all three groups engaged in self-regulatory talk, however, which was considerably more frequent than talk revealing comprehension monitoring. Children's metacognitive knowledge developed over the years for all three groups, but those with low metacognitive knowledge showed very little growth in metacognitive control. In contrast, those with high metacognitive knowledge showed considerable growth in metacognitive control. In addition, whereas no children with low metacognitve knowledge showed good metacognitive control, some children with higher levels of knowledge did not demonstrate control. These results suggest that metacognitive knowledge is necessary but not sufficient for metacognitive control.

## Developmental Changes in Adolescence and Adulthood

A substantial body of research has accumulated, showing better metacognitive knowledge and control among older, higher achieving students. However, it has also been shown that there remains considerable room for growth "at the top" (Baker, 1989). Thus, metacognitive growth is gradual throughout childhood, adolescence, and even into adulthood. As Pintrich and Zusho (2002) put it: "The active control of cognition may be a rather late-developing phenomenon, coinciding with a developmental shift in adolescence that enables students to have their own thoughts not just as objects of their thinking, but also to control their own thinking" (p. 261). Moreover, one cannot simply assert that an individual "has" or "does not have" metacognition. Metacognition is not a unitary construct, either across domains or within domains, nor is the deployment of a metacognitive strategy "all or none." There are degrees in the effectiveness with which strategies can be applied. This point was first articulated a long time ago by Brown (1980):

> It is therefore simplistic to speak of a particular age when children achieve certain [metacognitive] skills. Primitive precursors of the ability to plan and check one's activities against commonsense criteria probably emerge prior to the school years…, but when the task is a complex one, inadequate checking and planning may be manifested at a much later age. College students are by no means free of checking failures….
> The interaction of task complexity and age is an important issue that deserves further attention if we are to achieve a descriptive theory of the development of metacognitive skills. (p. 475)

The interconnections among age, reading ability, and type of task are illustrated in a study by Hacker (1997) of adolescents in Grades 7, 9, and 11 who had varied reading ability. Hacker used an error-detection paradigm to study age-related changes in the ability to identify different types of errors, namely, lexical, syntactic, and semantic. Students searched three times through a text. On the first search, monitoring levels were low for all readers, but there were age and ability-related differences in error detection, especially at the semantic level. Poorer readers at all grade levels performed at lower levels than more skilled readers. On the second search, some students were able to benefit from instruction to search for errors, but others were not. The third search showed that although some students had the knowledge necessary to monitor their understanding at the appropriate levels, they nevertheless did not use that knowledge. This latter finding illustrates the importance of examining *will* in addition to *skill*, an issue that will be discussed subsequently.

## Contributors to Metacognitive Development

*Automatic versus Deliberate Processing: A Developmental Challenge*

In a seminal paper on metacognitive development and reading, Brown (1980) distinguished between the automatic and deliberate processing alluded to by Pressley and Gaskins (2006) in the quotation presented earlier. Skilled readers:

> proceed merrily on automatic pilot, until a triggering event alerts them to a comprehension failure. While the process is flowing smoothly, their construction of meaning is very rapid, but when a comprehension failure is detected, they must slow down and allot extra processing capacity to the problem area. They must employ debugging devices and strategies, which take time and effort. (p. 455)

A central question for educators is how to help students make the transition from the slow, effortful processing characteristic of beginning readers *whenever* they read to effortful processing only when necessary. As Paris, Jacobs, and Cross (1987) have said: "The goal of development and education is not to produce people who reflect, orchestrate, plan, revise, and evaluate their every action" (p. 238). Similarly, Clay (1998) asserted: "We need to have children successfully monitoring and controlling their literacy acts, but with minimal conscious attention" (p. 68). Monitoring may take place at two different levels, according to Butterfield, Hacker, and Albertson (1996): "Readers can decide consciously which standards to use when monitoring comprehension, or...they may decide implicitly and automatically" (p. 277). When the decision is made at a conscious level, it competes for valuable working memory resources that are involved in comprehension per se.

That beginning readers experience difficulty due to limited resources was highlighted in a recent updating of the LaBerge and Samuels model of automaticity in reading to include metacognition (Samuels, Willcut, & Palumbo, 2006). Whereas previous conceptualizations focused on the need to develop automaticity of decoding, so that attention could be directed at comprehension, the new model calls for developing automaticity in comprehension monitoring as well. Beginning readers have only enough processing capacity to focus on one component at a time. With repeated experience, readers learn to decode and to monitor their comprehension sufficiently well that they do not have to allocate attention to the processes; it is only when an obstacle is noted that attention is directed to the problem area. Automaticity in metacognition as well as in decoding characterizes the skilled reader, as described earlier by Pressley and Gaskins (2006).

Pintrich and Zusho (2002) identified an interesting paradox with respect to the development of metacognition. To become more knowledgeable or skilled in a domain, children need to become more metacognitive and regulate their own learning. However, because young children do not yet have much knowledge and skill, performance of a task imposes high demands on working memory. Therefore, they have more trouble implementing regulatory strategies, which also require working memory resources. "Given this problem, it is not surprising that novices often have to be 'other regulated' initially through coaching, instructional supports, and teacher scaffolding before they can be self-regulating" (p. 258).

*The Contribution of Basic Cognitive Processes to Metacognition*

Working memory is the cognitive process most often implicated in the development of comprehension monitoring. Other cognitive components include fluency in word recognition and reading comprehension itself. Background knowledge also plays a role. Pintrich and Zusho (2002) argue that older students are better able to think about their own thinking and regulate it because "their cognitive resources are freed up for regulatory tasks in comparison to knowledge search or retrieval processes" (p. 258). Oakhill, Hartt, and Samols (2005) examined the contributions of working memory and reading comprehension to metacognition. Their study replicated previous studies showing differences in monitoring for same-age children (in this case, 9–10-year-olds) who differ in reading ability. In this research, the children were matched for reading vocabulary and word-recognition skills. In one study, the better comprehenders were better at identifying sentence-level anomalies, but not word-level problems. In a second study, they were better at detecting inconsistencies in the text, especially when the inconsistent sentences were more widely spaced and so put a greater burden on working memory. Children were given a numerical working memory test, and the poorer comprehenders performed more poorly on this test. Working memory performance was related to performance on some of the error-detection tasks. However, comprehension ability was also a good, and sometimes better, predictor of comprehension monitoring.

Oakhill et al. (2005) interpreted their data as evidence that better metacognitive control may be a consequence of better reading ability. On this view, comprehension influences metacognition, in contrast to the more commonly articulated view that metacognitive skill influences comprehension. In reality, reciprocal causation is most likely; that is, improvements in metacognition contribute to improvements in comprehension, which, in turn, contribute to further improvements in metacognition. Because the researchers controlled for children's word recognition and vocabulary skills, which are often confounded with comprehension ability, the study allowed for a test of the unique impact of comprehension per se on comprehension monitoring.

## Motivation as a Contributor to Performance on Metacognitive Tasks

A well-established finding in the cognitive development literature is that children initially do not use a strategy spontaneously, then they use the strategy but do not really benefit from it, and finally, after a considerable amount of practice and experience, they show more adaptive and successful strategy use. This phenomenon can be considered a variant of the competence-performance distinction revealed in many aspects of young children's cognitive development. That is, an important difference exists between a student having the competence to use a particular strategy and the student actually using that strategy. Older students become more capable of using strategies, but even if they know how to use them, they still might not do so, as in the Hacker (1997) study. This may reflect their failure to realize that the strategies are beneficial. But it also may reflect a lack of motivation to put forth the effort required for strategy use.

Although research suggests students in middle school are cognitively more prepared to benefit from instruction in metacognitive strategies than younger children, another well-established developmental difference may make these students less responsive. At the same time, students' ability to evaluate their own learning and performance increases, while their intrinsic motivation for learning decreases. Thus, it is important to examine the role of motivation, perceived competence, and attributional beliefs in the deployment of metacognitive strategies (Borkowski, Chan, & Muthukrishna, 2000; Pintrich & Zusho, 2002). For example, De Sousa and Oakhill (1996) demonstrated that interest level is a factor in comprehension monitoring. In a study of 8–9-year-olds, children participated in two tasks where they had to read short passages, some of which contained embedded problems. One task was a more traditional school-like reading task, whereas the other was more game-like and rated as more interesting. In both cases, children were asked to identify the embedded problems. The children were similar in single-word reading and vocabulary skills, but differed in comprehension skill. Poor comprehenders performed significantly better on the high-interest task than on the traditional task, whereas good comprehenders' performance did not differ across tasks. The study provided a clear demonstration that comprehension monitoring involves not only skill, but also will. If children who are poor readers are sufficiently motivated, they can demonstrate higher levels of competence than they otherwise would.

The longitudinal research by Roeschl-Heils et al. (2003) and Bouchard (1998) is also relevant to this issue. The strong, stable correlations among metacognition, motivation, self-concept, and comprehension provided further support for the position that the failure to demonstrate metacognitive control in a given situation does not necessarily mean that students lack metacognitve skill. Monitoring comprehension and deploying reading strategies is effortful, and students do not always believe the effort is warranted. The implications for classroom practice are spelled out in Baker, Dreher, and Guthrie (2000).

## Neurobiological Underpinnings of Metacognitive Development

As previously discussed, adolescence is a period of considerable metacognitive growth. Research in cognitive neuroscience is beginning to shed some light on the biological bases for these changes in adolescence. Adolescence is a period of major development in the prefrontal cortex, the portion of the brain involved in executive function. Executive function includes processes typically regarded as metacognitive in nature, such as planning, monitoring, and error correction and detection. Brain development is manifested in two ways, through changes in the gray matter (neuronal bodies and dendrites) as well as in white matter (myelination of the axons, which leads to faster processing speed). The prefrontal lobes are the last portions of the brain to develop, with maturation not complete until late adolescence or early adulthood (Sowell, Thompson, Holmes, Jernigan, & Toga, 1999). In a research synthesis that could be regarded as groundbreaking, Fernandez-Duque, Baird, and Posner (2000) provided compelling evidence for the biological basis of metacognition. Other researchers endorse the significance of these suggestions: "By relating metacognition to executive control, Fernandez-Duque et al. bring together an extraordinarily rich and useful pool of data not otherwise considered important for the analysis of metacognition" (Shimamura, 2000).

Let us consider one piece of evidence in further detail. Fernandez-Duque et al. (2000) identified the anterior cingulate as the portion of the brain that evaluates conditions in which conflict or errors are likely to occur; this information is relayed to lateral prefrontal areas for conflict resolution:

> This distinction between conflict monitoring and conflict resolution maps nicely on the distinction made in the metacognitive literature between cognitive monitoring and cognitive control. Moreover, the proposed role of the anterior cingulate in evaluating situations in which errors are likely to occur is consistent with neuroimaging data revealing anterior cingulate activation after the detection of an error. (p.293)

Although none of the supporting research involves reading tasks, the error-detection processes may very well be similar. Functional magnetic resonance imaging (fMRI) is now being used to study basic reading processes; a fruitful extension would be the study of comprehension monitoring and the use of other reading strategies.

The prefrontal area is important not only for metacognitive control, but also for metacognitive knowledge. Supporting evidence comes from studies of individuals with damage to this portion of the brain. For example, Hantan, Bartha, and Levin (2000) compared the performance of 9-year-old children with and without traumatic brain injury on a memory-monitoring task. The brain-injured children were less accurate in their predictions of the ease with which an item would be learned and in their predictions of recall of an item after a 2-hour delay, but not in recall performance itself. Adults with frontal lobe dysfunction, such as schizophrenia or Alzheimer's disease, also show difficulty assessing their own cognitive capacities, an important aspect of metacognitive knowledge (Fernandez-Duque et al., 2000).

Because maturation of the prefrontal lobes is not complete until late adolescence or early adulthood, it is easier to understand why lapses in metacognitive control during reading are still apparent in high school and college students (Baker, 1989). One should not conclude, however, that metacognitive abilities will not be present until that time. Indeed, as discussed earlier, there is ample evidence of metacognitive knowledge and control during the preschool years. Early childhood is another important period in the development of inhibitory and executive functions (Fernandez-Duque et al., 2000), with major changes occurring between the ages of 3 and 5. At the same time, there are advances in theory of mind, a form of metacognitive knowledge that involves knowing that people's behavior is guided by their beliefs, desires, and other mental states.

## Consequences of Metacognition

In the early research on ability-related differences in metacognition, students were typically divided into two or more groups based on reading test scores. Statistical comparisons of the groups would be conducted on whatever metacognitive measures were administered. Students in the higher ability groups would demonstrate higher levels of metacognition than those in the lower ability groups. What conclusions can one draw from such data? Is it that differences in metacognition cause differences in reading ability? Is it possible that differences in reading ability cause differences in metacognition? Many researchers selected the former interpretation and recommended that if metacognitive skills could be increased, students would become better readers. But consider that the same design is often used in studies of age-related differences. Two or more groups would be created, this time based on age rather than reading ability. Older students would perform better than younger students. Again, the conclusion one might draw is either that differences in metacognition cause differences in age or that differences in age cause differences in metacognition. In this example, going with the former conclusion is ludicrous. Age is simply a proxy for differences in life experiences, maturation, and education. It should be obvious that in neither design are causal interpretations appropriate.

Researchers today are still concerned with causal questions, but they are framed somewhat differently. Using multiple regression and other more sophisticated data analytic techniques, researchers are examining the extent to which metacognition predicts reading comprehension above and beyond other known predictors, such as word recognition, vocabulary, and working memory. Although these designs are still correlational, they acknowledge that metacognition is just one of many potential contributors to reading comprehension ability. A second approach is to conduct experiments in which students are randomly assigned to groups that do or not receive instruction in metacognition. To the extent that metacognition and reading comprehension increase over baseline in the intervention group more than in the comparison group, one is on firmer ground in concluding that metacognitive growth causes growth in reading comprehension.

## *Metacognition as a Predictor of Reading Comprehension*

Roeschl-Heils et al. (2003) examined interrelations among metacognition, motivation, and comprehension among seventh- and eighth-grade students (originally studied as third and fourth graders by van Kraanyord & Schneider, 1999). Reports of strategy use collected after reading were not associated with comprehension of the passage the students had read. However, students' evaluation of metacognitive strategies related to text recall, and their knowledge of strategies for text processing and recall were associated with reading comprehension. In addition, students' reported interest in reading and their self-concept in reading were associated with metacognitive knowledge and with reading comprehension, illustrating once again the important linkages among self-system variables. Analysis of variance showed that eighth graders had higher levels of metacognitive knowledge than seventh graders, and students who scored higher on the comprehension assessments had better meta-

cognitive knowledge than those who scored lower, replicating the typical finding of developmental and ability differences in metacognition. A
regression analysis showed that metacognitive knowledge accounted for
more than 25% of the variance in reading comprehension, with reading
self-concept accounting for an additional 5%.

Schoonen, Hulstijn, and Bossers (1998) also examined developmental differences among Dutch adolescents in metacognitive knowledge of
reading and in the relation of metacognitive knowledge to reading comprehension. Metacognitive knowledge concerning text characteristics,
reading strategies, and reading goals increased with age across Grades
6, 8, and 10, with the clearest increase for knowledge of text characteristics. Metacognitive knowledge predicted reading comprehension for the
children in Grades 8 and 10, but not in Grade 6. This latter finding is inconsistent with Roeschl-Heils et al. (2003), who found that metacognitive
knowledge predicted reading comprehension in Grades 3 and 4 as well
as in 7 and 8. Reasons for the discrepancy are unclear.

The contribution of comprehension monitoring to comprehension
was examined in conjunction with working memory and inference making by Cain, Oakhill, and Bryant (2004) in a longitudinal study of children
aged 8 through 11. Comprehension monitoring was assessed with error-
detection tasks using age-appropriate materials in which students needed
to find embedded inconsistencies. Working memory and comprehension
monitoring were significant predictors of comprehension. Comprehension monitoring accounted for unique variance once working memory
and other background variables (i.e., word-reading skill and verbal ability) were controlled. Comprehension-monitoring skill was significantly
correlated with most measures at all three time points. The authors suggested that if working memory, comprehension monitoring, and infer-
ence-making skills are inadequate, providing instruction in comprehension monitoring and inference making can help circumvent problems in
reading comprehension that are associated with working memory limitations, which are generally regarded as less amenable to intervention.

This notion of compensation serves as the foundation of a line of research by Walczyk and his colleagues (e.g., Walczyk, Marsiglia, Johns,
& Bryan, 2004). They proposed a model called the compensatory-
encoding model (C-EM), in which readers whose decoding of words or
verbal working memory capacities is inefficient can compensate so that
literal comprehension of text is not disrupted. However, the use of compensations may draw cognitive resources away from higher level reading activities, such as comprehension monitoring. The model was tested
in third graders who were recorded as they read aloud texts contain-
ing embedded anomalies. Literal comprehension was assessed, as were
the efficiency of word decoding, semantic encoding, and verbal working
memory. Consistent with the model, inefficient readers compensated by
pausing, looking back, rereading, and sounding out words more often
than efficient readers, but they had literal comprehension scores as good
as those of efficient readers.

## Evidence from Intervention Studies

Two influential national committees concluded that metacognition is important to reading comprehension and can and should be taught (The National Reading Panel, 2000; Snow, Burns, & Griffin, writing for the National Research Council, 1998). In drawing their conclusions, they drew, in part, on meta-analyses of early intervention research. Haller, Child, and Walberg (1988) conducted a meta-analysis to determine the effects of metacognitive instruction on reading comprehension. The 20 studies included in their analysis yielded a substantial mean effect size of .71. The most effective metacognitive strategies were monitoring for textual consistency and self-questioning. Rosenshine and Meister (1994) argued for the efficacy of reciprocal teaching in particular, which promotes the comprehension-fostering and comprehension-monitoring strategies of predicting, clarifying, summarizing, and questioning. Their analysis of 10 studies revealed a large median effect size of .88 on experimenter-developed comprehension assessments. The National Reading Panel meta-analysis concluded that interventions that included instruction of multiple comprehension strategies, including comprehension monitoring, were most promising.

These research syntheses suggested that metacognitively oriented reading strategies instruction is most effective with older students. Indeed, neurobiological evidence helps explain why significant metacognitive growth occurs during adolescence. Nevertheless, Trabasso and Bouchard (2002) concluded in a synthesis of the research examined by the National Reading Panel (2000) that training in comprehension monitoring can be successful as early as Grade 2. Pearson and Duke (2002) identified several studies showing that effective comprehension strategy instruction can take place in first- and second-grade classrooms, and that this instruction improves students' reading comprehension (e.g., Brown, Pressley, Van Meter, & Schuder, 1996).

Interventions that reduce some of the processing demands of reading are useful for teaching metacognitive strategies to young children and less successful readers whose decoding skills are weak. For example, using tape-assisted reciprocal teaching can be successful, as shown in a study by LeFevre, Moore, and Wilkinson (2003) with 9-year-old students whose decoding skills were weak. Students in the intervention showed an improved use of cognitive and metacognitive strategies, as well as improved comprehension, relative to a comparison group.

## Practical Implications of Studies on Metacognition: Changing Classroom Practices to Include Metacognitively-Oriented Instruction

Into the 1990s, classroom observations, teacher interviews, and analyses of literacy textbooks and curriculum materials revealed scant attention to metacognition (Baker, 1996). The lack of explicit attention to metacognition in the school curriculum has led many researchers to conclude that successful readers spontaneously acquire metacognitive knowledge and control (e.g., Annevirta & Vauras, 2001; Schnoonen, Hulstijn, & Bossers, 1998). But I ask: Why not attempt to facilitate its acquisition? Thanks, in part, to the report of the National Reading Panel (2000) and other educational initiatives on the international scene, renewed attention has been directed toward this topic. Publications on metacognition offer a number of practical strategies for teachers to use to foster metacognition (e.g., Israel et al., 2005), and the oft-lamented lack of explicit instruction in the classroom may be changing. Teachers themselves are implementing metacognitively oriented instruction in their classrooms. Pressley and Gaskins (2006) described the instruction that has been taking place at the Benchmark School, a school for struggling readers, for a number of years:

> Comprehension strategies instruction—and, frankly, all instruction—at the school is embellished with metacognitive information. Students learn where and when to use the strategies they are acquiring, how and when the strategies are helpful, and how learning and using strategies is part of general competence, not just at the school but in the larger world....By the end of a year of instruction, even primary-grades students can be practicing a basic repertoire of comprehension strategies, such as predicting, questioning, constructing representational images, seeking clarification when confused, and summarizing, with clear comprehension benefits for the students. (p. 110)

A comparison of two different approaches to teaching metacognitive skills was implemented by de Jager, Jansen, and Reezigt (2005). Seventh-grade teachers using a curriculum that emphasized metacognition took either a direct instruction or a cognitive apprenticeship approach with their students. Change in student metacognitive knowledge was assessed over the course of instruction and compared to that of students not receiving a metacognitively oriented curriculum. The assessment tapped students' self-reported use of reading strategies and strategies for repairing misunderstanding. It also tapped metacognitive knowledge about effective approaches to reading. Students receiving either type of instruction that had a metacognitve focus gained more in knowledge and skills over the year than students in the comparison group, who showed virtually no growth. Students benefited from the metacognitive instruction regardless of ability level. The lack of spontaneous metacognitive development in the comparison classrooms illustrates the importance of providing an instructional environment where metacognition is emphasized. Moreover, the study reveals that metacognition can be fostered using traditional instructional approaches as well as more student-centered ones.

The increased emphasis on metacognition in classroom literacy instruction is leading to increased teacher interest in evaluating the metacognitive knowledge and skills of their students. In a 1990s review of assessment tools intended for use by teachers, Baker and Cerro (2000) concluded that few good instruments were available for assessing metacognition, especially among younger students, and that teachers needed to interpret the results obtained from these instruments with caution.

However, since that time, questionnaires have been developed that appear very promising for teacher use (Mokhtari & Reichard, 2002). In addition, five chapters in the recent volume by Israel et al. (2005) on metacognition in literacy learning offer excellent practical suggestions for teachers. See, for example, Paris and Flukes' (2005) recommendation to use instruments that have ecological validity, reflecting processing that goes on during authentic reading tasks, rather than relying on assessments of static knowledge. See also Afflerbach and Meuwissen's (2005) recommendation for teaching students to engage in self-assessment of their comprehension. Not only will this help teachers gain greater understanding of their students' metacognitive strengths, but it will also be valuable to the students themselves as they encounter ever-increasing demands for challenging reading in the content areas.

## Conclusion

This chapter had a number of interconnected goals. One of the goals was to provide a brief overview of basic research findings on metacognitive development over the 25-plus-year history of research in this area of reading research. It was striking to me when I reread the early work, including my own, how extensively our current theory and research reflect issues and questions that were of concern at the outset. A second goal of the chapter was to provide a selective review of recent studies pertinent to metacognitive development, with an emphasis on those involving preschool children and adolescents. (The middle childhood period is much more often studied and much more often reviewed.) Two additional goals were highlighted in the subtitle of the chapter: to examine contributors to metacognitive development and consequences of metacognitive development. Much of the research is of a correlational nature and, therefore, remains rather speculative, although a growing number of experimental investigations provide clear evidence that by increasing a student's use of metacognitive strategies, one can increase that student's reading comprehension.

Evidence was presented in one section of the chapter that comprehension skill contributes to metacognition; evidence was presented in a subsequent section that metacognition contributes to comprehension. As with many aspects of psychological development, the pattern is most likely one of reciprocal causation. With the more sophisticated longitudinal modeling techniques now available to researchers, it may not be long before we have such evidence. One contributor to metacognitive development reviewed in this chapter most assuredly is not correlational: Specifically, maturation of the prefrontal cortex is strongly implicated in the development of executive function, which includes metacognitive control. To date, I am unaware of neuroimaging studies specifically focused on comprehension monitoring during reading, but examining patterns of brain activation at different ages would be a fascinating area for future inquiry.

The concluding section of this chapter has focused on how the knowl-

edge acquired through research is being translated into educational practice. Many researchers have called for metacognitive instruction in the
classroom, but researchers are also concerned that metacognition not become an end in itself. When teachers provide instruction in comprehension monitoring, the process must, of course, take place on a conscious
level. But the goal is for this "other regulation" to become internalized
as "self-regulation." Reading proceeds automatically until a problem is
detected; at that point, metacognitive skills are deployed to resolve the
difficulty. We have solid evidence that good readers behave this way,
but we still lack research demonstrating how they come to achieve this
capability.

# 4 | Measuring the Reading Strategies of First- and Second-Language Readers

**Kouider Mokhtari**
*Miami University, Ohio*

**Ravi Sheorey**
*Oklahoma State University*

**Carla Reichard**
*Miami University, Ohio*

## Introduction

As mentioned in the introductory chapter, a number of reading researchers have recognized and documented the important role of metacognitive awareness in reading comprehension, whether one is reading in the native language or a second language (e.g., Devine, 1993; Jiménez, Garcia, & Pearson, 1996; Kern, 1989; Kletzien, 1991; Mokhtari & Reichard, 2002; Paris, Lipson, & Wixon, 1983; Pressley, 2002; Pressley & Afflerbach, 1995; Sheorey & Mokhtari, 2001; Song, 1998; Zhicheng, 1992). Indeed, the consensus view is that strategic awareness *and* monitoring of the comprehension process are critically important aspects of skilled reading. Pressley (2002) described the text comprehension process as one consisting of *before-reading strategies* (e.g., setting a purpose and plan for reading so that it can be recalled later, skimming the text to get an overall view, and activating prior knowledge of the subject); *during-reading strategies* (e.g., reading or rereading selectively to make sure important parts are understood well, skipping parts that are not relevant to the reading goal, taking notes, interpreting and evaluating the information, and guessing the meaning of words); and *after-reading strategies* (e.g., continuing to reflect on the text, summarizing main ideas mentally or on paper, and discussing the text with someone else). In short, according to Pressley (2002), good readers are strategic, independent readers, and they are "extremely active [and aware] as they read, using a variety of comprehension strategies in an articulated fashion as they read challenging text" (p. 291). Such awareness and monitoring is often referred to in the literature as "metacognition" (Flavell, 1979), which can be thought of as the knowledge of the readers' cognition relative to the reading process and the self-control mechanisms they use to monitor and enhance comprehension. In this light, reading can be viewed as a complex interplay of cognition (the ability to comprehend what is read) and metacognition (the awareness of the need to use strategic aids to achieve a reading goal). Auerbach and Paxton (1997) and Carrell, Pharis, and Liberto (1989), for example, considered metacognitive awareness—planning and consciously executing appropriate actions to achieve a particular goal—to be a critical element of proficient, strategic reading. Such metacognition, according to Auerbach and Paxton (1997), "entails knowledge of strategies for processing texts, the ability to monitor comprehension, and the ability to adjust strategies as needed" (pp. 240–241). A similar view is expressed by Pressley and Afflerbach (1995), who, after examining 38 research studies on native English speakers' reading, theorized that proficient readers are strategic and "constructively responsive" and take conscious steps to comprehend what they are reading; such steps involve, according to Pressley and Afflerbach (1995), a careful orchestration of the cognitive resources to ensure maximum comprehension. "The metacognitively sophisticated reader," said Pressley (2002), "knows comprehension strategies, knows how to use them, and does use them" (p. 304).

More specifically, in the context of reading, metacognitive knowledge or metacognitive awareness refers to the knowledge readers have about themselves and about the particular tasks they are engaged in while reading a text. In this sense, reading, whether in the first (L1) or a second (L2) language, would be considered a "cognitive enterprise" which occurs, in part, as a result of the interaction among the reader, the text, and the context in which reading takes place. Furthermore, to successfully accomplish the task of comprehending the text, the reader must utilize metacognitive knowledge—that is, be consciously aware of whether comprehension is occurring or not—and must invoke conscious and deliberate reading strategies. The reader's metacognitive knowledge about reading may be influenced by a number of factors, including previous experiences, beliefs, culture-specific instructional practices, and, in the case of non-native readers, proficiency in L2, and it may be triggered, consciously or unconsciously, when the reader encounters a specific reading task. We suggest that the reader's metacognitive knowledge about reading includes an awareness of a variety of reading strategies and that the cognitive enterprise of reading is influenced by this metacognitive awareness of the reading strategies used. In our view, it is the combination of conscious awareness of the strategic reading processes and the actual utilization of reading strategies that distinguish the skilled from unskilled readers.

Such a view is consistent with current literacy research, which stresses the active, constructive nature of reading, suggests the need for all students (especially struggling ones) to become "constructively responsive" readers (Pressley & Afflerbach, 1995) and "thoughtfully literate" individuals (Allington, 2000) who are "highly engaged, self-determining readers who are the architects of their own learning" (Alvermann & Guthrie, 1993). This type of constructively responsive, thoughtful, and engaged literacy clearly involves much more than simply having good decoding skills, an adequate reading vocabulary, and an ability to recall what the text said. It involves readers who are strategically engaged in reading. According to Alexander and Jetton (2000): "All learning, and certainly learning from text, demands a reader who is *strategically* engaged in the construction of meaning" (p. 295). Pressley and Afflerbach (1995) have noted that skilled readers approach the reading task with some general tendencies. These tendencies are shaped into specific responses, depending on the goals of reading and the nature of the text being read. Although there are potentially hundreds, perhaps thousands, of such responses, researchers generally agree on several important strategies that have been shown to play a critical role in proficient reading comprehension. Some of the most commonly cited strategies include inferencing, identifying important information in text, comprehension monitoring, summarizing, question generating, and evaluating one's understanding. This work has been very important in prompting reading researchers to examine readers' awareness of the reading processes, monitoring of reading comprehension, and the use of strategies before, during, and after reading.[1] In addition, such research has provided teacher educators and practicing teachers with practical suggestions for helping readers increase their awareness and use of reading strategies.

As mentioned above, in our opinion, effective use of reading strategies is closely related to the awareness and control of the cognitive processes involved in reading. Such metacognitive awareness is considered to be an important first step toward achieving the type of constructively responsive and thoughtful reading that is emphasized by current pedagogical models of reading. Studies investigating reading comprehension monitoring among expert and novice readers have long recognized the importance of metacognitive awareness in reading comprehension because it distinguishes between skilled and nonskilled readers. Paris and Jacobs (1984) provided an illustration of the differences between these two types of readers:

> Skilled readers often engage in deliberate activities that require planful thinking, flexible strategies, and periodic self-monitoring. They think about the topic, look forward and backward in the passage, and check their own understanding as they read. Beginning readers or poor readers do not recruit and use these skills. Indeed, novice readers often seem oblivious to these strategies and the need to use them. (p. 2083)

Unskilled readers (typically young developing readers and some inexperienced adolescents and adults) are quite limited in metacognitive knowledge about their reading processes (Kletzien, 1991; Paris & Winograd, 1990). They do relatively little monitoring of their own memory, comprehension, and other cognitive tasks and tend to focus on reading as a decoding process, rather than as a meaning-based process (Baker & Brown, 1984). In addition, they are less likely than skilled readers to detect contradictions or resolve inconsistencies in understanding text (Snow, Burns, & Griffin, 1998). Finally, they seem not to realize that they do not understand (Garner & Reis, 1981) and, consequently, fail to

---

1. See Pressley and Afflerbach (1995) for an excellent review of research studies devoted to these aspects of reading

exercise control of their reading processes (Wagner & Sternberg, 1987), as well as lose interest in reading (Alexander & Jetton, 2000).

The recent emphasis on the need to help students become thoughtful, constructive, and strategic readers has prompted some researchers and practitioners to devise ways of measuring students' metacognitive awareness and use of reading strategies while reading, in part because of the strong interface between one's ability to read strategically and one's ability to excel academically. Because the awareness and use of reading strategies has been shown to be characteristic of superior comprehenders and, therefore, successful learners, it would be helpful for teachers to assess their students' awareness of such strategies. Such information will be helpful to readers in developing an awareness of their own reading strategies; also, it will help teachers to teach to the needs of their students.

In this chapter, we describe two instruments that teachers at the school and college levels can use to evaluate adolescent and adult readers' awareness and use of reading strategies while reading academic or school-related materials: The Metacognitive Awareness of Reading Strategies Inventory (MARSI), and its ESL adapted version the Survey of Reading Strategies (SORS). The former was designed to identify or uncover the reading strategies of native speakers of English, while the latter attempts to do the same for non-native readers of English (commonly referred to as English as a second language [ESL] students). Because a number of studies included in this volume utilize one of these instruments, we devote this chapter to a detailed explanation of how these two self-report instruments were developed and how they can be used to identify the reading strategies that L1 and L2 readers report using when they read academic texts. The instruments are presented as useful assessment and research tools, along with a discussion of their development and suggestions for how teachers can interpret and use the information derived from them.

## Development of MARSI

The MARSI (Mokhtari & Reichard, 2002) is intended to measure students' metacognitive awareness and use of reading strategies while reading academic materials, such as textbooks or other academic publications, not newspapers or general-interest magazines. MARSI builds upon existing instruments of strategy use and awareness (e.g., Jacobs & Paris, 1987; McLain, Gridley, & McIntosh, 1991; Miholic, 1994; Pereira-Laird & Deane, 1997; Schmitt, 1990). It is also grounded in Pressley and Afflerbach's model of "constructively responsive reading" (1995), which is consistent with recognized theories of reading, such as Rosenblatt's (1978) reader response theory, which emphasizes the interaction between readers and texts. It also embraces key principles of the top-down processing model of reading reflected in schema theory (Anderson & Pearson, 1984), bottom-up text-processing strategies emphasized by van Dijk and Kintsch (1983), and comprehension-monitoring processes advocated by many of the researchers cited in this chapter.

MARSI is a 30-item inventory aimed at measuring students' awareness and use of reading strategies while reading academic materials (see Appendix A). The set of strategies are aimed at measuring the comprehension processes and actions that native English-speaking readers invoke when reading academic materials. These strategies were classified (using factor analyses) into three broad categories or subscales as follows: (i) global reading strategies, which can be thought of as generalized, or global, reading strategies aimed at setting the stage for the reading act (e.g., setting purpose for reading, previewing text content, predicting what the text is about, etc.); (ii) problem-solving reading strategies, which are localized, focused, problem-solving, or repair strategies used when problems develop in understanding textual information (e.g., checking one's understanding upon encountering conflicting information, rereading for better understanding, etc.); and (iii) support reading strategies, which provide the support mechanisms or tools aimed at sustaining responsiveness to reading (e.g., use of reference materials, such as dictionaries, and other support systems). These three types of strategies are assumed to interact with, and support, each other in the process of reading comprehension.

## Instrument Development, Reliability, and Validity

The statements used in MARSI were subjected to several cycles of development, field-testing, evaluation, and revision. To construct the final version of the instrument, we followed standard measurement criteria for developing valid, reliable, and sensitive instruments proposed by measurement experts (e.g., Crocker & Algina, 1986; Sax, 1997). First, we reviewed four published reading strategies instruments (Jacobs & Paris, 1987; Miholic, 1994; Pereira & Deane, 1997; Schmitt, 1990) for ideas regarding general format and content. Second, we examined several reading methods textbooks and other literacy resources for ideas that could be used in statements about metacognitive reading strategies (e.g., Alexander & Jetton, 2000; Baker & Brown, 1984; Paris & Winograd, 1990; Garner, 1987; Pressley & Afflerbach, 1995, to name only a few) who have provided much of what is currently known about strategic behaviors exhibited by adolescent and adult readers when they read in their native language. One of major sources consulted was Pressley and Afflerbach's *Verbal Protocols of Reading: The Nature of Constructively Responsive Reading* (1995), which provides a compendium of ideas on reading strategy research and instruction based on an extensive synthesis of some 38 self-report studies of reading. Third, we solicited the assistance of three expert judges (two professional research colleagues and a research assistant) who were knowledgeable and experienced in the area of literacy. The judges reviewed items in each successive drafts of the instrument for appropriateness, redundancy, and clarity. They also helped in refining its readability, format, administration, scoring, and interpretation.

After the semifinal draft of the inventory was completed, it was field-tested with a large sample of students ($N = 825$) in Grades 6–12 in 10 school districts in the midwestern United States. The schools consisted of urban, suburban, and rural schools, including students representing various ethnic minorities. In addition to completing the inventory, students were asked to mark the items that were unclear or confusing to them. They were also asked to provide written feedback, if any, about any aspect of the instrument, including the clarity of instructions, wording of items, time devoted to completing the inventory, response format, and content. The feedback obtained throughout these phases resulted in additional enhancements to the final version of the instrument, which was then administered to a representative sample of nearly 450 students in Grades 6–12. Estimates of reliability as well as evidence of validity were based on the larger sample. Cronbach's alpha, a measure of internal consistency, was calculated for each subscale and for the entire inventory. Coefficients ranged from .89 to .93 and reliability for the total sample was .93, indicating a reasonably reliable measure of metacognitive awareness of reading strategies.

Content validity was determined by having two raters rewrite and revise the statements until they were reasonably clear and unambiguous. Each statement was scrutinized for appropriateness and clarity, and disagreements were discussed until reasonable consensus among the raters was reached. The raters were qualified to judge the appropriateness of the statements used by virtue of being experienced educators and researchers themselves in the area of literacy. Throughout the revision and refinement process, student feedback was also continually sought relative to clarity and ease of understanding the strategy statements. The feedback was used to produce the final draft of the inventory, which is displayed in Appendix A. After MARSI was developed, we felt that it could be easily adapted to serve the needs of teachers of ESL, who are equally interested in identifying the reading strategies of their students and teaching them the ones that would improve their proficiency in reading academic texts.

## Development of SORS

The development of SORS (Mokhtari & Sheorey, 2002) is an attempt to assist ESL teachers in helping their students increase metacognitive awareness and become thoughtful, constructively responsive, and strategic readers while reading academic materials—one of the major reasons for their learning of English. Three compelling reasons motivated the development of the SORS: First, there is strong research support for the positive relationship between students' metacognitive awareness of reading processes and their ability to read and excel academically (e.g., Alderson, 1984; Carrell, 1991; Clarke, 1979; Cziko, 1978). Second, we could not find any published instruments that are specifically designed to assess ESL students' metacognitive awareness and perceived use of reading strategies while reading for academic purposes. Third, we have found that even though there is some agreement among researchers that a number of reading strategies are transferable from one language to another

(Alderson, 1984; Carrell, 1991), the existing instruments do not take into account some of the strategies that are unique to students who are literate in more than one language, such as translating from English into one's native language. Consequently, such instruments may not be appropriate for an ESL population. Finally, given the recent and projected increases in cultural and linguistic diversity in schools, colleges, and university classrooms in the United States (August & Hakuta, 1997), ESL instructors will be in need of adequate tools for identifying the reading strategies of their students and teaching the strategies most frequently used by proficient ESL readers. Instruments such as SORS should fit quite well within a comprehensive reading assessment for ESL learners at all levels, but especially at the secondary school and college levels. Like MARSI, we present SORS as an easily administered and interpreted, yet effective, tool for enabling students to develop an awareness of their reading strategies, for helping teachers assess such awareness, and for assisting their students in becoming constructively responsive readers.

The adaptation of SORS from MARSI was further inspired by our own experiences teaching language and literacy skills to college-level ESL students. Such experiences are highlighted by a series of observations concerning the mental processes some ESL students go through and the actions they take when reading for academic purposes. Auerbach and Paxton (1997) provide the following illustration of such processes:

> I used to believe that I have to know all the words in the English readings in order to understand the readings. Therefore, I read in English with the dictionary beside me all the time. I read English readings only for homework before I came to this reading class. I never read any English readings because I wanted to read them. I read them because they were my homework. I like to read in my first language, but I just could not read in English with the same feeling as I read in Chinese. The belief that I have to know all the words in order to understand the reading made me lose interest—*Li.* (p. 237)

The above statements reveal some of the conscious and unconscious thought processes students like Li go through when reading in a second language. These processes shed light on the struggles as well as the successes of L2 readers and provide essential information not only for understanding how they construct meaning from text, but also how they can become thoughtful, strategic readers. For example, Li appears to make sense of what she reads and what strategies she deploys in order to overcome reading difficulties and to facilitate reading comprehension. Li's statements are consistent with the findings from research studies, which have focused on the reading process and about the ways in which students respond to reading and learning to read in both their first and second language. According to Auerbach and Paxton (1997), there is a direct relationship between ESL students' reading strategies and their conceptions of literacy. Thus, readers such as Li, who are in the beginning stages of developing their reading skills in L2:

> ...feel they have to know all the words in a text in order to understand

it, rely heavily on the dictionary, are unable to transfer productive L1 [native language] strategies or positive feelings about reading, spend long hours laboring over sentence-by-sentence translation, and attribute their difficulties to a lack of English proficiency. (p. 238)

Similar findings have been reported for L1 readers by Garner and Alexander (1989), who found that "younger and poorer readers often rely on a single criterion for textual understanding: Understanding of individual words" (p. 145).

L2 reading research has also shown that reading difficulties are closely associated with L2 readers' level of proficiency in the target language. Alderson (1984), for example, pointed out that "proficiency in a foreign language may be more closely associated with foreign-language reading ability [than reading ability in the native language]" (p. 20). Alderson does not, of course, imply that high proficiency in the second language equals higher level reading skills; rather, as Cziko (1978) suggested, once L2 learners reach higher levels of overall competence in the target language, there is concurrent improvement in their reading ability in that language. In addition, there is evidence that good L2 readers can compensate for a lack of English proficiency by increasing awareness of reading strategies and learning how to use these strategies while reading to enhance comprehension (Carrell, Pharis, & Liberto, 1989).

Since our initial reporting of the adaptation of SORS from MARSI (Mokhtari & Sheorey, 2002), we have tweaked and modified some of the statements in the instrument, changes deemed necessary after having administered the original SORS to large numbers of ESL students in various countries (e.g., India, Japan, and Hungary) and having interviewed several of the subjects after the SORS was administered. The latest version of SOS is presented in Appendix B. Throughout the initial adaptation and subsequent modification of SORS, we made sure that the instrument as a whole is consistent with current research on the reading processes and strategies of L2 learners (such as that of Jiménez, Garcia, & Pearson, 1996). Several of the strategy statements from MARSI were reworded for SORS so that they are easily comprehensible to ESL students. Second, we added a couple of key strategies which are clearly not used by L1 readers, but which are often invoked by L2 learners (e.g., "translating from English into native language") and ones that L2 readers mentioned during interviews (e.g., "looking at the title to get a hint about content"). We also removed two of the items (namely, "summarizing information read" and "discussing what one reads with others") which do not specifically constitute reading strategies as conceived in the current research literature on metacognition and reading comprehension. SORS was pilot-tested on a population of ESL students studying at two universities in the United States ($N = 147$) and found consistent results relative to the instrument's overall reliability (Cronbach's alpha = .89), indicating a reasonable degree of consistency in measuring awareness or perceived use of reading strategies among native and non-native speakers of English. The results of this study were reported in Sheorey, Mahar, and Miller (2001) as well as Sheorey and Mokhtari (2001). Also, the initial version of SORS and its development was reported in Mokhtari and Sheorey (2002).

## Description of the Instrument

The SORS, like MARSI, is intended to measure the type and frequency of reading strategies perceived to be used by adolescent and adult ESL students while reading academic materials in English (such as textbooks, journal articles, class notes, etc.). The SORS consists of 30 items, each of which uses a 5-point Likert scale ranging from 1 ("I never or almost never do this") to 5 ("I always or almost always do this"). Students are asked to read each statement and circle the number that applies to them, indicating the frequency with which they use the reading strategy implied in the statement. Thus, the higher the number, the more frequent the use of the strategy concerned. A short background questionnaire, which can be administered along with the SORS statements, can include items requesting information about age, gender, and self-rated ability in reading English; students can also be asked to self-rate their proficiency in English as well as to report the overall score they might have obtained on a standardized test, such as the Test of English as a Foreign Language (TOEFL). The SORS measures three broad categories of reading strategies, namely, global reading strategies, cognitive strategies, and support strategies. These categories (or subscales) were based on MARSI's factor analyses and theoretical considerations. A brief description of each SORS category and the number of items within each category are given below (the latest version of SORS can be found in Appendix B):

- *Global reading strategies* are those intentional, carefully planned techniques by which learners monitor or manage their reading, such as having a purpose in mind, previewing the text as to its length and organization, or using typographical aids as well as tables and figures (13 items).
- *Problem-solving strategies* are the actions and procedures that readers use while working directly with the text. These are localized, focused techniques used when problems develop in understanding textual information; examples include adjusting one's speed of reading when the material becomes difficult or easy, guessing the meaning of unknown words, and rereading the text to improve comprehension (9 items).
- *Support strategies* are basic support mechanisms intended to aid the reader in comprehending the text, such as using a dictionary, taking notes, underlining, or highlighting textual information (8 items).

## Administration, Scoring, and Interpretation of MARSI and SORS

*Administering*

Both MARSI and SORS can be administered individually as well as to groups of adolescent and adult students. However, while MARSI can be used with grade-level equivalents ranging from fifth grade through college, SORS, if administered in English, is appropriate for high school or college-level ESL students who have high intermediate to advanced levels of proficiency in English; for lower levels of proficiency, it should be translated into the students' native language. We suggest that either instrument be administered after removing strategy category identifications (i.e., global, problem-solving, and support strategies), as it may confuse the students. The total administration time is estimated to be approximately 10–12 minutes, depending on the students' overall language and reading ability and grade level. After explaining the purpose of the inventory, teachers should direct students to read each statement and indicate how often they use the strategy described in that statement, using the 5-point Likert scale provided after each statement. It is important to remind the students that their responses are to refer only to the strategies they use when reading school-related materials, not leisure materials, such as newspapers or magazines. They should also be encouraged to respond honestly to each statement in the inventory and to ask questions about any aspect of the inventory they do not understand. The following outline delineates the steps we have used when administering MARSI and SORS to our students:

1. Distribute copies of the inventory to each student.
2. Ask students to write their names, grade levels, and school in the spaces provided.
3. Read the directions aloud and work through the example provided with the students.
4. Discuss the response options and make sure the students understand the rating scale.
5. Ask if anyone has any questions about any aspect of the inventory.
6. Instruct the students to read each statement carefully and circle the appropriate responses.
7. Encourage students to work at their own pace.

*Scoring*

Scoring either inventory is quite easy and can be done by the students themselves. Students simply transfer the scores obtained for each strategy to the scoring sheet, which accompanies each instrument. After the individual scores are recorded, they should be added up in each column to obtain a total score for the entire instrument as well as for each strategy subscale (i.e., global, problem-solving, and support strategies). These scores can then be interpreted using the interpretation key provided.

*Interpreting Scores*

The interpretation of the information obtained from either instrument is based on benchmarks used in published instruments and studies (e.g., Henk & Melnick, 1995; Oxford, 1990; Oxford & Burry-Stock, 1995). Three levels of reading strategy usage are identified: high (mean = 3.5 or higher), moderate (mean = 2.5–3.4), and low (mean = 2.4 or lower). These usage levels provide a convenient standard that can be used for interpreting the score averages obtained by students. The scores obtained should be interpreted using the high-, moderate-, and low-usage designations shown on the scoring sheet that accompanies each instrument. These levels were also reflected in the scores obtained by students in the "norming groups" used in developing MARSI and SORS.

As a general rule of thumb, the overall score averages indicate how often students report using all the strategies in the inventory when reading academic materials. The averages for each subscale in each inventory show which group of strategies (i.e., global, problem-solving, and support strategies) they report using when reading academic materials. This information will serve as a useful means of raising learner awareness of their reading processes when reading and will enable them to tell if they are very high or very low in any of these strategy groups. A low score on any of the subscales or parts of the inventory indicates that there may be some strategies in these parts that they might want to learn about and consider using when reading. It is important to note, however, that the best possible use of these strategies will ultimately depend, to a great extent, on the students' age, their reading ability, text difficulty, type of material read, and other related factors.

## Using MARSI and SORS for Assessment, Research, and Instruction Purposes[2]

The assessment information derived from MARSI and SORS has important uses for students, teachers, and researchers. First, the information derived from these instruments can be helpful to students in increasing their awareness of reading strategies while reading, improving their understanding of the reading process, and gaining confidence in their own reading ability, and also to amend the conceptions they hold about reading and learning from text. Students who have always held on to the belief that reading requires knowing the pronunciation and the meaning of each and every word (especially non-native readers) would appreciate learning about the various strategies that can be used before reading (e.g., previewing text), during reading (e.g., using context clues), and after reading (e.g., evaluating one's reading). Becoming aware of

---

2. Both MARSI and SORS have been used extensively for assessment, teaching, and research purposes by several researchers and practitioners around the world (see, e.g., chapters by Sheorey for information on the use of the SORS instrument in Hungary, and Mokhtari for information on the use of the MARSI instrument in Arabic and French—this volume). Because of this level of interest in using the instrument, both instruments have been translated in several languages, including Arabic, French, Spanish, and Hungarian. Copies of the translated versions of these instruments may be obtained from the authors upon request.

one's cognitive processes while reading is a first important step toward achieving the type of constructively responsive and thoughtful reading that is emphasized by current models of reading. According to Paris and Winograd (1990), such "consciousness-raising" has twin benefits: "(a) it transfers responsibility for monitoring learning from teachers to students themselves, and (b) it promotes positive self-perceptions, affect, and motivation among students. In this manner, metacognition provides personal insights into one's own thinking and fosters independent learning" (p. 15).

Second, the information derived from these instruments can provide teachers with convenient, useful tools for assessing, monitoring, and documenting the type and number of the reading strategies used by students when reading. For example, teachers can examine the overall responses to get a general sense of the students' awareness and use of the individual reading strategies invoked using the guidelines provided. Over- or underreliance on a particular strategy while reading may provide a hint about how the students approach the reading task. The research evidence now available suggests that students' internalized conceptions of the reading process are often related to the textual information they attend to. A student who reports overusing support strategies, such as "using the dictionary" to look up every word in text, may have a restricted view of reading. Support for this observation comes from Garner and Alexander (1989), who found that "children, particularly younger and poorer readers, often rely on a single criterion for textual understanding: Understanding of individual words" (p. 145). On the other hand, underusing problem-solving strategies, such as "re-reading or re-inspecting text for better understanding" may indicate lack of awareness of reading strategies and inadequate control of one's comprehension processes. Research tells us that certain strategies, particularly text "re-inspection" and "summarization," are often difficult to learn and easy to abandon. Garner and Alexander (1989) have noted that students often avoid reinspecting text to answer questions because it takes time and effort, as well as evade summarization because it is difficult.

Third, both MARSI and SORS can serve as useful tools for teacher-researchers in investigating the impact of teaching strategic reading on students' reading comprehension under a variety of conditions, including reading for different purposes (e.g., reading to answer questions on a test vs. reading to research a particular topic), reading texts varying in length, difficulty, structure, and topic familiarity (e.g., reading a book chapter vs. reading a computer manual), and assigned reading versus self-selected reading. Teachers and researchers can use the data obtained from the instruments as a means of monitoring students' progress in becoming constructively responsive readers. They can administer it as a pre- and post-test in studies aimed at evaluating the impact of strategy instruction on students' awareness and use of strategies while reading. They can use the individual and group average scores to derive a profile designating students along the three subscales of the inventory. Depending on the students' individual profiles, teachers might consider devising specific instructional strategies for addressing the specific weaknesses and needs. Some educators recommend maintaining performance data in portfolios, which can be used to demonstrate changes in the meta-cognitive awareness and use of strategies over time. Differences in performance can be documented, along with other measures of reading in portfolios for individual students (Henk & Melnick, 1995).

Finally, and perhaps more importantly, the information derived from MARSI and SORS should be helpful to teachers in addressing the instructional needs of struggling L1 and L2 readers. In addition to using the information to gain insights about the strategies used by individual students, they can also plan for meaningful instruction that will support students in becoming strategic and thoughtful readers. We have known for some time now that awareness and regulation of one's cognitive processing develops with age and experience, that strategic reading can and should be taught to students, and that when taught successfully, strategies can help improve students' academic performance. Educators agree that strategic reading can be taught to students who need it through carefully devised instructional approaches, including, but not limited to: direct explanation, teacher modeling, and feedback. Paris and Winograd (1990) make several excellent suggestions for reading strategy instruction, which can be used for all readers, and particularly the struggling ones. For example, when teaching a particular reading strategy, such as setting purpose for reading or adjusting reading rate, they recommend using the following steps: (i) describing what the strategy is, (ii) explaining why the strategy should be learned and used, and (iii) providing examples of the circumstances under which the strategy should be used. Constructing the meaning of unfamiliar words from the context (rather than relying constantly on a dictionary), for example, is one of several strategies that can be easily taught through this type of direct explanation approach; in turn, such instruction can provide a useful way of increasing students' metacognitive awareness and use of reading strategies when coping with academic reading tasks. Steps like these are aimed at showing students how one thinks when reading. They are helpful in teaching reading strategies so that students can use them when learning from text. The direct explanation approach has been applied in classrooms by researchers and practitioners as a useful way of helping all readers, and particularly less skilled readers, to interact with text and to become constructively responsive, strategic, and thoughtful readers. Templeton (1991) emphasizes that young children and poor readers do not spontaneously monitor their reading to the extent adults or skilled readers do; as a result, they have to be taught to do so:

> Strategies for approaching different types of reading have different purposes. We will not leave our students to discover these strategies on their own, because most of them won't. Rather, we will forthrightly show them. For example, you can effectively model out loud for students the way to determine the main idea or most important point of a text. We

also model reading itself, not only during read alouds, but also by reading ourselves during Sustained Silent Reading (SSR) time. (p. 272)

It is important for all readers, both native or non-native, to be aware of
some of the key strategies proficient readers use before reading (e.g., setting purpose for reading, using prior knowledge, paraphrasing, monitoring one's comprehension, and using fix-up strategies when encountering
reading problems). Teachers can play a key role in increasing students'
awareness of such strategies and in helping them become "constructively responsive" readers (Pressley & Afflerbach, 1995). According to Chi-
borowski (1999, p. 46), the success of strategy instruction depends, to a
large degree, on three important criteria, including (i) the commitment
teachers make to arm themselves with a set of strategies that have shown
promise with all readers, particularly the struggling ones, (ii) how well
they can model their own strategic thinking while reading, and (iii) how
well they can convince their students that such strategies are useful in
improving their reading comprehension.

In our experiences in teaching native English-speaking and ESL students, we consistently find that students who lack metacognitive awareness and control of reading strategies often have difficulties coping with
academic reading materials, such as textbooks. They tend to expend
more time and energy struggling with individual words than on constructing meaning from the text—a condition which often results in a
slow, labored, and choppy reading style that strains their attention and
interest. We believe that strategy instruction can be helpful to all students
and that MARSI and SORS can be utilized in an overall plan for improving students' reading skills. Indeed, the need to teach students to become
thoughtful, strategic readers has already been expressed by literacy educators. For example, Allington (2000) has pointed out that developing
thoughtful literacy through strategy instruction has been overlooked in
schools. He has called for restructuring the school day and reorganizing
reading instruction in an attempt to help all readers, particularly struggling readers, to become thoughtfully literate:

> For too long we have relied more on the assign-and-assess lessons and
> materials and provided too little successful strategy teaching and offered
> too few opportunities to engage in and develop literate talk. Changing
> in-school environments so that thoughtful literacy is fostered is one of
> the things that really matters for struggling readers. (p. 110)

## Concluding Thoughts and Cautions

The MARSI and the SORS are offered here as practical tools for assessing students' metacognitive awareness of reading strategies while reading academic materials. The information they provide can also be helpful
to teachers in understanding and addressing the needs of students who
encounter difficulties reading constructively and thoughtfully. We invite
practicing teachers and researchers to use them for helping adolescent and
adult readers to develop awareness of their own comprehension processes
and to become constructively responsive to their reading. However, while

teachers may find them to be useful assessment and research tools, they should exercise caution when using them in their classrooms. First, like other measures of reading, these surveys should be used to *supplement*, rather than to supplant, existing assessment measures of students' reading comprehension. Teachers should consider them as only one source of information about students' reading abilities that must be analyzed in conjunction with other measures of reading ability.

Second, although there is psychometric support for the adequacy of MARSI and SORS as measures of metacognitive awareness of reading strategies, they are essentially self-report measures, and as such, results should be interpreted with vigilance. For instance, one cannot tell from the instrument alone whether students actually engage in the strategies they report using. In other words, invoking certain strategies through an inventory such as MARSI or SORS may indicate that the students know about, or are aware of, those strategies. However, mere awareness of certain reading strategies does not always translate into actual use of the strategies concerned. According to Baker and Brown (1984), it is not enough to simply know appropriate reading strategies. Students must also be able to "regulate" or monitor the use of such strategies to ensure success in reading comprehension. Teacher judgment and common sense are clearly required to validate the discrepancy between students' beliefs about using the strategies and actual practice. Teachers should carefully scrutinize the responses to the reading strategies students report using while reading, and interpret them in light of their own experiences observing and working with their students before they make instructional decisions. Such caution is consistent with prior research on reading strategies, which has shown that there is a need for triangulation (with qualitative methodology, such as observation and in-depth interviews) of data in order to get complete and reliable results (Merriam, 1998).

Third, while there is widespread agreement that constructively responsive reading is amenable to assessment and instruction, teachers who have helped students learn to become strategic readers often say that this process is work-intensive and time consuming on the part of teachers and students alike. Some estimate that it takes several months, perhaps as much as 1 year or more, for students to become strategic readers (Pressley, El-Dinary, & Brown, 1992). Others caution that metacognition should not be regarded as a final objective for curriculum or instruction. Instead, it should be regarded as an opportunity to "provide students with knowledge and confidence that *enables* them to manage their own learning and *empowers* them to be inquisitive and zealous in their pursuits" (Paris & Winograd, 1990, p. 22). Ciborowski (1999) also states that reading strategy instruction requires careful reflection on the teachers' part about "how to teach: why, when, and in what problems or circumstances to use a strategy. It involves frequent modeling, and reteaching specific strategies when necessary" (p. 46). In other words, as teachers, we should strive first to better understand the thinking processes that support students' attempts to learn from texts; we should also help all readers, particularly struggling readers, learn to become actively engaged in reading. Increasing students' awareness of their comprehension processes while reading is an important first step toward becoming constructively responsive, strategic, and thoughtful readers.

# Appendix A

## Metacognitive Awareness of Reading Strategies Inventory (MARSI)

**Directions**: Listed below are statements about what people do when they read **academic or school-related materials** such as textbooks, library books, etc. Five numbers follow each statement (1, 2, 3, 4, 5) and each number means the following:

- **1** means "I **never or almost never** do this."
- **2** means "I do this **only occasionally**."
- **3** means "I **sometimes** do this." (about **50%** of the time)
- **4** means "I **usually** do this."
- **5** means "I **always or almost always** do this."

After reading each statement, **circle the number** (1, 2, 3, 4, or 5) that applies to you using the scale provided. Please note that there are **no right or wrong answers** to the statements in this inventory.

| Type | Strategies | Scale | | | | |
|------|-----------|---|---|---|---|---|
| GLOB | 1. I have a purpose in mind when I read. | 1 | 2 | 3 | 4 | 5 |
| SUP | 2. I take notes while reading to help me understand what I read. | 1 | 2 | 3 | 4 | 5 |
| GLOB | 3. I think about what I know to help me understand what I read. | 1 | 2 | 3 | 4 | 5 |
| GLOB | 4. I preview the text to see what it's about before reading it. | 1 | 2 | 3 | 4 | 5 |
| SUP | 5. When text becomes difficult, I read aloud to help me understand what I read. | 1 | 2 | 3 | 4 | 5 |
| SUP | 6. I summarize what I read to reflect on important information in the text. | 1 | 2 | 3 | 4 | 5 |
| GLOB | 7. I think about whether the content of the text fits my reading purpose. | 1 | 2 | 3 | 4 | 5 |
| PROB | 8. I read slowly but carefully to be sure I understand what I'm reading. | 1 | 2 | 3 | 4 | 5 |
| SUP | 9. I discuss what I read with others to check my understanding. | 1 | 2 | 3 | 4 | 5 |
| GLOB | 10. I skim the text first by noting characteristics like length and organization. | 1 | 2 | 3 | 4 | 5 |
| PROB | 11. I try to get back on track when I lose concentration. | 1 | 2 | 3 | 4 | 5 |

| SUP | 12. I underline or circle information in the text to help me remember it. | 1 | 2 | 3 | 4 | 5 |
|---|---|---|---|---|---|---|
| PROB | 13. I adjust my reading speed according to what I'm reading. | 1 | 2 | 3 | 4 | 5 |
| GLOB | 14. I decide what to read closely and what to ignore. | 1 | 2 | 3 | 4 | 5 |
| SUP | 15. I use reference materials such as dictionaries to help me understand what I read. | 1 | 2 | 3 | 4 | 5 |
| PROB | 16. When text becomes difficult, I pay closer attention to what I'm reading. | 1 | 2 | 3 | 4 | 5 |
| GLOB | 17. I use tables, figures, and pictures in text to increase my understanding. | 1 | 2 | 3 | 4 | 5 |
| PROB | 18. I stop from time to time and think about what I'm reading. | 1 | 2 | 3 | 4 | 5 |
| GLOB | 19. I use context clues to help me better understand what I'm reading. | 1 | 2 | 3 | 4 | 5 |
| SUP | 20. I paraphrase (restate ideas in my own words) to better understand what I read. | 1 | 2 | 3 | 4 | 5 |
| PROB | 21. I try to picture or visualize information to help remember what I read. | 1 | 2 | 3 | 4 | 5 |
| GLOB | 22. I use typographical aids like boldface and italics to identify key information. | 1 | 2 | 3 | 4 | 5 |
| GLOB | 23. I critically analyze and evaluate the information presented in the text. | 1 | 2 | 3 | 4 | 5 |
| SUP | 24. I go back and forth in the text to find relationships among ideas in it. | 1 | 2 | 3 | 4 | 5 |
| GLOB | 25. I check my understanding when I come across conflicting information. | 1 | 2 | 3 | 4 | 5 |
| GLOB | 26. I try to guess what the material is about when I read. | 1 | 2 | 3 | 4 | 5 |
| PROB | 27. When text becomes difficult, I reread to increase my understanding. | 1 | 2 | 3 | 4 | 5 |
| SUP | 28. I ask myself questions I like to have answered in the text. | 1 | 2 | 3 | 4 | 5 |
| GLOB | 29. I check to see if my guesses about the text are right or wrong. | 1 | 2 | 3 | 4 | 5 |
| PROB | 30. I try to guess the meaning of unknown words or phrases. | 1 | 2 | 3 | 4 | 5 |

# Metacognitive Awareness of Reading Strategies Inventory Scoring Rubric

Student Name:_____ Age: _____ Date: _____

Grade in School:  □ 6th  □ 7th  □ 8th  □ 9th  □ 10th  □ 11th
 □ 12th  □ College  □ Other

1. Write your response to each statement (i.e., 1, 2, 3, 4, or 5) in each of the blanks.
2. Add up the scores under each column. Place the result on the line under each column.
3. Divide the score by the number of statements in each column to get the average for each subscale.
4. Calculate the average for the inventory by adding up the subscale scores and dividing by 30.
5. Compare your results to those shown below.
6. Discuss your results with your teacher or tutor.

| Global Reading Strategies (GLOB Subscale) | Problem-Solving Strategies (PROB Subscale) | Support Reading Strategies (SUP Subscale) | Overall Reading Strategies |
|---|---|---|---|
| 1._____ | 8._____ | 2._____ | GLOB _____ |
| 3._____ | 11._____ | 5._____ | |
| 4._____ | 13._____ | 6._____ | PROB _____ |
| 7._____ | 16._____ | 9._____ | |
| 10._____ | 18._____ | 12._____ | SUP _____ |
| 14._____ | 21._____ | 15._____ | |
| 17._____ | 27._____ | 20._____ | |
| 19._____ | 30._____ | 24._____ | |
| 22._____ | | 28._____ | |
| 23._____ | | | |
| 25._____ | | | |
| 26._____ | | | |
| 29._____ | | | |
| _____ GLOB Score | _____ PROB Score | _____ SUP Score | _____ Overall Score |
| _____ GLOB Mean | _____ PROB Mean | _____ SUP Mean | _____ Overall Mean |

**Key to averages**:  3.5 or higher = High   2.5 – 3.4 = Medium   2.4 or lower = Low

**Interpreting your scores**: The overall average indicates how often you use reading strategies when reading academic materials. The average for each subscale of the inventory shows which group of strategies (i.e., global, problem-solving, and support strategies) you use most when reading. With this information, you can tell if you are very high or very low in any of these strategy groups. It is important to note, however, that the best possible use of these strategies depends on your reading ability in English, the type of material read, and your purpose for reading it. A low score on any of the subscales or parts of the inventory indicates that there may be some strategies in these parts that you might want to learn about and consider using when reading (adapted from Oxford, 1990, pp. 297–300).

# Appendix B

## SURVEY OF READING STRATEGIES (SORS)

The purpose of this survey is to collect information about the various strategies you use when you read **school-related academic materials in English** (e.g., reading textbooks for homework or examinations, reading journal articles, etc.). Each statement is followed by five numbers, 1, 2, 3, 4, and 5, and each number means the following:

- **1** means that "I **never or almost never** do this."
- **2** means that "I do this **only occasionally**."
- **3** means that "I **sometimes** do this." (about **50%** of the time)
- **4** means that "I **usually** do this."
- **5** means that "I **always or almost always** do this."

After reading each statement, **circle the number** (1, 2, 3, 4, or 5) which applies to you. Note that there are **no right or wrong responses** to any of the items on this survey.

| Category | Strategy | Never | | | | Always |
|----------|----------|-------|---|---|---|--------|
| GLOB | 1. I have a purpose in mind when I read. | 1 | 2 | 3 | 4 | 5 |
| SUP | 2. I take notes while reading to help me understand what I read. | 1 | 2 | 3 | 4 | 5 |
| GLOB | 3. I think about what I know to help me understand what I read. | 1 | 2 | 3 | 4 | 5 |
| GLOB | 4. I take an overall view of the text to see what it is about before reading it. | 1 | 2 | 3 | 4 | 5 |
| SUP | 5. When text becomes difficult, I read aloud to help me understand what I read. | 1 | 2 | 3 | 4 | 5 |
| GLOB | 6. I think about whether the content of the text fits my reading purpose. | 1 | 2 | 3 | 4 | 5 |
| PROB | 7. I read slowly and carefully to make sure I understand what I am reading. | 1 | 2 | 3 | 4 | 5 |
| GLOB | 8. I review the text first by noting its characteristics like length and organization. | 1 | 2 | 3 | 4 | 5 |
| PROB | 9. I try to get back on track when I lose concentration. | 1 | 2 | 3 | 4 | 5 |
| SUP | 10. I underline or circle information in the text to help me remember it. | 1 | 2 | 3 | 4 | 5 |
| PROB | 11. I adjust my reading speed according to what I am reading. | 1 | 2 | 3 | 4 | 5 |

| GLOB | 12. When reading, I decide what to read closely and what to ignore. | 1 | 2 | 3 | 4 | 5 |
|------|------|---|---|---|---|---|
| SUP | 13. I use reference materials (e.g., a dictionary) to help me understand what I read. | 1 | 2 | 3 | 4 | 5 |
| PROB | 14. When text becomes difficult, I pay closer attention to what I am reading. | 1 | 2 | 3 | 4 | 5 |
| GLOB | 15. I use tables, figures, and pictures in text to increase my understanding. | 1 | 2 | 3 | 4 | 5 |
| PROB | 16. I stop from time to time and think about what I am reading. | 1 | 2 | 3 | 4 | 5 |
| GLOB | 17. I use context clues to help me better understand what I am reading. | 1 | 2 | 3 | 4 | 5 |
| SUP | 18. I paraphrase (restate in my own words) to better understand what I read. | 1 | 2 | 3 | 4 | 5 |
| PROB | 19. I try to picture or visualize information to help remember what I read. | 1 | 2 | 3 | 4 | 5 |
| GLOB | 20. I use typographical features like boldface and italics to identify key information | 1 | 2 | 3 | 4 | 5 |
| GLOB | 21. I critically analyze and evaluate the information presented in the text. | 1 | 2 | 3 | 4 | 5 |
| SUP | 22. I go back and forth in the text to find relationships among ideas in it. | 1 | 2 | 3 | 4 | 5 |
| GLOB | 23. I check my information when I come across new information. | 1 | 2 | 3 | 4 | 5 |
| GLOB | 24. I try to guess what the content of the text is about when I read. | 1 | 2 | 3 | 4 | 5 |
| PROB | 25. When text becomes difficult, I reread it to increase my understanding. | 1 | 2 | 3 | 4 | 5 |
| SUP | 26. I ask myself questions I like to have answered in the text. | 1 | 2 | 3 | 4 | 5 |
| GLOB | 27. I check to see if my guesses about the text are right or wrong. | 1 | 2 | 3 | 4 | 5 |
| PROB | 28. When I read, I guess the meaning of unknown words or phrases. | 1 | 2 | 3 | 4 | 5 |
| SUP7 | 29. When reading, I translate from English into my native language. | 1 | 2 | 3 | 4 | 5 |
| SUP | 30. When reading, I think about information in both English and my mother tongue. | 1 | 2 | 3 | 4 | 5 |

# Scoring Guidelines for the Survey of Reading Strategies

Student Name: _____     Date: _____

1.  Write the number you circled for each statement (i.e., 1, 2, 3, 4, or 5) in the appropriate blanks below.
2.  Add up the scores under each column and place the result on the line under each column.
3.  Divide the subscale score by the number of statements in each column to get the average for each subscale.
4.  Calculate the average for the whole inventory by adding up the subscale scores and dividing by 30.
5.  Use the interpretation guidelines below to understand your averages.

| Global Reading Strategies (GLOB Subscale) | Problem-Solving Strategies (PROB Subscale) | Support Reading Strategies (SUP Subscale) | Overall Reading Strategies |
|---|---|---|---|
| 1. _____ | 7. _____ | 2. _____ | GLOB _____ |
| 3. _____ | 9. _____ | 5. _____ | |
| 4. _____ | 11. _____ | 10. _____ | PROB _____ |
| 6. _____ | 14. _____ | 13. _____ | |
| 8. _____ | 16. _____ | 18. _____ | SUP _____ |
| 12. _____ | 19. _____ | 22. _____ | |
| 15. _____ | 25. _____ | 26. _____ | |
| 17. _____ | 28. _____ | 29. _____ | |
| 20. _____ | | 30. _____ | |
| 21. _____ | | | |
| 23. _____ | | | |
| 24. _____ | | | |
| 27. _____ | | | |
| ___ GLOB Score | ___ PROB Score | ___ SUP Score | ___ Overall Score |
| ___ GLOB Average | ___ PROB Average | ___ SUP Average | ___ Overall Average |

**Key to averages:**    3.5 or higher = High    2.5 – 3.4 = Medium    2.4 or lower = Low

**Interpreting your scores:** The overall average indicates how often you use reading strategies when reading academic materials. The average for each subscale shows which group of strategies (i.e., global, problem-solving, or support reading strategies) you use most often when reading. It is important to note, however, that the best possible use of these strategies depends on your reading ability in English, the type of material read, and your reading purpose. A low score on any of the subscales or parts of the inventory indicates that there may be some strategies in these parts that you might want to learn about and consider using when reading (adapted from Oxford, 1990, pp. 297–300).

# 5 | Using Rasch Analysis to Calibrate Students' Metacognitive Awareness and Use of Reading Strategies

**Kouider Mokhtari and Bruce Perry**
*Miami University, Oxford, Ohio*

## Introduction

A significant problem encountered by many of our nation's at-risk students in public schools and colleges is that while many can read (i.e., they can decode words rapidly and accurately), they often have difficulty comprehending what they read. This problem has been well documented over the years in national reports, such as the National Assessment of Educational Progress (NAEP). For example, two recent national reading reports indicate that 37% of fourth graders, 26% of eighth graders, and 26% of twelfth graders cannot read at the "basic level" (National Center for Education Statistics, 2003). According to these reports, when reading grade-appropriate materials, these students find it hard to understand the main idea of the text, make simple inferences based on what is read, or evaluate the information presented. Simply stated, they can read but they cannot understand what they have read. As a result, too many students need remediation in reading when they enroll in their first year of college.

The concerns about students' reading comprehension ability have been exacerbated by two major conflicting forces, including (i) the ever-increasing number of school-age children with family characteristics that put them at risk for reading difficulties (e.g., living in poverty, reading in English as second language [ESL], or having a learning or reading disability) and (ii) the ever-increasing demands for sophisticated literacy skills among adolescents and young adults (see Allington, 2006, for an extended discussion of these conflicting demands). Demands for higher levels of comprehension skills are articulated in recent research and policy reports such as the RAND Reading Study Group report, *Reading For Understanding* (Snow, 2001), *Reading Next* (Biancarosa & Snow, 2004), and *Rising to the Challenge* (Achieve, Inc., 2005). The following excerpt provides a sample statement for the concerns for literacy among adolescents and young adults articulated in these reports:

> American youth need strong literacy skills to succeed in school and in life. Students who do not acquire these skills find themselves at a serious disadvantage in social settings, as civil participants, and in the

working world. Yet approximately eight million young people between fourth and twelfth grade struggle to read at grade level. Some 70 percent of older readers require some form of remediation. Very few of these older struggling readers need help to read the words on a page; their most common problem is that they are not able to comprehend what they read. (*Reading Next,* Summary Statement, p. 1)

The call for the need to increase students' reading comprehension skills has been demonstrated in at least two ways. First, at least 25 states now require high school students to pass tests that tap sophisticated reading skills (i.e., inferential and other higher order reading comprehension skills) in order to graduate (Center on Education Policy, 2004), despite the concern that these exams are associated with higher risks of dropping out among low-performing students (Reardon & Galindo, 2002). Demand for raising adolescents' reading skills has also come from the No Child Left Behind Act of 2001, which currently requires adequate yearly progress for all students in reading and math. The No Child Left Behind Act has put incredible pressure on teacher educators, researchers, and teachers to develop and disseminate methods for increasing the literacy proficiency of young adolescents in the United States.

The fact that such significant numbers of students across all grade levels are unable to comprehend what they read highlights the pressing need for (i) developing assessment instruments aimed at identifying students with reading comprehension problems, (ii) increasing our understanding of the nature and underlying causes of comprehension difficulties encountered by these students, and (iii) developing instructional strategies aimed at improving these students' ability to comprehend what they read.

An examination of the reading research reports, such as the RAND *Reading for Understanding* report and others, indicates that researchers had clearly identified a need for basic research to understand reading comprehension in adolescents, specifically research on different components of reading comprehension, including assessment strategies for such components. The Metacognitive Awareness of Reading Strategies Inventory (MARSI) was developed in response to calls for the development of valid, reliable measures of assessing students' awareness of reading strategies, which has been shown to play a critical role in assessing reading comprehension performance. The MARSI instrument was developed specifically to measure adolescent and adult students' awareness of reading strategies when reading school-related materials, such as textbooks, journal articles, and other related materials. Its development was informed by several research findings, including but not limited to, the following:

## Good Readers Are Active Readers

In reading comprehension, proficient readers have been found to engage in a wide range of cognitive and metacognitive activities. These include summarizing or paraphrasing what was read, generating questions and answering them, activating relevant prior knowledge, monitoring their own level of understanding, and then rereading or engaging in problem-solving activities when text was not properly understood (e.g., Pressley, 2000). Collectively, these mental activities have been termed comprehension strategies, and include both cognitive strategies (e.g., searching and summarizing) and metacognitive or self-monitoring strategies (e.g., feeling of knowing). According to Pressley (2000), in contrast to poor readers, good readers are extremely active when they read, as is apparent whenever they are asked to think aloud and demonstrate their thought processes while reading. He writes that:

> Good readers are aware of why they are reading a text, gain an overview of the text before reading, make predictions about the upcoming text, read selectively based on their overview, associate ideas in text to what they already know, note whether their predictions and expectations about text content are being met, revise their prior knowledge when compelling new ideas conflicting with prior knowledge are encountered, figure out the meanings of unfamiliar vocabulary based on context clues, underline and reread and make notes and paraphrase to remember important points, interpret the text, evaluate its quality, review important points as they conclude reading, and think about how ideas encountered in the text might be used in the future. (Pressley, 2000, p. 549)

Awareness and use of reading strategies improves reading comprehension. Research has shown that students' metacognitive awareness and use of reading strategies for planning, regulating, and evaluating text understanding are quite effective in improving reading comprehension and enjoyment (e.g., Alexander & Jetton, 2000; Baker & Brown, 1984; Garner, 1987; Jiménez, Garcia, & Pearson, 1995, 1996; Kletzien, 1991; Paris, Lipson, & Wixon, 1994; Pressley, 2000; Sheorey & Mokhtari, 2001). Awareness of one's cognitive processes while reading has been found to be a useful tool for learners across various cognitive domains, in that learners with high levels of awareness are better able to organize what they know and use that knowledge to learn what they need to know. As a result, metacognition has been considered an important domain for literacy research and assessment, and it is increasingly being incorporated into academic or content-area reading instruction.

Variability in reader characteristics can be used to partially explain differences in reading comprehension performance. Reading strategy awareness and use have been found to differ as a function of language ability (e.g., Jiménez, Garcia, & Pearson, 1995; Sheorey & Mokhtari, 2001; Mokhtari & Reichard, 2004), gender (e.g., Sheorey & Mokhtari, 2001; Mokhtari & Reichard, 2004), background knowledge (e.g., Chiesi, Spilich, & Voss, 1979), and reading perspective (e.g., Anderson & Pichert, 1978). An additional important source of variability in reading comprehension is a reader's perception of how competent he or she is as a reader. According to members of the RAND Reading Study Group (Snow, 2001), for developing and mature readers, "it is the belief in the self (or lack of such a belief) that makes a difference in how competent they feel" (p.

22). The RAND Reading Study Group summarized research on the relationship between individual capabilities and comprehension outcomes, indicating that "providing those who are experiencing reading difficulties with clear goals for a reading comprehension task and then giving them feedback on the progress they are making can lead to increased self-efficacy and a greater use of comprehension strategies" (p. 22).

Effective use of reading strategies transfers across languages. Research on the reading of first- (L1) and second-language (L2) learners has shown that important reading strategies that deal with planning, controlling, and evaluating one's understanding while reading (e.g., setting purpose for reading, prediction, summarization, questioning, use of text structural features, self-monitoring, etc.) are widely used by L1 and L2 readers (e.g., Jiménez, Garcia, & Pearson, 1995, 1996; Sheorey & Mokhtari, 2001). In addition, the supply of reading strategies used by L2 readers often includes some strategies (e.g., translation or use of cognates) that may be unique and particularly useful to different types of, and purposes for, reading (e.g., Mokhtari & Reichard, 2004). For instance, the reading strategies used when reading to study for a test may be quite different from those used when reading for recreational purposes.

Metacognitive awareness of reading strategies can be increased through guided reading and scaffolding. Reading researchers have developed approaches to stimulating active reading by teaching readers to use comprehension strategies. Of the many possible strategies, the following have often been shown to produce improved memory and comprehension of text in children: generating questions about ideas in text while reading; constructing mental images representing ideas in text; summarizing; and analyzing stories read into story grammar components of setting, characters, problems encountered by characters, attempts at solution, successful solution, and ending (e.g., Pearson & Fielding, 1991).

Becoming strategic readers takes time and effort. One major line of reading strategy research has considered how strategy use develops over time and as readers progress from novice to expert—for example, Brown and Day (1983) compared the ability of middle school, high school, undergraduate, and graduate students to summarize science texts. They found that the ability to summarize developed over many years, with simple rules, such as deleting redundant information emerging early and more complex rules, such as generating a new topic sentence emerging late. Overall, this line of developmental research shows that proficiency in using strategies improves as students progress through school, and that patterns of strategy use differ between more- and less proficient readers (for a summary of developmental studies, see Garner, 1987; for a review of novice-expert studies, see Pressley & Afflerbach, 1995).

There is a need for the development of valid and reliable strategy assessment measures. Researchers investigating metacognition and reading comprehension—whether from developmental, expert-novice, or intervention perspectives (e.g., Snow, 2001)—have called for the need for high-quality measures of strategic knowledge and strategy use. This research has also called for more research work aimed at increasing our understanding of the nature and underlying causes of comprehension difficulties encountered by these students and developing instructional strategies aimed at improving these students' ability to comprehend what they read. It is important to note that while self-report measures serve the useful purpose of assessing students' *perceived* strategy use, they should be used with a great deal of caution because (i) they are highly context-, task-, and goal-dependent, and (ii) they are not designed to assess students' *actual* use of reading strategies, which can and should be assessed through other appropriate means, such as verbal reports or think-aloud techniques. (For a more detailed discussion of the limitations of self-report measures of reading strategies, see Baker & Cerro, 2000; Hadwin, Winne, Stockley, Nesbit, & Woszczyna, 2001; Veenman, 2005; Veenman, Elshout, & Groen, 1993).

## The Present Study

In this study, we used Rasch measurement techniques (Bond & Fox, 2001) to evaluate the unidimensionality of the three scales on the MARSI (Mokhtari & Reichard, 2002). The application of Rasch analysis provides crucial diagnostic information, which enables us to scrutinize items (reading strategies) that do not adequately fit the Rasch model. This reevaluation constitutes an important preliminary step in revising and updating the MARSI instrument as a measure of students' metacognitive awareness of reading strategies when applied to academic or school-related readings.

*Subjects*

The participants in this study consisted of 305 junior high, high school, and college students enrolled in schools and colleges located in the midwestern United States. Participants were included in the study because their teachers responded favorably to a call for participation in a study aimed at determining students' awareness and use of reading strategies when reading for school purposes. The junior high students ($n = 75$) included 32 males (43%) and 43 females (57%), with the great majority (98%) being Caucasian. These students ranged in age from 13 to 15 years, and the mean age of the group was 13.87 ($SD = .475$). The high school students ($n = 95$) included 42 females (44.22%) and 53 males (55.78%), with the great majority (97%) being Caucasian. The students ranged in age from 15 to 17, with a mean age of 15.5 ($SD = .613$). The college students ($n = 161$) consisted of mostly freshmen and a few sophomores and included 81 males (50.3%) and 80 females (49.7%), representing Caucasian (87%), African-American (3%), Hispanic (2%), American-Indian (3.3%), Asian-American (2.2%), and other (2.5%). School records indicated that the students shared similar linguistic, cultural, and socioeconomic backgrounds. None of the students was identified as having any specific learning or reading disability.

*Data Collection*

The data were collected by using the MARSI (Mokhtari & Reichard, 2002), which was specifically designed for measuring students' metacognitive awareness and use of reading strategies while reading academic materials. The MARSI instrument measures three broad categories of strategies, including (i) global reading strategies, which can be thought of as generalized or global reading strategies aimed at setting the stage for the reading act (e.g., setting purpose for reading, previewing text content, predicting what the text is about, etc.); (ii) problem-solving strategies, which are localized, focused, problem-solving or repair strategies used when problems develop in understanding textual information (e.g., checking one's understanding upon encountering conflicting information, rereading for better understanding, etc.); and (iii) support reading strategies, which provide the support mechanisms or tools aimed at sustaining responsiveness to reading (e.g., use of reference materials, such as dictionaries, and other support systems). These three classes of strategies interact with and support each other when used in the process of constructing meaning from text. Table 5.1 contains an abbreviated inventory of the strategies used in the MARSI instrument. A detailed description of the MARSI instrument, including its psychometric properties as well as its theoretical and research foundations, can be found in Mokhtari, Sheorey, and Reichard (this volume, chapter 4).

*Procedures*

All students completed the MARSI instrument in the three institutions under similar conditions. The MARSI instrument was administered to the subjects at the beginning of a class period, with the help of the classroom instructor who was familiar with the purpose of the study and the instrument. After a brief overview about the purpose of the study, a description of the instrument, and an explanation of the steps involved in completing it, the students were instructed to read each statement in the inventory, and circle the number that best described their responses to the statements. They were also advised to work at their own pace and instructed to keep in mind the reading of academic or school-related materials while responding to the strategy statements. Finally, they were told that there are no right or wrong responses to the statements, and that they could take as much time as they needed to complete the inventory. On average, the students completed it in about 10–12 minutes.

*Data Analyses*

The MARSI has already been evaluated using the standard techniques of classical test theory, namely, factor analysis and psychometric statistics. In this study, we take a preliminary step in the process of reevaluating the MARSI instrument using Rasch analysis, a particular form of item-response theory. The Rasch model (Bond & Fox, 2001) is based on the premise that data are represented on a single unitary construct or latent trait (in our case, awareness of reading strategies) in accordance with a particular theory of reading (e.g., metacognition and reading), which supports that construct. The model analyzes both the items (strategies) and persons (readers) on the same ruler or metric. The fit statistic generated is based on the reader's ability to determine his or her level of strategy awareness or frequency of use, as well as his or her response to the strategies as predicted by the Rasch model. In other words, the greater awareness a reader shows when responding to a given strategy, the greater the probability that reader has reached the desired goal for that strategy.

Table 5.1. Abbreviated Outline of the Metacognitive Awareness of Reading Strategies Inventory

| Global reading strategies | Problem-solving strategies | Support reading strategies |
|---|---|---|
| • Setting purpose for reading<br>• Using prior knowledge<br>• Previewing text before reading<br>• Check how text content fits purpose<br>• Skim to notice text characteristics<br>• Decide what to read closely<br>• Using text features (e.g., graphs)<br>• Using context clues<br>• Using typographical aids<br>• Critically analyzing information<br>• Checking one's understanding<br>• Predicting text meaning<br>• Checking to verify understanding | • Reading slowly but carefully<br>• Getting back on track while reading<br>• Adjusting reading rate<br>• Paying close attention to reading<br>• Stopping and thinking about reading<br>• Visualizing information read<br>• Rereading for better understanding<br>• Guessing meaning of unknown words | • Taking notes while reading<br>• Reading text aloud<br>• Summarizing and reflecting<br>• Discussing reading with others<br>• Underlining information in text<br>• Using reference materials<br>• Paraphrasing for better understanding<br>• Going back and forth in text<br>• Asking oneself questions |

The Rasch model represents an idealized structure or a standard against which the data obtained are evaluated, to see whether the data fit the expectations of the model. The model uses mathematical formulas (or fit statistics) to calculate the probability that a person (a student) will respond to a given item (i.e., is able to determine their level of strategy awareness or frequency of strategy use) and that an item (or a reading strategy) will receive the expected response by the reader. When the probabilities are quite different from what actually occurs, the results will show that the data do not fit the expectations of the model. The fit statistics (Infit and Outfit) are used to identify any items that do not seem to fit the model, and any subjects whose responses to the items do not appear to be consistent with the expectations of the model, thereby decreasing the validity and reliability of the instrument. The results can be used to identify subjects who may have been anxious or who did not complete the instrument as intended as well as items or strategies that are less likely to be known to, or used by, readers thereby allowing them to consider increasing their awareness and use of such strategies when reading, with the goal of enhancing reading comprehension performance.

# Results

The statistical tests presented in Appendix A were used to examine the "test of fit" or level of correspondence of data with the Rasch model. In general, the results of this analysis indicate that while a majority of the strategies in the inventory showed an overall good fit to the model, a few of the items in each of the three strategy scales (i.e., global, problem-solving, and support strategies) did not exhibit good model data fit for the three student populations studied, indicating some perceived redundancy on the part of the subjects, as shown by their responses to the strategies, and possibly a lack of item independence among the strategies in the inventory. Removal of these potentially redundant items in each scale resulted in better unidimensionality or enhanced fit for the remaining strategy items. Person Item analyses were then conducted utilizing the modified scales to assure construct validity. Appendix A provides more details about these analyses.

*Comparison of Person-Item Maps*

Person and Item Response maps for the reading strategy response patterns in each of the three modified scales of the MARSI instrument for the three student groups are shown in Figures 5.1–5.3. An item (strategy)-person (reader) map illustrates where responses place each person with respect to those items. Item-person figures are useful in recognizing the potential match between expected level of response for each strategy (awareness levels range from 1 [low] to 5 [high]) and actual response relative to each reading strategy as perceived by readers, identifying gaps in the trait or attribute being measured—in this case, level of awareness and strategy use when reading. In general, persons with a closely matched level of awareness, as indicated by their response, have a 1:1 odds of using that strategy "sometimes." Persons with higher reported strategy use have greater odds of using the strategy more frequently ("usually" or "always or almost always"), and persons with lower reported strategy use have greater odds of using the strategy "occasionally" or "never or almost never." In a well-constructed one-dimensional instrument or scale, the levels of awareness are spread evenly over the entire range of strategies in the inventory.

An examination of the Person and Item Response maps for the strategies in each of the three modified scales for the three student groups indicates that the distribution of persons is on the left side of the vertical line and item numbers from the MARSI for each scale on the right. Each "X" or "#" represents a person or persons in each figure. "M" marks the person and item mean, "S" is one standard deviation away from the mean, and "T" is two standard deviations away from the mean. On these maps, item-response estimates are regarded as a balance point for the response distribution across the strategies in the inventory. The variation of item-

Figure 5.1. Person and item maps for global strategies.

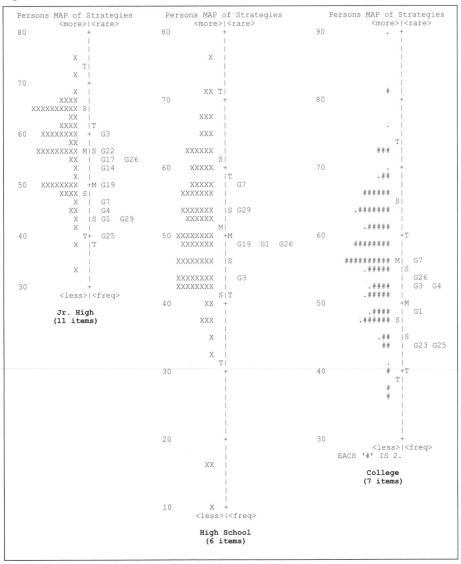

response estimates shows the level of awareness of the strategies relative to each other and to the person distribution (Bond & Fox, 2001). For any person location, the model indicates that items or strategies represented on the scale at or below this position were used more frequently (50% of the time or greater) and that those above this position were used only "occasionally" or "never or almost never." Items located at the upper end of the item scale represent those strategies that persons or readers indicated to be used less frequently than others; that is, readers reported a relatively low level of awareness and use of these strategies when reading.

Figure 5.2. Person and item maps for problem-solving strategies.

```
Persons MAP of Strategies    Persons MAP of Strategies    Persons MAP of Strategies
        <more>|<rare>                <more>|<rare>                <more>|<rare>
 100     XXX  +               90       X  +               90         .  +
              |                           |                             |
              |               XXXXXXXXXX  |                       .     |
              |                           |                             |
         XX   |                           |                             |
  90          +               80          +               80            +
              |                   XXX     |                             |
         T|                              |                             |
         XX   |                         S|                             |
              |                           |                        .#   |
         XX   |               XXXXXXXXXX  |               70            +
  80          +                           |                       #     |
              |               70          +                       T|
              |                           |                      ###   |T
         S|               XXXXXXXX  |                             |
      XXXXX   |                           |                      .##   |  P30
              |               XXXXXXX   |               60      .####  +
  70 XXXXXXX  +                          |T                     .###   |S
      XXX     |                          |                    .###### |
       X      |               60 XXXXXXXXXX  + P18    60  .######  |
      XXXXX   |                         M|                 ########## |
       X      |               XXXXXXX   |                     ##### M|  P18
   XXXXXXX  M|                          |S              50 .######### +M
  60    XX    +                   XXX    |  P8                  ######  |  P16 P21
         |T P21          XXXXXX  |               .######### |
      XXXX    |               50          +M                   #####   |
         |S                   XXX   |  P16              ##### S|S
      XXXXX   |               XXXXXX  |                     #####   |
      XXXX    | P27 P8         XX  |S P27          40      #  +
  50      +M P11              | P11                        |  P11
       X S|   P16            XXX S|                      ###   |
   XXXXXX  |               40          +                       . T|T
         |S P13  P30          XXXX   |                       |
       X      |                   XX    |T                            .  |
         |T                  XXX   |               30            +
  40     XXX  +               30          +                   <less>|<freq>
              |                   XX    |                      EACH '#' IS 2.
         T|                       |
              |                         T|                      College
       X      |                   X     |                      (6 items)
  30          +               20          +
      <less>|<freq>                       |
                                          |
       Jr. High                     XX    |
       (7 items)                          |
                                          |
                              10       X  +
                              <less>|<freq>

                                 High School
                                  (5 items)
```

Figure 5.3. Person and item maps for support strategies.

```
Persons MAP of strategies      Persons MAP of Strategies       Persons MAP of Strategies
        <more>|<rare>                  <more>|<rare>                   <more>|<rare>
  90        X  +                       X   |               90                +
                 |                      X   |                                 |
                 |             60            +                         .      |
         XX  |                     XXX  |                                 |
                 |                      X   |                                 |
       .         |                     XX  |T                                |
         X  T|                     XXXXX  |                                 |
  80             +                    XX  S|   S15                           |
                 |                 XXXXX   |S  S9             80              +
         X  |                       XXX   |   S12   S6                      |
                 |              50   XXXXX   +M  S24                  .#      |
        XX  |                 XXXXXXXX   |   S28                             T|
                 |                         |S                      .#   |
         X  |                     XXXXXX   |                       ####    |
  70      XXX  S+                      XX   |               70             +
                 |                 XXXXXXXX M|T S20                   ####    |
         X  |                                |                                 |
        XXX  |                            |                    .## S|
                 |              40 XXXXXXXXXXX   +                       ######    |
      XXXXXXX   |                            |                       ######   |T
       XXXXXX   |                     XXXX   |               60     .        +
  60      XXX  +T                          |                      #######   |
                 |                     XXX   |                               |   S12   S2
        XX  M|                       S|                           ##### M|S
     XXXXXXXX   |S  S9             XXXXXXX   |                  ##########    |
        XXXX  |   S20   S2                 |                      .#####   |
                 |   S15             30            +                       |
        XXXX  |                     XXX   |                        ####### |   S6   S9
  50      XXXX  +M  S12                     |               50       .####    +M
         X  |   S28                     |                       .        |
                 |                    XX   |                       .##### S|
       XXX  S|                        T|                         .#   |
        XX  |S                           |                         ##   |   S20   S24
                 |   S6             20            +                              |S  S15
                 |   S24                      |                         ##   |
  40             +T                         |               40                +
        XX  |                     XXX   |                          #  T|T
                 |                          |                                 |
         X  |                           |                         .#   |
         X  T|                           |                               |
        XX  |                           |                               |
                 |             10            |               30                +
  30             +                   XXXX   +                         .        |
        <less>|<freq>                <less>|<freq>                             |
                                                                               |
       Jr. High                   High School                                 |
      (8 items)                    (7 items)                                   |
                                                                 20            +
                                                                      <less>|<freq>
                                                               EACH '#' IS 2.

                                                                     College
                                                                    (7 items)
```

An examination of the person-item maps further shows that all but one of the distributions of person-item logit positions for the three scales are negatively skewed to some degree; only the map for the Support Strategy scale for the High School subjects is positively skewed. Generally, in a negatively skewed distribution, the mean value for the persons is greater than the mean value for the item-response (frequency of use) estimate. In this type of distribution, there are numerous persons whose position is above where items are measuring, indicating that there are several strategies that appear to match these readers' level of the scale trait very well.

The negatively skewed distribution of persons or readers relative to the frequency of use of the strategies is an indication that the readers were generally aware of the strategies represented on the MARSI scales and reported using these strategies frequently (more than 50%) while reading. In other words, readers in all three groups could easily identify with the strategies and reported using them fairly often when reading academic or school-related materials. The exception to this person-item response pattern is the support strategy scale for the high school student group.

## Discussion

This diagnostic information obtained from this preliminary reexamination of the MARSI instrument from a Rasch measurement perspective is quite helpful to us as we prepare to refine and update the MARSI instrument as a measure of students' metacognitive awareness of reading strategies when applied to academic or school-related readings. In general, we were encouraged by the results, which indicate that a majority of the 30 strategies in the instrument appear to be functioning quite well; that is, they appear to fit the unidimensional Rasch measurement model in each of the three strategy scales (i.e., global, problem solving, and support) for each of the student populations in this study.

However, we were also intrigued by the response patterns among the three student populations, which seem to indicate that there is a certain level of redundancy perceived by the subjects, indicating that some of the reading strategies within the three strategy scales may be either redundant in that they may be measuring the same type of strategies. An examination of the data shown in Appendix A (Table 5.2) indicates that a few of the items or strategy statements showed differential item functioning indicating either redundancy in the responses among the students and/or a lack of item independence. For instance, when examining the data in the High School group, it is conceivable that students failed to see the fine distinctions between those strategies, which focus on "previewing text to see how it's organized" (G10) or structured and "previewing text to get the gist or the main idea" (G4). Similarly, it is quite conceivable that college students saw no discernable difference between strategies of "asking questions when trying to understand text" (S28) and "discussing text with others" (S9) after reading. These response patterns appear to be similar in some parts of the inventory but different in others when examining response patterns across the three student populations. For instance, note that several of the strategies that did not appear to fit the Rasch model (4 for Junior High; 7 for High School; and 4 for College) were found in the global strategies scale of the inventory, which has the highest number of strategies ($n = 13$). Of these 13 strategies, only two (namely, G10 "checking text organization" and S5 "reading aloud") did not fit the model's expected structure in all three data sets among the Junior High, High School, and College readers. The response patterns in the remaining strategies within the global scale were different for the three student populations.

Second, with the exception of the Support Strategy scale for College students, almost all of the strategies in the Problem-Solving and Support strategies scales appear to fit the model quite well. Those strategies that did not fit the model were different for different groups of students, as can be seen from the data in Appendix A (see Table 5.2). It is also interesting to note that far fewer strategies showed "misfits" among students in the Junior High group than among those in the High School or College groups. It is unclear why the Junior High data set had a better model fit than those in the High School and College data set. Our goal is to explore this issue further with a greater number of students representing the three student populations while controlling for factors (e.g., reading ability), which may shed some light on these discrepancies.

The technical data shown in Appendix A (see Table 5.3) reflect a reanalysis of the data following the removal of the strategies that did not quite meet the expectations of the Rasch model. The reanalyzed data indicate an active level of strategy awareness and reported use among students in all three groups. This level of awareness and use is calibrated with item "difficulty" and student "ability." As we prepare to refine and update this version of the MARSI instrument, we plan to take into account the diagnostic information obtained through the Rasch analysis, which includes the "misfit" data found across the three scales as well as across the three student groups. These data enable us to closely examine differential item functioning for different groups of students across the latent trait, which focuses on students' metacognitive awareness and use of reading strategies while reading.

The Rasch analysis findings will also be helpful in designing research studies aimed at exploring some of the critical variables, which can explain differences among students when measuring their level of awareness and use of reading strategies when reading for multiple purposes and under various conditions. We plan to utilize the information obtained from this initial pilot study, and subsequent studies, to further explore the functioning of the instrument as a useful metacognitive reading strategy awareness measure. Our strategy is to apply applicable theoretical and methodological tools provided by the Rasch family of measurement models when examining the instruments' functionality.

While there are many issues and variables, which are critically important in designing instruments aimed at measuring student awareness of reading strategies while reading, our research plans are currently focused on the issues of reader ability, readers' developmental levels, and reader diversity. We believe a careful study of these, and other variables,0 will enable us to further explore the functioning of the MARSI instrument as a useful metacognitive reading strategy awareness measure.

## Reader Ability

Current and established research indicates that proficient readers, unlike their less proficient counterparts, engage in a wide range of cognitive and metacognitive strategic activities when reading (Baker & Cerro,

2000; Garner, 1987; Pressley, 2000). However, it is not clear the extent to which high comprehending readers differ significantly in their ability to accurately self-report their strategic reading activities when reading. The range of reader abilities that could be reliably measured by the item pool in the present study was restricted to the range of ability that typically exists among readers varying by grade levels or within the same grade levels. The role of reading ability in determining readers' metacognitive awareness and strategy use is critical in interpreting students' awareness or perceived use of reading strategies while reading.

*Reader Developmental Level*

The ability to monitor one's thinking when engaged in a cognitive task such as reading (metacognitive monitoring), to regulate or control one's thoughts and thinking strategies (metacognitive control), and to express or describe one's knowledge or awareness of what one does when reading (metacognitive awareness) develop gradually and often unevenly in different areas through childhood and across the life span (Alexander & Jetton, 2000; Pressley, 2000; Flavell, 1979; Schraw, 1998). These developmental levels indicate that the achievement of ability and competence is developmental, complex, and varies across readers. Taking into account developmental differences relative to metacognitive awareness will be helpful in interpreting students' perceived or reported use of reading strategies when reading.

*Reader Diversity*

Current and established research has shown that students' reading performance across grade levels differs a great deal among students representing diverse cultural and linguistic groups (e.g., Baker, this volume; Grigg, Daane, Jin, & Campbell, 2003. Cross-comparisons of students' reading performance on tests such as the NAEP indicate that students representing minority groups (e.g., African-American, Hispanic, and Asian) are generally lower than those from mainstream groups. Students' awareness and use of reading strategies has been shown to differ based on cultural and linguistic backgrounds. Such information will be helpful when interpreting student-reported use of reading strategies when reading. Taking student diversity into consideration will be helpful in determining the functionality of the MARSI instrument for all students, including students from culturally and linguistically diverse readers.

# Appendix A

## MARSI Item-Fit Analysis

Tables 5.2 and 5.3 show the results of the WINSTEPS (Linacre, 2006) item-fit analysis for all 30 items on the MARSI instrument for the Junior High School (JrHi), High School (High), and College (Coll) data sets. The INFIT and OUTFIT columns combine the mean square (MNSQ) and standardized fit index (ZSTD). INFIT is associated with response patterns that are similar and the OUTFIT measures are associated with response patterns that help to identify unexpected response patterns. Combined, INFIT and OUTFIT help assess the fit of the data to the Rasch model. A "rule of thumb" for assessing item fit is to closely scrutinize any item or strategy with a ZSTD value outside the boundaries of ±2.0 (Bond & Fox, 2001): A ZSTD greater than 2.0 indicates an unexpected (irregular) response pattern and a ZSTD less than -2.0 could indicate redundancy in the item responses.

An analysis of the data obtained shows that while a majority of the strategies in the inventory appear to fit the model fairly well, a few of the items within each scale highlighted (in italics; see Table 5.2) show INFIT and/or OUTFIT ZSTD values beyond ±2.0, indicating unexpected or irregular response patterns. However, note that only a few of these items showed consistent misfit across all of the data sets, suggesting that in general, items have an overall good fit to the model. Interpretations based on specific items or strategies should incorporate a more detailed analysis of item fit to the Rasch model. An examination of the fit statistics for each of the data sets follows.

For the Junior High data set, 4 of the 13 Global Scale items, namely, G3 (Using prior knowledge), G23 (Critically evaluating what is read), G10 (Checking text organization), and G19 (Using context clues), show misfit, indicating unexpected responses to these strategies on the part of respondents. These data indicate that the Junior High students either are not aware of the importance of these four strategies in reading comprehension or that they believe they are redundant or irrelevant as reading strategies. One strategy on the Problem Solving scale shows similar misfit characteristics. P18 (Stop and think) shows marginal misfit on the INFIT and substantial misfit on the OUTFIT measures, indicating some redundancy in responses and a lack of item independence. On the Support scale, S5 (Reading aloud) has an INFIT ZSTD = -2.5 and an OUTFIT ZSTD = -2.6, indicating a lack of fit and an absence of unidimensionality with the other eight strategies on the scale. A reanalysis of the Junior High school population responses for the three scales, with the misfit items removed, reveals INFIT and OUTFIT statistics that show a considerably improved match with the rest of the strategies and better overall unidimensionality (see Table 5.3).

An examination of the High School data set indicates that seven of

the Global Scale strategies show misfit statistics greater than ±2.0 on either or both the INFIT or OUTFIT measures. These strategies include G23
(Critically evaluating what is read), G10 (Checking text organization),
G14 (Deciding what to read or ignore), G17 (Using tables and figures),
G25 (Resolving conflicts in understanding), G22 (Using typographical
aids), and G4 (Previewing text). Also, two of the strategies on the Problem Solving scale, namely, P30 (Guessing unknown words) and P21 (Vi-
sualizing), and one item on the Support Scale, S5 (Reading aloud), show
fit statistics greater than ±2.0 on either or both the INFIT or OUTFIT measures, indicating some unexpected responses relative to these strategies
due to either perceived redundancy or other factors. The reanalysis of the
High School data with these strategies removed (see Table 5.3) shows a
better fit of the data to the model.

An examination of the College student data reveals fit statistics
greater than ±2.0 on either or both the INFIT or OUTFIT measures for
the following four strategies on the Global Strategy scale: G14 (Deciding what to read or ignore), G3 (Using prior knowledge), G19 (Using
context clues), and G10 (Checking text organization). In addition, a similar pattern was found for two strategies on the Problem Solving scale,
including P8 (Stop and think) and P13 (Adjusting reading rate). Finally,
three strategies on the Support Scale showed misfit on one or both the
INFIT or OUTFIT measures, including S28 (Asking questions), S5 (Reading aloud), and S9 (Discussing what is read with others). A reanalysis of
the data with these items removed from the scale (see Table 5.3) provides
a significant improvement in unidimensionality or enhanced fit of the
data to the model.

**Table 5.2. Item-Fit Statistic (WINSTEPS, 2006)**

Junior high data

| INFIT MNSQ | ZSTD | OUTFIT MNSQ | ZSTD | Strategy |
|---|---|---|---|---|
| .68 | -2.1 | .72 | -1.8 | G3-KNOWLEDGE |
| .80 | -1.3 | .81 | -1.2 | G22-TextAids |
| .96 | -.2 | .96 | -.2 | G17-Figures |
| .97 | -.1 | .97 | -.1 | G26-Guess |
| .75 | -1.7 | .74 | -1.7 | G14-Decision |
| 1.51 | 2.9 | 1.50 | 2.8 | G23-ANALYZE |
| 1.81 | 4.3 | 1.83 | 4.3 | G10-ORGANIZATION |
| .64 | -2.6 | .65 | -2.5 | G19-CONTEXT |
| 1.11 | .8 | 1.09 | .6 | G7-Content |
| .94 | -.3 | .97 | -.1 | G4-Preview |
| .85 | -1.0 | .88 | -.7 | G1-Purpose |
| .87 | -.8 | .83 | -1.0 | G29-Check |
| .91 | -.5 | .96 | -.2 | G25-Conflicting |
| .85 | -.9 | .84 | -.9 | P21-Visualize |
| .97 | -.1 | 1.13 | .8 | P8-Carefully |
| 1.06 | .4 | 1.03 | .2 | P27-Re-Read |
| .85 | -.9 | .82 | -1.0 | P11-On-Track |
| .97 | -.1 | .89 | -.6 | P16-Attention |
| 1.35 | 1.9 | 1.60 | 2.9 | P18-STOP |
| .82 | -1.1 | .81 | -1.0 | P13-Adjust |
| 1.03 | .2 | 1.03 | .2 | P30-Unknown |
| .62 | -2.5 | .60 | -2.6 | S5-ALOUD |
| 1.28 | 1.6 | 1.23 | 1.3 | S9-Discus |
| 1.04 | .3 | 1.18 | 1.1 | S20-Paraphrase |
| 1.11 | .7 | 1.11 | .7 | S2-Notes |
| .81 | -1.2 | .79 | -1.2 | S15-Reference |
| .88 | -.7 | .91 | -.5 | S12-Underline |
| 1.12 | .8 | 1.23 | 1.3 | S28-Questions |
| 1.05 | .4 | 1.11 | .7 | S6-Summarize |
| 1.03 | .3 | .95 | -.2 | S24-Relationships |

High school data

| INFIT MNSQ | ZSTD | OUTFIT MNSQ | ZSTD | Strategy |
|---|---|---|---|---|
| .68 | -2.6 | .68 | -2.5 | G23-ANALYZE |
| 1.38 | 2.6 | 1.43 | 2.8 | G10-ORGANIZATION |
| .80 | -1.6 | .78 | -1.7 | G7-Content |
| 1.40 | 2.8 | 1.38 | 2.6 | G14-DECISION |
| .98 | -.1 | .97 | -.2 | G29-Check |
| 1.32 | 2.3 | 1.26 | 1.9 | G17-FIGURES |
| .57 | -4.0 | .59 | -3.6 | G25-CONFLICTING |
| 1.26 | 1.9 | 1.38 | 2.6 | G22-TEXTAIDS |
| .80 | -1.6 | .83 | -1.3 | G1-Purpose |
| .84 | -1.2 | .83 | -1.3 | G19-Context |
| .80 | -1.6 | .79 | -1.6 | G26-Guess |
| 1.36 | 2.5 | 1.41 | 2.8 | G4-PREVIEW |
| .89 | -.8 | .84 | -1.1 | G3-Knowledge |
| .77 | -1.8 | .84 | -1.1 | P18-Stop |
| .94 | -.4 | .98 | -.1 | P8-Carefully |
| 1.30 | 2.0 | 1.34 | 2.1 | P30-UNKNOWN |
| 1.21 | 1.4 | 1.24 | 1.5 | P13-Adjust |
| .82 | -1.2 | .77 | -1.5 | P16-Attention |
| .82 | -1.2 | .74 | -1.7 | P27-Re-Read |
| .90 | -.6 | .85 | -.9 | P11-On-Track |
| 1.49 | 2.8 | 1.33 | 1.8 | P21-VISUALIZE |
| 1.15 | .9 | 1.29 | 1.4 | S2-Notes |
| 1.03 | .3 | 1.12 | .8 | S15-Reference |
| .87 | -.9 | .84 | -1.0 | S9-Discus |
| .94 | -.4 | .90 | -.6 | S6-Summarize |
| .89 | -.7 | .83 | -1.1 | S12-Underline |
| 1.01 | .1 | .94 | -.4 | S24-Relationships |
| .78 | -1.7 | .78 | -1.6 | S28-Questions |
| 1.47 | 3.1 | 1.72 | 4.3 | S5-ALOUD |
| .99 | -.1 | 1.03 | .3 | S20-Paraphrase |

College data

| INFIT MNSQ | ZSTD | OUTFIT MNSQ | ZSTD | Strategy |
|---|---|---|---|---|
| 1.17 | 1.7 | 1.18 | 1.7 | G29-Check |
| 1.06 | .7 | 1.06 | .6 | G17-Figures |
| 1.30 | 2.7 | 1.34 | 3.1 | G14-DECISION |
| .89 | -1.1 | .87 | -1.3 | G7-Content |
| .93 | -.7 | .93 | -.7 | G22-TextAids |
| .89 | -1.1 | .88 | -1.2 | G26-Guess |
| .75 | -2.6 | .79 | -2.1 | G3-KNOWLEDGE |
| .82 | -1.8 | .81 | -1.9 | G4-Preview |
| .70 | -3.1 | .71 | -3.0 | G19-CONTEXT |
| 1.37 | 3.2 | 1.35 | 3.0 | G10-ORGANIZATION |
| .82 | -1.7 | .81 | -1.8 | G1-Purpose |
| 1.15 | 1.4 | 1.12 | 1.0 | G23-Analyze |
| 1.17 | 1.5 | 1.16 | 1.3 | G25-Conflicting |
| .79 | -2.0 | .81 | -1.8 | P30-Unknown |
| .88 | -1.2 | .93 | -.6 | P27-Re-Read |
| .67 | -3.7 | .71 | -3.2 | P8-CAREFULLY |
| 1.01 | .2 | 1.02 | .2 | P18-Stop |
| 1.42 | 3.7 | 1.37 | 3.2 | P13-ADJUST |
| 1.03 | .3 | 1.04 | .4 | P16-Attention |
| 1.18 | 1.7 | 1.12 | 1.2 | P21-Visualize |
| .92 | -.7 | .97 | -.2 | P11-On-Track |
| .80 | -2.0 | .79 | -2.1 | S28-QUESTIONS |
| 1.08 | .8 | 1.07 | .7 | S12-Underline |
| .95 | -.4 | .93 | -.7 | S2-Notes |
| .70 | -3.2 | .71 | -3.0 | S5-ALOUD |
| 1.03 | .4 | 1.04 | .4 | S6-Summarize |
| 1.26 | 2.3 | 1.24 | 2.2 | S9-DISCUS |
| 1.11 | 1.0 | 1.10 | .9 | S20-Paraphrase |
| .94 | -.5 | .91 | -.8 | S24-Relationships |
| 1.14 | 1.3 | 1.10 | .9 | S15-Reference |

## Table 5.3. Item-Fit Statistic for Retained Items

Junior high data

| INFIT MNSQ | ZSTD | OUTFIT MNSQ | ZSTD | Strategy |
|---|---|---|---|---|
| .80 | -1.2 | .85 | -.9 | G3—Knowledge |
| .96 | -.2 | 1.00 | .1 | G22—TextAids |
| 1.17 | 1.0 | 1.15 | .9 | G17—Figures |
| 1.12 | .8 | 1.11 | .7 | G26—Guess |
| .88 | -.8 | .87 | -.8 | G14—Decision |
| .78 | -1.4 | .80 | -1.3 | G19—Context |
| 1.27 | 1.6 | 1.26 | 1.5 | G7—Content |
| .96 | -.2 | .98 | -.1 | G4—Preview |
| .96 | -.2 | .97 | -.1 | G1—Purpose |
| .90 | -.6 | .87 | -.8 | G29—Check |
| 1.05 | .4 | 1.15 | .9 | G25—Conflicting |
| .89 | -.6 | .90 | -.5 | P21—Visualize |
| 1.00 | .0 | 1.13 | .8 | P8—Carefully |
| 1.04 | .3 | 1.02 | .2 | P27—Re-Read |
| .98 | -.1 | .96 | -.3 | P11—On-Track |
| .99 | .0 | .93 | -.3 | P16—Attention |
| .96 | -.2 | .98 | .0 | P13—Adjust |
| 1.05 | .4 | 1.11 | .7 | P30—Unknown |
| 1.23 | 1.4 | 1.17 | 1.0 | S9—Discus |
| 1.00 | .0 | 1.10 | .6 | S20—Paraphrase |
| 1.12 | .7 | 1.11 | .7 | S2—Notes |
| .74 | -1.6 | .73 | -1.7 | S15—Reference |
| .85 | -.9 | .89 | -.6 | S12—Underline |
| 1.06 | .4 | 1.13 | .8 | S28—Questions |
| .98 | -.1 | 1.05 | .3 | S6—Summarize |
| .98 | .0 | .90 | -.5 | S24—Relationships |

High school data

| INFIT MNSQ | ZSTD | OUTFIT MNSQ | ZSTD | Strategy |
|---|---|---|---|---|
| 1.07 | .6 | 1.03 | .3 | G7—Content |
| 1.11 | .8 | 1.09 | .6 | G29—Check |
| .92 | -.5 | .98 | -.1 | G1—Purpose |
| 1.14 | 1.1 | 1.13 | 1.0 | G19—Context |
| .88 | -.8 | .90 | -.7 | G26—Guess |
| .89 | -.8 | .85 | -1.1 | G3—Knowledge |
| 1.07 | .5 | 1.24 | 1.4 | P18—Stop |
| 1.12 | .8 | 1.18 | 1.1 | P8—Carefully |
| .74 | -1.8 | .73 | -1.8 | P16—Attention |
| .81 | -1.2 | .71 | -1.8 | P27—Re-Read |
| 1.23 | 1.4 | 1.13 | .8 | P11—On-Track |
| 1.08 | .5 | 1.27 | 1.6 | S15—Reference |
| .99 | .0 | .92 | -.4 | S9—Discus |
| 1.11 | .8 | 1.05 | .4 | S6—Summarize |
| 1.04 | .3 | .98 | -.1 | S12—Underline |
| 1.03 | .2 | .94 | -.3 | S24—Relationships |
| .83 | -1.2 | .83 | -1.1 | S28—Questions |
| .98 | -.1 | 1.02 | .2 | S20—Paraphrase |

College data

| INFIT MNSQ | ZSTD | OUTFIT MNSQ | ZSTD | Strategy |
|---|---|---|---|---|
| 1.01 | .2 | 1.00 | .1 | G7—Content |
| .94 | -.5 | .93 | -.6 | G26—Guess |
| .93 | -.7 | .98 | -.1 | G3—Knowledge |
| .89 | -1.0 | .89 | -1.0 | G4—Preview |
| .90 | -.9 | .87 | -1.2 | G1—Purpose |
| 1.23 | 2.0 | 1.17 | 1.5 | G23—Analyze |
| 1.20 | 1.7 | 1.17 | 1.5 | G25—Conflicting |
| .80 | -.9 | .82 | -1.6 | P30—Unknown |
| .83 | -1.8 | .88 | -1.2 | P27—Re-Read |
| .99 | -.1 | .99 | -.1 | P18—Stop |
| 1.08 | .8 | 1.10 | 1.0 | P16—Attention |
| 1.15 | 1.4 | 1.10 | 1.0 | P21—Visualize |
| .99 | .0 | 1.08 | .7 | P11—On-Track |
| 1.00 | .1 | 1.00 | .1 | S12—Underline |
| .94 | -.6 | .91 | -.8 | S2—Notes |
| .95 | -.5 | .98 | -.2 | S6—Summarize |
| 1.07 | .7 | 1.05 | .5 | S9—Discus |
| 1.03 | .3 | 1.00 | .0 | S20—Paraphrase |
| .91 | -.8 | .89 | -1.0 | S24—Relationships |
| 1.13 | 1.2 | 1.09 | .8 | S15—Reference |

# 6 | The Impact of Reading Purpose on the Use of Reading Strategies

**Kouider Mokhtari and Carla A. Reichard**
*Miami University, Ohio*

## Introduction

A review of current and established research on reading comprehension indicates that there are three closely interconnected variables or dimensions that have been shown to affect reading comprehension performance, namely, the *reader*, the *text*, and the *context* (e.g., Alexander & Jetton, 2000; Gaskins & Elliott, 1991; National Reading Panel Report, 2000; Pressley, 2000; Pressley & Gaskins, 2006; Snow, 2002; Snow & Sweet, 2003). The first key element, the reader, refers to the knowledge, abilities, and experiences (the schemata) that the person doing the reading brings to the act of reading. The second element, the text, refers to any and all texts that are read, including printed, electronic, or symbolic. The third element, the context, refers to the contextual variables (e.g., the reader's prior knowledge, purpose, and interest) that are related to the construction of meaning of the text. While researchers vary somewhat in defining the roles and contributions of each of these dimensions to reading comprehension, they concur that the reader is the central element in this transaction. The RAND Reading Study Group Report (Snow & Sweet, 2003) provides a detailed discussion of the similarities and differences among researchers with respect to the role of these three dimensions in defining reading comprehension.

In the study reported here, we focus on the ways in which readers take advantage of the reading task and context variables when engaged in the act of reading comprehension. We do this by examining how one reader attribute, namely, purpose for reading, influences students' use of reading strategies when reading for two different purposes: reading for school and reading for enjoyment. Following a brief overview of the research evidence focusing on the role of purpose for reading comprehension, we report the results of a study that was designed to examine the relationship between (i) reading purpose and metacognitive awareness and (ii) the use of reading strategies among a heterogeneous group of high school students.

# Reading Purpose and Reading Comprehension Processes

A great deal of research has focused on the effects of reader characteristics (e.g., prior knowledge, reading ability, reading purpose, and native language) on the reading comprehension processes among various types of readers, including children and adults, when reading in English as a first or a second language. For example, comprehension-monitoring processes have been found to differ as a function of students' language and reading ability levels (e.g., Anderson, 1991; Jiménez, Garcia, & Pearson, 1995; Sheorey & Mokhtari, 2001; Mokhtari & Reichard, 2004), background, domain, or topic knowledge (e.g., Afflerbach, 1990; Alexander, Pate, Kulikowich, Farrell, & Wright, 1989; Baker, 2002; Chiesi, Spilich, & Voss, 1979), as well as reading orientation or perspective (e.g., Anderson & Pichert, 1978). However, whereas these studies have focused on the differences in metacognitive control of reading processes across different types of readers, less attention has been paid to the fact that such processes might also differ within individual readers. Research focusing on individual differences in metacognition and reading has shown that skilled readers demonstrate more knowledge and control of reading processes than less skilled readers (e.g., Baker, 2005; Baker & Brown, 1984; Vellutino, 2003).

One reader characteristic that is thought to play a key role in determining intraindividual variation in the pattern of reading comprehension activity during reading is reading purpose (e.g., Anderson & Pichert, 1978; Braten & Samuelstuen, 2004; Hadwin, Winne, Stockley, Nesbitt, & Woszczyna, 2001; Lorch, Lorch, & Klusewitz, 1993; Narvaez, van der Broek, & Ruiz, 1999; Rowe & Rayford, 1987). The role of reading purpose in the comprehension process is supported by theory and research suggesting that one's orientation to, or goal for, reading text influences comprehension processes, including recall, inferential thinking, and control of reading processes. In one study, for example, Rowe and Rayford (1987) investigated readers' prior knowledge activation through answering purpose-driven questions among students in Grades 1, 6, and 10. They showed students a set of three prereading, purpose-setting questions from the Metropolitan Achievement Test and asked them to make predictions about the passage and end-of-passage comprehension questions that might go with each purpose-oriented question. They also asked students to put themselves in the test taker's position and describe what they would try to find out while reading the passage. Analysis of the students' responses to the three prereading purpose-setting questions showed that students were able to activate background knowledge under these conditions, an indication that purpose-setting questions may serve as helpful cues for activating students' background knowledge while reading. The authors suggested that teachers can facilitate student activation of background knowledge by having them answer questions before and/or while they read new material.

Lorch, Lorch, and Klusewitz (1993) studied college students' conditional knowledge about reading and its impact on strategic reading comprehension activity. They provided participants with a rich description of text types and asked them to sort them according to how they believed they read in each situation. The results indicated that college students identified a total of ten distinct reading categories or situations, including four types of school reading (i.e., required school-related reading) and six types of out-of-school reading (i.e., voluntary reading by personal choice). A particularly important point made in the study was that the participants perceived the two types of reading as quite different in their cognitive demands. When students were asked to describe their text-processing strategies in relation to the different reading types, they clearly distinguished between school reading and personal-choice reading with regard to processing demands, with school reading being perceived as less enjoyable and much more cognitively demanding than reading by personal choice. Moreover, students perceived reading in preparation for an examination to be different from the other types of school reading. Specifically, exam preparation reading was perceived to be slower and to involve more reading and rereading, memorization, attention to details, thinking, testing of understanding, and use of supports than other school reading tasks. The implication of these findings is that students modulate or adapt their reading comprehension strategies based upon text type and cognitive demands of the reading situations.

Narvaez, van den Broek, and Ruiz (1999) studied the influence of two reading purposes (namely, reading for study and reading for entertainment) on students' inference generation and comprehension performance. They asked 20 undergraduate students to read narrative and expository texts and analyzed their thinking-aloud and comprehension performance. The results showed that reading purpose did not influence reading comprehension performance but did influence strategic reading processes. Specifically, they found that readers with a study purpose produced more repetitions, more acknowledgments of knowledge breaks, and more evaluations of text content and writing than did readers with an entertainment purpose. This pattern of strategic reading was stronger for expository than for narrative text reading. They concluded that "reading purpose, and possibly text type, affects the kinds of inferences that readers generate. Hence, inferential activities are at least partially under the reader's strategic control" (Narvaez et al., 1999, p. 488). In another study designed to ascertain whether participant awareness of reading strategies was affected by reading purpose, Narvaez et al. (1999) asked participants to complete a questionnaire on metacognitive reading strategies in relation to reading for enjoyment and reading for study purposes. The authors did not find any significant differences between readers with different reading purposes in their responses to the questionnaire on reading strategies and concluded that while "the reading purpose did not affect the strategies that readers considered relevant to comprehension, the small size in this study may have contributed to the null effect" (Narvaez et al., 1999, p. 492).

Hadwin, Winne, Stockley, Nesbitt, & Woszczyna (2001) examined the extent to which three study contexts (namely, reading for learning, completing a brief essay, and studying for an exam) and diverse goals influence students' use of study strategies using a self-report questionnaire. The authors asked participants to rate the frequency with which they applied 26 study tactics, used 20 textbook features and other resources, and adopted 30 goals for studying. The results showed significant context effects in students' self-reports of study activity, indicating that students' application of study strategies, use of textbook features, and goals for studying were closely related to the context of study.

Braten and Samuelstuen (2004) examined the impact of reading purpose on different types of reading strategies that students reportedly used for learning from text. They also examined whether this effect was moderated by students' prior knowledge of the topic of the text they had read. They asked tenth-grade Norwegian students in different schools to read expository texts in three different reading purpose conditions, including (i) reading to prepare for a test, (ii) reading to write a text summary, and (iii) reading to discuss text content with peers. They found that the effect of reading purpose on reported use of memorization and elaboration strategies depended on students' level of topic knowledge. Specifically, they found that for participants who read for the purpose of discussing text content, reported use of memorization and elaboration was positively related to topic knowledge, whereas no relation between reported use of such strategies and topic knowledge was found for participants who read for the purposes of test taking or summary writing. They suggested that "students' flexible use of text-processing strategies may depend on their topic knowledge" (Braten & Samuelsten, 2004, p. 324).

Individual differences in metacognitive awareness have also been found among students varying in ability levels. Research has shown that high-ability readers tend to exhibit higher levels of metacognitive awareness about reading processes than do low-ability readers. For example, in a study aimed at examining differences in the metacognitive awareness of reading strategies among 350 U.S. and English as a second language (ESL) university students, Sheorey and Mokhtari (2001) found that both the U.S. and ESL students demonstrated a high level of awareness of nearly 30 reading strategies. They also found that U.S. female students reported a significantly higher use of reading strategies than did their male counterparts, and that the use of reading strategies was associated with higher levels of reading ability for both groups of students. These findings are consistent with other studies (e.g., Jiménez, Garcia, & Pearson, 1995, 1996), which have shown that efficient bilingual readers exhibit an awareness of a rich supply of strategies when reading in English and Spanish, and that they do make use of such strategies when reading English.

Definite answers regarding completeness and accuracy of students' cognitive processes while reading remain uncertain and should be subjected to further research and exploration. Whether students actually use the reading strategies they may have some knowledge of or profess to use depends, to a large extent, on a variety of factors, including, but not limited to, the type of material read, the reader's overall reading proficiency, and the measures used for assessing awareness and actual strategy use. As some researchers have pointed out, learning is a complex process affected by personal and contextual variables, and students' perceptions of themselves, teachers, and peers are influential during learning (e.g., Pintrich & de Groot, 1990; Pintrich, 2000); additionally, because reading is highly individual in nature, no two readers approach any reading task in exactly the same way (e.g., Baker, 2005; Anderson, 1991). Although the relationships between students' perceived self-efficacy and various cognitive and motivational outcomes have been extensively studied, with few exceptions (e.g., Kruger & Dunning, 1999; Phiffer & Glover, 1982), almost all the research work has been limited to cognitive domains, such as mathematics, and we know little about whether similar patterns of relationships hold for reading comprehension processes. Research is, therefore, needed to explore the relationships that might exist between students' perceptions of their own metacognition and reading comprehension performance. Such research will help a great deal in diagnosing students' awareness of their own reading processes, documenting their actual usage of reading strategies while reading, and teaching them to become strategic, thoughtful, and constructively responsive readers.

## The Present Study

In this study, we sought to examine the relationship of reading purpose to metacognitive awareness and use of reading strategies among a group of high school students. In light of current and established research on the influence of reader attributes, such as prior knowledge, interest, and reader orientation, we predicted that students would modify their reading strategy use depending on whether they were asked to read for school-related purposes or for entertainment purposes. Informed by research on the impact of reading ability and gender on students' reading comprehension processes, we further predicted that students' reading ability and gender would have some impact on the strategy choices students make when reading for these two purposes.

### Subjects

The participants in this study included 65 eleventh-grade students enrolled in a public school located in the midwestern United States. The students consisted of 34 males (52.3%) and 31 females (47.7%). Their ethnicities were Caucasian (89.2%), African-American (3.4%), and Hispanic (4.3%). The students ranged in age from 15 to 18 years, with a mean age of 16.03 ($SD$ = .67). School records indicated that the students shared similar linguistic, cultural, and socioeconomic backgrounds. None of the students were identified as having any specific learning or reading disability.

*Data Collection*

The materials used to collect the data for this study consisted of a 30-item instrument—the Metacognitive Awareness of Reading Strategies Inventory (MARSI; Mokhtari & Reichard, 2002), which was specifically designed for measuring students' metacognitive awareness and use of reading strategies while reading academic materials.

The MARSI measures three broad categories of strategies, including (i) global reading strategies, which can be thought of as generalized, or global, reading strategies aimed at setting the stage for the reading act (e.g., setting purpose for reading, previewing text content, predicting what the text is about, etc.); (ii) problem-solving strategies, which are localized, focused, problem-solving or repair strategies used when problems develop in understanding textual information (e.g., checking one's understanding upon encountering conflicting information, rereading for better understanding, etc.); and (iii) support reading strategies, which provide the support mechanisms or tools aimed at sustaining responsiveness to reading (e.g., use of reference materials, such as dictionaries, and other support systems). These three classes of strategies interact with and support each other when used in the process of constructing meaning from text. For a detailed description of the strategies used in the MARSI instrument and its development, see Mokhtari, Reichard, & Sheorey (chapter 4, this volume).

*Procedures*

The data for this study were collected within a 3-week period. During the first week, students were briefed about the purposes and procedures of the study and completed a demographic survey, which requested information about their age, gender, ethnicity, and perceptions of reading ability, using a scale ranging from 5 ("I am an excellent reader") to 1 ("I am a very poor reader"). Students were told that the intent of the study was to find out about what readers do when they read in general and what strategies they use when reading for different purposes, such as reading for fun or for study, and that their participation was completely voluntary.

During the second week, students completed the MARSI instrument with specific instructions to do so while reading for school purposes. They were asked to identify the strategies they use when completing assignments, such as reading an article or a book chapter in preparation for a homework assignment or an exam. In the third week, they completed the MARSI instrument a second time, with specific instructions to do so while reading materials, such as a newspaper or magazine article or story, freely and voluntarily. They were asked to read each of the strategies and identify the ones they used when reading for pleasure or entertainment purposes.

During each of the sessions, students were advised to work at their own pace and that they could take as much time as they needed to complete each of the tasks. On average, the students completed each of the tasks in about 15 minutes. Data pertaining to students' reading ability were obtained from school records, which consisted of students' performance on the Gates-MacGinite reading test, which was administered approximately 3 weeks following the completion of the above tasks.

*Data Analyses*

The data obtained were analyzed using *t*-tests as well as repeated measures analyses of variance (ANOVAs), with purpose (study vs. entertainment), gender (male vs. female), and ability (high vs. low) as independent variables, and reported strategy use as the dependent or repeated measure variables. The main variable of interest was purpose: Does reading purpose influence students' reported use of reading strategies? Gender and ability were added to check for possible interactions that may exist between students' gender and reading ability and their use of reading strategies when reading for different purposes. The predicted outcome was that there would be significant differences in strategy use as a function of reading purpose, indicating that students would adjust their strategy use depending on whether they were reading for study or for entertainment purposes.

*Results*

The results are presented in Tables 6.1–6.3. Table 6.1 presents results pertaining to whether students' purpose for reading (reading for study vs. reading for entertainment) influenced their selection of reading strategies when reading. *T*-test analyses revealed a significant difference in overall strategy use between students' reported strategy use when they read for study purposes ($M = 3.27$; $SD = .78$) and for entertainment purposes ($M = 3.09$; $SD = .78$). These data indicate that while students reported using a range of strategies when reading for both purposes, they reported using these strategies more frequently when reading for study purposes than when reading for entertainment purposes.

A closer examination of the data in Table 6.1 also shows that in general, students reported using certain types of strategies, namely, global reading strategies ($M = 3.4$ vs. 3.18) and support reading strategies ($M = 2.90$ vs. 2.66) significantly more when reading for study purposes than when reading for entertainment purposes ($p < .05$). On the other hand, while the mean reported strategy use for problem-solving strategies was slightly higher for study purposes ($M = 3.51$) than for entertainment purposes ($M = 3.44$), it did not reach significance ($p = .365$). Finally, these data show that regardless of reading purpose, students reported using the problem-solving strategies with greater frequency ($M = 3.51$ and 3.44) than the global reading strategies ($M = 3.40$ and 3.18) or the support reading strategies ($M = 2.90$ and 2.66). Individual items showing strongly significant differences included: setting a purpose for reading ($p = .001$); checking how text content fits purpose ($p = .012$); using text features (e.g., graphs) ($p = .008$); using typographical aids ($p = .020$); taking notes ($p = .001$); summarizing and reflecting ($p = .001$); underlining information in text ($p = .001$); and using reference materials ($p = .004$).

Table 6.1 Differences in Reported Strategy Use When Reading for Study and for Entertainment

| | Reading for study M (SD) | Reading for entertainment M (SD) | t (64) | P-value |
|---|---|---|---|---|
| **Global Reading Strategies** | **3.40 (.805)** | **3.18 (.838)** | **3.28** | **.002** |
| Setting purpose for reading | 4.12 (1.02) | 3.29 (1.40) | 4.83 | .001 |
| Using prior knowledge | 3.74 (1.08) | 3.49 (1.30) | 1.95 | .055 |
| Previewing text before reading | 3.62 (1.17) | 3.70 (1.28) | -.574 | .568 |
| Check how text content fits purpose | 3.31 (1.22) | 2.91 (1.20) | 2.59 | .012 |
| Skim to notice text characteristics | 3.26 (1.25) | 3.18 (1.37) | .743 | .460 |
| Decide what to read closely | 3.22 (1.21) | 2.98 (1.34) | 2.03 | .046 |
| Using text features (e.g., graphs) | 2.98 (1.30) | 2.60 (1.40) | 2.75 | .008 |
| Using context clues | 3.36 (1.24) | 3.34 (1.19) | .123 | .902 |
| Using typographical aids | 3.27 (1.29) | 2.89 (1.37) | 2.39 | .020 |
| Critically analyzing information | 3.40 (1.16) | 3.32 (1.29) | .637 | .526 |
| Checking one's understanding | 3.37 (1.07) | 3.12 (1.23) | 2.08 | .041 |
| Predicting text meaning | 3.26 (1.18) | 3.22 (1.26) | .370 | .713 |
| Checking to verify understanding | 3.31 (1.13) | 3.28 (1.22) | .341 | .735 |
| **Problem-Solving Strategies** | **3.51 (.845)** | **3.44 (.887)** | **.912** | **.365** |
| Reading slowly but carefully | 3.43 (1.17) | 3.23 (1.20) | 1.85 | .068 |
| Getting back on track while reading | 3.52 (1.12) | 3.38 (1.28) | 1.10 | .275 |
| Adjusting reading rate | 3.57 (1.10) | 3.49 (1.23) | .712 | .479 |
| Paying close attention to reading | 3.62 (1.23) | 3.42 (1.31) | 1.66 | .102 |
| Stopping and thinking about reading | 3.40 (1.27) | 3.43 (1.19) | -.265 | .792 |
| Visualizing information read | 3.72 (1.11) | 3.80 (1.18) | -.515 | .608 |
| Rereading for better understanding | 3.28 (1.21) | 3.34 (1.24) | -.475 | .636 |
| Guessing meaning of unknown words | 3.54 (1.15) | 3.49 (1.26) | .417 | .678 |
| **Support Reading Strategies** | **2.90 (.820)** | **2.66 (.802)** | **3.71** | **.001** |
| Taking notes while reading | 2.79 (1.19) | 1.59 (1.03) | 7.18 | .001 |
| Reading text aloud | 3.09 (1.48) | 3.02 (1.46) | .617 | .539 |
| Summarizing and reflecting | 3.18 (1.17) | 2.78 (1.31) | 3.46 | .001 |
| Discussing reading with others | 3.11 (1.20) | 2.82 (1.30) | 1.74 | .087 |
| Underlining information in text | 2.92 (1.23) | 2.23 (1.26) | 4.51 | .001 |
| Using reference materials | 2.62 (1.25) | 2.18 (1.14) | 2.96 | .004 |
| Paraphrasing for better understanding | 3.23 (1.20) | 2.98 (1.24) | 2.05 | .045 |
| Going back and forth in text | 3.28 (1.23) | 3.17 (1.21) | .926 | .358 |
| Asking oneself questions | 3.05 (1.11) | 3.08 (1.27) | -.299 | .766 |
| **Overall Reading Strategies** | **3.27 (.780)** | **3.09 (.781)** | **2.96** | **.004** |

Table 6.2 presents results concerning whether students' reported strategy use differed by gender. Repeated measures ANOVAs revealed no significant differences in students' strategy use as determined by gender ($p > .05$). However, this lack of significance notwithstanding, females reported using all strategies more often across all three strategy categories (i.e., global, problem-solving, and support reading strategies) than did their male counterparts when reading for study and for entertainment purposes.

Table 6.2 Effects of Reading Purpose on Reports of Strategy Use by Gender

| | Reading for study | | Reading for entertainment | | Significance tests | | |
|---|---|---|---|---|---|---|---|
| | M (n = 34) M (SD) | F (n = 30) M (SD) | M (n = 34) M (SD) | F (n = 30) M (SD) | Purpose F (1, 62) | Gender F (1, 62) | Interaction F (1, 62) |
| **Global Reading Strategies** | **3.35 (.75)** | **3.44 (.88)** | **3.06 (.84)** | **3.29 (.83)** | **10.745 (.002)** | **0.687 (.410)** | **1.145 (.289)** |
| Setting purpose for reading | 4.06 (1.04) | 4.20 (1.03) | 3.18 (1.40) | 3.40 (1.43) | 22.554 (.000) | 0.507 (.479) | 0.055 (.816) |
| Using prior knowledge | 3.71 (1.09) | 3.73 (1.08) | 3.44 (1.40) | 3.50 (1.20) | 3.714 (.059) | 0.025 (.874) | 0.015 (.904) |
| Previewing text before reading | 3.45 (1.18) | 3.73 (1.14) | 3.42 (1.30) | 3.93 (1.20) | 0.359 (.552) | 1.909 (.172) | 0.673 (.415) |
| Checking how text content fits purpose | 3.41 (1.13) | 3.17 (1.34) | 3.09 (1.11) | 2.63 (1.22) | 7.486 (.008) | 1.867 (.177) | 0.449 (.505) |
| Skimming to notice text characteristics | 3.09 (1.22) | 3.40 (1.28) | 2.97 (1.34) | 3.37 (1.38) | 0.506 (.479) | 1.319 (.255) | 0.158 (.692) |
| Deciding what to read closely | 3.15 (1.18) | 3.27 (1.26) | 2.85 (1.40) | 3.13 (1.31) | 3.437 (.068) | 0.440 (.510) | 0.486 (.488) |
| Using text features (e.g., graphs) | 2.94 (1.27) | 3.03 (1.38) | 2.61 (1.46) | 2.59 (1.38) | 7.594 (.008) | 0.014 (.907) | 0.164 (.687) |
| Using context clues | 3.29 (1.22) | 3.47 (1.25) | 3.18 (1.19) | 3.57 (1.17) | 0.007 (.935) | 0.984 (.325) | 0.730 (.396) |
| Using typographical aids | 3.21 (1.19) | 3.30 (1.42) | 2.76 (1.37) | 3.00 (1.37) | 5.542 (.022) | 0.306 (.582) | 0.232 (.631) |
| Critically analyzing information | 3.47 (1.08) | 3.33 (1.27) | 3.21 (1.30) | 3.43 (1.31) | 0.468 (.497) | 0.025 (.875) | 2.293 (.135) |
| Checking one's understanding | 3.26 (1.02) | 3.50 (1.14) | 2.94 (1.13) | 3.27 (1.31) | 5.802 (.019) | 1.130 (.292) | 0.152 (.698) |
| Predicting text meaning | 3.21 (1.04) | 3.27 (1.31) | 2.91 (1.24) | 3.50 (1.20) | 0.060 (.807) | 1.411 (.239) | 4.549 (.037) |
| Checking to verify understanding | 3.26 (1.08) | 3.33 (1.21) | 3.15 (1.21) | 3.45 (1.24) | 0.068 (.796) | 0.535 (.467) | 0.996 (.322) |
| **Problem-Solving Strategies** | **3.46 (.83)** | **3.54 (.88)** | **3.38 (.94)** | **3.50 (.84)** | **0.830 (.366)** | **0.220 (.640)** | **0.110 (.741)** |
| Reading slowly but carefully | 3.44 (1.19) | 3.37 (1.16) | 3.12 (1.23) | 3.30 (1.15) | 3.180 (.079) | 0.038 (.845) | 1.378 (.245) |
| Getting back on track while reading | 3.50 (1.05) | 3.50 (1.20) | 3.12 (1.27) | 3.63 (1.25) | 0.996 (.322) | 0.901 (.346) | 4.273 (.043) |
| Adjusting reading rate | 3.62 (1.05) | 3.47 (1.17) | 3.53 (1.21) | 3.40 (1.25) | 0.488 (.488) | 0.268 (.606) | 0.009 (.923) |
| Paying close attention to reading | 3.56 (1.28) | 3.67 (1.21) | 3.35 (1.32) | 3.47 (1.33) | 2.697 (.106) | 0.138 (.712) | 0.001 (.981) |
| Stopping and thinking about reading | 3.38 (1.26) | 3.47 (1.31) | 3.47 (1.16) | 3.43 (1.22) | 0.053 (.818) | 0.007 (.935) | 0.262 (.610) |
| Visualizing information read | 3.53 (1.05) | 3.93 (1.16) | 3.71 (1.19) | 3.83 (1.23) | 0.209 (.649) | 1.442 (.234) | 0.462 (.499) |
| Rereading for better understanding | 3.21 (1.15) | 3.33 (1.30) | 3.35 (1.30) | 3.27 (1.17) | 0.094 (.761) | 0.005 (.941) | 0.662 (.419) |
| Guessing meaning of unknown words | 3.47 (1.08) | 3.60 (1.25) | 3.35 (1.35) | 3.63 (1.16) | 0.139 (.710) | 0.528 (.470) | 0.446 (.507) |
| **Support Reading Strategies** | **2.82 (.78)** | **3.00 (.88)** | **2.51 (.77)** | **2.81 (.83)** | **12.884 (.001)** | **1.523 (.222)** | **0.893 (.348)** |
| Taking notes while reading | 2.71 (1.27) | 2.90 (1.09) | 1.44 (.860) | 1.79 (1.20) | 47.420 (.000) | 1.353 (.249) | 0.209 (.649) |
| Reading text aloud | 2.91 (1.51) | 3.27 (1.46) | 2.85 (1.50) | 3.17 (1.44) | 0.386 (.537) | 0.925 (.340) | 0.026 (.873) |
| Summarizing and reflecting | 3.18 (.999) | 3.17 (1.38) | 2.71 (1.27) | 2.87 (1.38) | 10.713 (.002) | 0.067 (.797) | 0.525 (.471) |
| Discussing reading with others | 3.21 (1.18) | 3.00 (1.26) | 2.85 (1.37) | 2.70 (1.18) | 3.759 (.057) | 0.461 (.500) | 0.025 (.876) |
| Underlining information in text | 2.71 (1.14) | 3.10 (1.27) | 2.00 (1.18) | 2.47 (1.33) | 18.456 (.000) | 2.630 (.110) | 0.054 (.817) |
| Using reference materials | 2.65 (1.23) | 2.50 (1.23) | 2.12 (1.15) | 2.27 (1.17) | 7.201 (.009) | 0.000 (.997) | 1.085 (.302) |
| Paraphrasing for better understanding | 3.12 (1.12) | 3.37 (1.30) | 2.76 (1.18) | 3.23 (1.31) | 3.945 (.051) | 1.627 (.207) | 0.805 (.373) |
| Going back and forth in text | 3.26 (1.24) | 3.33 (1.24) | 3.06 (1.18) | 3.33 (1.24) | 0.754 (.389) | 0.368 (.546) | 0.754 (.389) |
| Asking oneself questions | 2.88 (1.07) | 3.23 (1.17) | 2.79 (1.27) | 3.33 (1.18) | 0.003 (.953) | 2.586 (.113) | 0.888 (.350) |
| **Overall Reading Strategies** | **3.21 (.74)** | **3.32 (.83)** | **2.98 (.79)** | **3.20 (.77)** | **8.451 (.005)** | **0.784 (.379)** | **0.772 (.383)** |

Table 6.3 presents results concerning whether students' reported strategy use differed by reading ability. An examination of these data using repeated measures ANOVAs revealed no significant differences in students' strategy use as determined by reading ability ($p > .05$). While these differences were not statistically significant, less skilled readers reported using nearly all the strategies they identified more often across all three strategy categories (i.e., global, problem-solving, and support reading strategies) than did their higher skilled reader counterparts when reading for study and for entertainment purposes.

## Discussion

In this study, we sought to ascertain the extent to which a group of eleventh-grade students adjust their strategic reading activity based upon whether they read for school or for entertainment purposes. The results revealed three important findings. First, the participants' reports indicate that reading purpose plays an important role in their use of reading strategies. When reading for study purposes, they were more likely to use reading strategies more frequently than when reading for fun or entertainment purposes. A close examination of the patterns of strategy use (see Table 6.1) further suggests that students were likely to use "global" and "support" reading strategies significantly less frequently when reading for fun than when reading for study purposes. However, they reported using "problem-solving" strategies to the same degree regardless of reading purpose.

The above patterns of strategy use appear to be consistent with findings from Lorch et al. (1993), whose subjects reported finding school reading to be more challenging than reading for fun. We concur that in terms of processing demands, school reading is often required, not voluntary, and can be perceived as less enjoyable and more cognitively demanding than reading by personal choice. Consequently, it requires a greater degree of intensity and is likely to require readers to invoke a larger variety of reading strategies than reading for entertainment.

Students in this study reported using problem-solving strategies (e.g., reading slowly but carefully, getting back on track while reading, stopping and thinking about reading, and rereading for better understanding) to the same degree regardless of reading purpose. One possible explanation for this usage is that while a particular purpose for reading may influence the overall frequency or volume of strategy use, it does not seem to have a significant impact on the type of strategies that are invoked when reading for understanding (Lorch, Lorch, & Klusewitz, 1993). It is also conceivable that reading purpose influences how the reader allocates his or her attention while reading and hence what type of strategies are invoked. For example, the cognitive demands expected in summarizing the content of a chapter in a science textbook might result in slower reading and a greater use of a number of reading strategies than would reading a news story in a popular magazine. It is also conceivably possible that the influence of reading purpose on reports

Table 6.3 Impact of Reading Purpose on Reports of Strategy Use as a Function of Reading Ability

| | Reading for study | | Reading for entertainment | | Significance tests | | |
|---|---|---|---|---|---|---|---|
| | High (n = 23) M (SD) | Low (n = 23) M (SD) | High (n = 23) M (SD) | Low (n = 23) M (SD) | Purpose F (1, 44) | Ability F (1, 44) | Interaction F (1, 44) |
| **Global Reading Strategies** | **3.30 (.89)** | **3.47 (.69)** | **3.14 (.87)** | **3.32 (.67)** | **4.155 (.048)** | **0.647 (.425)** | **0.002 (.964)** |
| Setting purpose for reading | 4.00 (1.00) | 4.26 (.86) | 3.22 (1.48) | 3.43 (1.24) | 16.530 (.000) | 0.720 (.401) | 0.012 (.913) |
| Using prior knowledge | 3.39 (1.20) | 4.04 (.93) | 3.30 (1.43) | 3.91 (1.04) | 0.564 (.457) | 4.108 (.049) | 0.023 (.881) |
| Previewing text before reading | 3.77 (1.11) | 3.43 (1.27) | 3.59 (1.22) | 3.74 (1.25) | 0.110 (.741) | 0.151 (.700) | 2.086 (.156) |
| Checking how text content fits purpose | 3.13 (1.25) | 3.52 (1.12) | 2.74 (1.05) | 3.04 (1.22) | 5.087 (.029) | 1.491 (.229) | 0.051 (.823) |
| Skimming to notice text characteristics | 2.78 (1.24) | 3.35 (1.27) | 2.91 (1.35) | 3.30 (1.33) | 0.139 (.711) | 1.727 (.196) | 0.555 (.460) |
| Deciding what to read closely | 3.00 (1.28) | 3.48 (1.12) | 2.78 (1.54) | 3.26 (1.14) | 2.402 (.128) | 1.864 (.179) | 0.000 (1.00) |
| Using text features (e.g., graphs) | 3.23 (1.23) | 2.91 (1.35) | 2.77 (1.41) | 2.52 (1.41) | 6.535 (.014) | 0.590 (.446) | 0.037 (.849) |
| Using context clues | 3.39 (1.27) | 3.22 (1.28) | 3.61 (1.41) | 3.41 (1.22) | 3.323 (.075) | 0.270 (.606) | 0.026 (.872) |
| Using typographical aids | 3.14 (1.28) | 3.35 (1.40) | 2.87 (1.29) | 3.13 (1.60) | 1.752 (.193) | 0.401 (.530) | 0.022 (.882) |
| Critically analyzing information | 3.17 (1.27) | 3.48 (1.04) | 3.17 (1.37) | 3.61 (1.12) | 0.249 (.620) | 1.251 (.270) | 0.249 (.620) |
| Checking one's understanding | 3.39 (1.12) | 3.39 (.89) | 3.35 (1.30) | 3.13 (1.06) | 1.190 (.281) | 0.137 (.713) | 0.607 (.440) |
| Predicting text meaning | 3.26 (1.18) | 3.13 (1.14) | 3.22 (1.20) | 3.22 (1.24) | 0.019 (.891) | 0.043 (.836) | 0.170 (.683) |
| Checking to verify understanding | 3.13 (1.06) | 3.52 (1.04) | 3.26 (1.18) | 3.45 (1.01) | 0.001 (.981) | 1.243 (.271) | 1.179 (.284) |
| **Problem-Solving Strategies** | **3.44 (.98)** | **3.61 (.60)** | **3.47 (.95)** | **3.65 (.64)** | **0.162 (.689)** | **0.565 (.456)** | **0.001 (.971)** |
| Reading slowly but carefully | 3.57 (1.34) | 3.30 (1.11) | 3.17 (1.34) | 3.30 (1.11) | 2.820 (.100) | 0.036 (.850) | 2.820 (.100) |
| Getting back on track while reading | 3.57 (.99) | 3.87 (.92) | 3.39 (1.16) | 3.83 (1.07) | 0.476 (.494) | 1.977 (.167) | 0.171 (.681) |
| Adjusting reading rate | 3.39 (1.23) | 3.74 (.86) | 3.57 (1.34) | 3.61 (1.08) | 0.024 (.878) | 0.407 (.527) | 1.174 (.284) |
| Paying close attention to reading | 3.48 (1.28) | 3.78 (1.09) | 3.30 (1.49) | 3.83 (.89) | 0.194 (.661) | 1.633 (.208) | 0.540 (.466) |
| Stopping and thinking about reading | 3.17 (1.40) | 3.30 (1.19) | 3.35 (1.27) | 3.52 (1.12) | 1.793 (.187) | 0.203 (.655) | 0.022 (.882) |
| Visualizing information read | 3.57 (1.20) | 3.91 (.85) | 3.87 (1.14) | 3.91 (1.08) | 0.887 (.352) | 0.513 (.478) | 0.887 (.352) |
| Rereading for better understanding | 3.30 (1.22) | 3.30 (1.11) | 3.61 (1.23) | 3.43 (1.16) | 2.200 (.145) | 0.076 (.785) | 0.352 (.556) |
| Guessing meaning of unknown words | 3.52 (1.12) | 3.70 (.93) | 3.52 (1.20) | 3.74 (.92) | 0.035 (.851) | 0.465 (.499) | 0.035 (.851) |
| **Support Reading Strategies** | **2.80 (.84)** | **2.92 (.65)** | **2.63 (.86)** | **2.63 (.63)** | **8.546 (.005)** | **0.085 (.772)** | **0.732 (.397)** |
| Taking notes while reading | 2.91 (1.20) | 2.70 (1.11) | 1.57 (.99) | 1.45 (.86) | 56.170 (.000) | 0.421 (.520) | 0.123 (.727) |
| Reading text aloud | 3.00 (1.48) | 3.09 (1.41) | 3.17 (1.37) | 3.04 (1.49) | 0.305 (.584) | 0.003 (.958) | 0.846 (.363) |
| Summarizing and reflecting | 3.13 (1.06) | 3.22 (1.17) | 2.74 (1.42) | 2.74 (1.20) | 8.462 (.006) | 0.019 (.892) | 0.085 (.773) |
| Discussing reading with others | 2.96 (1.33) | 3.17 (.94) | 2.83 (1.37) | 2.57 (1.12) | 2.938 (.094) | 0.006 (.939) | 1.230 (.273) |
| Underlining information in text | 3.00 (1.24) | 3.00 (1.31) | 2.30 (1.30) | 2.17 (1.37) | 17.707 (.000) | 0.037 (.849) | 0.130 (.720) |
| Using reference materials | 2.17 (1.15) | 2.83 (.98) | 1.83 (1.07) | 2.35 (.94) | 5.316 (.026) | 5.565 (.023) | 0.133 (.718) |
| Paraphrasing for better understanding | 3.17 (1.19) | 3.22 (1.00) | 3.00 (1.24) | 2.96 (1.19) | 3.716 (.060) | 0.000 (1.00) | 0.149 (.702) |
| Going back and forth in text | 3.17 (1.19) | 3.17 (1.23) | 3.22 (1.13) | 3.13 (1.14) | 0.000 (1.00) | 0.018 (.895) | 0.148 (.703) |
| Asking oneself questions | 3.00 (1.21) | 3.09 (1.04) | 3.04 (1.36) | 3.13 (1.29) | 0.101 (.752) | 0.067 (.797) | 0.000 (1.00) |
| **Overall Reading Strategies** | **3.17 (.86)** | **3.33 (.61)** | **3.08 (.84)** | **3.19 (.57)** | **3.030 (.089)** | **0.440 (.511)** | **0.092 (.763)** |

of strategic text processing may depend on students' topic knowledge and the type of reading assignment at hand. This question was recently explored by Braten and Samuelstuen (2004), who found a significant relationship between students' reported use of certain types of strategies and their level of topic knowledge. However, while students' use of certain strategies (e.g., memorization and elaboration) depended on how well they knew the topic, the use of other strategies (e.g., test taking or summary writing) did not.

The second finding related to whether reported strategy use is impacted by students' gender. Using repeated measures ANOVAs with interaction terms, we found that students' gender did not have any influence on their ability to adjust their strategy use depending on reading purpose. While female students had a tendency to invoke a greater number of reading strategies when reading for either purpose than male students, no significant differences were found in the ways they modulated their strategy use across reading purposes. It is conceivable that students' use of reading strategies is moderated not so much by their gender as by their level of awareness of the cognitive and metacognitive processes involved in text comprehension. This finding is consistent with early research on metacognition and reading, indicating that older, mature students have more knowledge and control of their reading processes than younger students. The consistent pattern in this early research (see Baker, this volume) is that that younger readers have little awareness that they must attempt to make sense of text; they focus on reading as a decoding process, rather than as a meaning-getting process (Baker & Brown, 1984; Garner, 1987).

The third important finding of this study pertains to whether the influence of reading purpose was related to students' reading ability. Again using repeated measures ANOVAs with interaction terms, we found that students' reading ability did not have any influence on their tendency to adjust their strategy use depending on reading purpose. In other words, both the skilled and less skilled readers students reported modulating their strategy use when reading for study as well as for entertainment. This finding appears to be inconsistent with prior research which focused on individual differences in metacognition, typically involving comparisons of better and poorer readers, with better readers demonstrating more knowledge and control of reading than poorer readers (Baker & Brown, 1984; Baker, 2005). This finding may be explained by the fact that students are able to distinguish between reading for study, which is required and often more cognitively demanding, and reading for fun, which is often voluntary and, therefore, perceived to be less demanding.

## Conclusion

The findings of this study should be interpreted with caution as they pertain to students' reported, not actual, use of reading strategies when reading for study and for entertainment purposes. We should note that we examined students' perceived, rather than actual, strategy use to vary across two different reading purposes. Presumably, students' ability to modify their text-processing strategies according to reading purpose may be quite different when asked to report on their strategy use while reading or in the context of recently completed reading tasks. A discussion of the differences between perceived general versus perceived specific use of reading strategies when reading for school purposes can be found in the next chapter.

# 7 | Metacognitive Awareness and Use of Reading Strategies among Adolescent Readers

**Kouider Mokhtari and Carla A. Reichard**
*Miami University, Ohio*

**Ravi Sheorey**
*Oklahoma State University*

## Introduction

Research within the domains of cognition and reading comprehension has led to an increasing emphasis on the role of metacognitive awareness and control of one's cognitive and motivational processes while engaged in cognitive tasks such as reading (e.g., Flavell, 1979; Garner, 1987; Pressley, 2000; Schunk, 1992). This research has contributed a great deal to our understanding of students' cognitive and metacognitive strategy development. It has also shed a new light on the influence in classrooms of student perceptions of their metacognitive knowledge, cognitive skills, and reading strategies; we define the latter as systematic cognitive plans that assist in the acquisition of information and task performance.

Research conducted over the past two decades indicates that several important variables (e.g., linguistic knowledge, content knowledge, cognitive and metacognitive knowledge about reading, etc.) account for variability in reading comprehension among mature and developing readers. One critically important source of variability in reading comprehension is a reader's perception of how competent he or she is as a reader. According to members of the RAND Reading Study Group (Snow, 2001), for developing and mature readers: "It is the belief in the self (or lack of such a belief) that makes a difference in how competent they feel" (p. 22). The RAND Reading Study Group summarized research on the relationship between self-perceived individual capabilities and comprehension outcomes, indicating that "providing those who are experiencing reading difficulties with clear goals for a reading comprehension task and then giving them feedback on the progress they are making can lead to increased self-efficacy and a greater use of comprehension strategies" (p. 22).

There is considerable consensus among researchers that variation in reader characteristics can be used to partially explain differences in reading comprehension performance. The process of reading is greatly influenced by the beliefs, attitudes, and values that readers possess. We know from research that what learners believe and know about their own abilities and skills may affect whether they succeed or fail in school (Paris &

Winograd, 1990). Students' beliefs cannot be ignored, since beliefs often lead to actions consonant with those beliefs. Indeed, the development of metacognitive beliefs about reading and the understanding of the parameters and complexities involved in reading tend to develop whenever and wherever students receive instruction in reading.

In recent years, researchers have investigated the importance of metacognitive awareness as a condition for thoughtful, constructively responsive reading by first- (L1) and second-0language (L2) learners. This research has shown that important reading strategies which deal with planning, controlling, and evaluating one's understanding while reading (e.g., setting purpose for reading, prediction, summarization, questioning, use of text structural features, self-monitoring, etc.) are widely used by L1 and L2 readers (Sheorey & Mokhtari, 2001). In addition, the supply of reading strategies used by L2 readers often includes some strategies (e.g., translation and use of cognates) that may be unique and particularly useful to different types of, and purposes for, reading. For instance, the reading strategies used when reading to study for a test may be quite different from those used when reading for recreational purposes.

This research has also shown that students' metacognitive awareness and use of reading strategies for planning, regulating, and evaluating text understanding are quite effective in improving reading comprehension (e.g., Alexander & Jetton, 2000; Baker & Brown, 1984; Devine, 1993; Garner, 1987; Jiménez, Garcia, & Pearson, 1995, 1996; Kletzien, 1991; Paris, Lipson, & Wixon, 1994; Pressley, 2000; Pressley, Beard El-Dinary, & Brown, 1992; Sheorey & Mokhtari, 2001). As a result, metacognition has been considered an important domain for literacy research and assessment, and it is increasingly being incorporated into academic or content-area reading instruction. Awareness of one's cognitive processes while reading has been found to be a useful tool for learners across various cognitive domains, in that learners with high levels of awareness are better able to organize what they know and use that knowledge to learn what they need to know.

Individual differences in metacognitive awareness have been found among students who were varying in ability levels. Research has shown that high-ability readers tend to exhibit higher levels of metacognitive awareness about reading processes than do low-ability readers. For example, in a recent study aimed at examining differences in the metacognitive awareness of reading strategies among 350 U.S. and English as a second language (ESL) university students, Sheorey and Mokhtari (2001) found that both U.S. and ESL students demonstrated a high level of awareness of nearly 30 reading strategies. They also found that U.S. female students reported a significantly higher usage of reading strategies than did their male counterparts, and that the use of reading strategies was associated with higher levels of reading ability for both groups of students. These findings are consistent with other studies (e.g., Jiménez, Garcia, & Pearson, 1995, 1996) that have shown that efficient bilingual readers exhibit an awareness of a rich supply of strategies when reading in English and another language, and that they do make use of such strategies when reading in English.

Support for the above research findings comes from a particularly active area of research concerned with the development of students' achievement self-perceptions and the role of these perceptions in cognitive domains, such as mathematics. This rather extensive area of research, which has grown quite rapidly during the past three decades, has shown that student "perceived self-efficacy" or beliefs about their abilities and skills in various domains are related to their academic achievement, persistence, and task engagement. Perceived self-efficacy, as used in the literature, refers to "judgments of one's capabilities to organize and implement actions necessary to attain designated performance" (Schunk, 1992, p. 8). Researchers in this area tend to differ in the theoretical perspectives, research assumptions, constructs, and measurements criteria used to study these constructs. However, they share at least two important assumptions, namely, that (i) students' academic performance represents a complex process that is influenced by various perceptions and cognitions and that (ii) student self-perceptions may be quite useful in explaining differences in achievement-related outcomes beyond the effects of student abilities and classroom-related factors (Schunk, 1992; an in-depth analysis is available in Schunk & Meece, 1992). Although there are various types of student perceptions that operate in the classroom (e.g., perceptions of self, others, and classroom-related tasks), we emphasize in this chapter only one major type of perception—namely, students' beliefs regarding their metacognitive reading processes—as it is central to reading comprehension performance. Research on the development of student achievement has shown that student-perceived self-efficacy can explain ability and gender differences in various areas, including thoughtful, reflective learning, academic help-seeking, and overall academic performance. We know from research that there is a strong, positive relationship between students' self-perceptions of their abilities and their willingness to seek academic help to obtain information relevant to learning. For instance, Newman and Schwager (cited in Schunk, 1992) provide a helpful summary of an extensive body of research in this area, indicating that academic help seeking depends on perceptions of ability, classroom control, and learning goals. In other words, students who perceive themselves as academically competent tend to view help seeking as an effective learning strategy.

In a recent study, Schmeck (2000) synthesized research findings on thoughtful learners—namely, students who engage in highly reflective or "deep and elaborative information processing" (p. 79). Consistent with other work, Schmeck and his colleagues (e.g., Meier, McCarthy, & Schmeck, 1984) found that reflective students have more highly developed and integrated self-concepts and tend to be more accurate at estimating their own cognitive skills. In addition, they "tend to have high self-efficacy, self-esteem, and self-assertion, as well as an internal locus of control, low anxiety, and low fear of failure" (p. 89). The authors concluded that students who are high on reflecting on their beliefs and/or actions are generally more self-aware, and "know themselves better" than less reflective students. These findings have been supported by reading researchers whose research has shown that skilled readers are not only "thoughtfully literate" (Allington, 2000), but they also engage in highly reflective "constructively responsive" reading (Pressley & Afflerbach, 1995). In another study, Zimmerman and Martinez-Ponz (1992) explored the relationship between self-efficacy and learning strategy usage during self-regulated learning. The authors reviewed research indicating that students differ in efficacy and strategy use as a function of academic ability and grade level. In other words, they found that academically competent students report greater use of effective learning strategies and hold higher perceived self-efficacy when compared to less academically able students. Zimmerman and Martinez-Ponz agree with other researchers (e.g., Paris, Newman, & McVey, 1982), suggesting that "one of the most important accomplishments during children's cognitive development is the acquisition of learning strategies" (p. 190), which enable them to control and regulate cognitive resources when solving problems. According to Schunk (1992), children begin to perceive ability as a factor of underlying performance around the third grade and that students show an increase in strategy use and self-efficacy from the fifth to the eleventh grade.

The research reviewed above has shown that students' perceived self-efficacy is strongly associated with students' academic performance. However, it should be noted that some researchers, who have argued that people tend to hold overly favorable views of their abilities in many social and intellectual domains, have recently questioned the reliability of students' perceptions of their metacognitive knowledge, skills, and abilities. For example, in four related studies, aimed at exploring why people tend to hold overly optimistic and miscalibrated views about their own abilities and skills, Kruger and Dunning (1999) found that subjects performing poorly on tests of humor, grammar, and logic grossly overestimated their test performance and overall ability. The authors noted that unskilled readers are unaware that they are unskilled. They tend to have difficulties in recognizing their own incompetence, which leads to inflated self-assessments of their own reading abilities. They state:

> This overestimation occurs, in part, because people who are unskilled in these domains suffer a dual burden: Not only do these people reach erroneous conclusions and make unfortunate choices, but their incompetence robs them of the metacognitive ability to realize it. (p. 1121)

These observations appear to be consistent with findings from other researchers who have found that people are generally poor at accurately estimating how able they are at specific cognitive tasks, such as reading. For instance, Phiffer and Glover (1982), who investigated the metacognitive knowledge and use of reading strategies by college students, found that "students did not consistently apply the metacognitive strategies they professed to use or they were not proficient in applying them" (p. 194). We suggest that whether students actually use the reading strategies they profess to use depends, to a large extent, on a variety of factors, such as the type of material read, the reader's overall reading proficiency, and the measures used for assessing awareness and actual strategy use. Although the relationships between students' perceived self-efficacy and various cognitive and motivational outcomes have been extensively studied, with few exceptions (namely, Kruger & Dunning, 1999; Phiffer & Glover, 1982), almost all the research work has been limited to cognitive domains, such as mathematics, and we know little about whether similar patterns of relationships hold for reading comprehension processes. Research is, therefore, needed to explore the relationships that might exist between students' perceptions of their own metacognition and reading comprehension performance. This chapter attempts to respond to that need. The research study we report here sought to examine the individual differences in perceived (or professed) versus specific use of reading strategies among adolescent readers. The following two research questions are used to conceptualize the relationship between students' perceived and specific use of reading strategies when reading for academic purposes:

1. Are there any significant differences between perceived general and specific reading strategy use by high school students?
2. Do the discrepancies in perceived general and specific reading strategy use vary by gender?

# Method

## Subjects

The participants in this study were 51 high school students who were enrolled in a public school located in the midwestern United States. The sample included 22 males (43%) and 29 females (57%), with the great majority (98%) being Caucasian native English speakers. The students ranged in age from 16 to 19 years, and the mean age of the group was 17.5 ($SD = 17.34$). School records indicated that the students shared similar linguistic, cultural, and socioeconomic backgrounds. None of the students were identified as having any specific learning or reading disability. The subjects were enrolled in three sections of a 1-year-long high school business class, which was a part of the overall school curriculum.

## Study Materials

The materials used to collect the data for this study consisted of (i) a 30-item instrument—the Metacognitive Awareness of Reading Strategies Inventory[1] (MARSI; Mokhtari & Reichard, 2002)—which is specifically designed for measuring students' metacognitive awareness and use of reading strategies while reading academic materials, and (ii) a set of readings—two intact textbook chapters (approximately 3,000 words) selected from the students' regularly assigned class readings. A complete

---

1. See chapter 4 (this volume) for a copy of this instrument.

description of the strategies used in the MARSI instrument and its development can be found in Mokhtari, Sheorey and Reichard (this volume, chapter 4).

A modified version of the MARSI instrument (referred to hereafter as MARSI Version 2) was created for students to use when indicating which reading strategies they actually used when reading the assigned textbook chapters (i.e., specific use). The only difference between the published MARSI and MARSI Version 2 is that the latter specifies the reading material, in its directions and in the items, to refer to the textbook chapters used in this study.

The assigned reading materials included two intact chapters from a textbook published by McGraw-Hill (Farese, Kimbrell, & Woloszyk, 1997), which was used by the students in a marketing class. The two selected chapters, entitled "The Global Marketplace" and "World Economies," respectively, were divided into three major sections and deal with various related issues, including import and exports, economic interdependence between nations, international trade, different types of market economies, and business involvement in international trade. The chapters were comparable in length (approximately 14 pages each), with an average grade-level equivalent of 10.8, as estimated by the Flesch-Kincaid Readability formula. The information in each of the chapters resembled standard textbook material in terms of textual features, such as text type, headings, boldface type, and other elements. In addition to regular text, each chapter included two to three tables, graphs, boxes, and a short case study. The chapters were assigned to be read and discussed in class following a regular class schedule.

*Data Collection*

The data for this study were collected during a 3-week period. During the first week, students were told about the purposes of the study and were asked to provide demographic information, such as age, gender, ethnicity, and self-perceptions of reading ability. In addition, they completed the MARSI instrument, which was used to assess their perceived use of reading strategies. The MARSI instrument was administered to the subjects at the beginning of each class period, with the help of the classroom instructor, who was quite familiar with the purposes of the study. The students were instructed to read each statement in the inventory and circle the number that best described their response to each statement. They were also advised to work at their own pace and to keep in mind their reading of academic or school-related materials while responding to the strategy statements. Finally, they were told that there were no right or wrong responses to the statements, and that they could take as much time as they needed to complete the inventory. On average, the students completed this task in about 10–12 minutes.

For the second week's task, the subjects were instructed to read a book chapter. In connection with the reading of the book chapter, the subjects participated in two related tasks: The first task was designed to check the students' comprehension of what they had read; the second was to determine what specific strategies were actually used while reading the assigned chapter. Immediately following the completion of the chapter reading, the subjects were instructed to indicate which strategies they actually used when reading the assigned textbook chapter by completing Version 2 of the MARSI instrument. The strategy statements in this version of the instrument were stated in the past tense, allowing the subjects to indicate which strategies they *actually did use*, and to rate how often they actually used the strategies while reading the chapters, using a scale from 1 ("rarely or never used") to 5 ("always or almost always used"). Finally, the subjects were instructed to provide a written summary of the main ideas in the chapter read. This task took approximately 20 minutes. The tasks completed during week 2 (namely, chapter reading, written summary, and responding to MARSI Version 2) were replicated during week 3 using a similar reading activity in an attempt to provide corroboration of data relative to perceived versus specific use of reading strategies while reading academic materials. The written summaries of chapters were used to verify that students had actually read the chapters. Two students provided no usable summaries and their strategy use data were excluded from all analyses.

*Data Analyses*

The analyses consisted of descriptive statistics and correlations, as well as analysis of variance (ANOVA) with repeated measures, which were conducted to examine whether there were any significant between-group differences regarding their perceived general and perceived specific reading strategy usage when reading academic materials (Research Question #1). Similar procedures were used to determine whether differences in perceived general versus perceived specific strategy use were found by gender (Research Question #2).

# Results

The data obtained were analyzed using repeated measures ANOVAs, with gender and reading ability as independent variables. The subjects' perceived general and perceived specific strategy use were used as repeated measures—each subject provided one perceived general strategy use rating before reading and two perceived specific strategy use ratings immediately following the completion of assigned reading. The main variables of interest were perceived general and perceived specific strategy use: Did the subjects' perceived general strategy use differ significantly from their perceived specific use when reading? In addition, gender and ability were checked for any possible interactions: Did the subjects' perceived general and perceived specific strategy use vary by gender and reading ability?

The results obtained are presented in Tables 7.1–7.3. Tables 7.1 and 7.2 contain data pertaining to whether the subjects' perceived general strategy use differed significantly from their perceived specific strategy use. The data also pertain to differences in perceived general versus perceived specific strategy use by gender. The students' perceived general and perceived specific strategy use were analyzed for overall strategy usage as well as for strategy usage within each of the categories or subscales (i.e., global reading strategies, problem-solving strategies, and support strategies).

Table 7.1 Means and Standard Deviations for Perceived General and Perceived Specific Strategy Use by Gender

| Strategy category | Perceived general use M (SD) | Perceived specific use 1 M (SD) | Perceived specific use 2 M (SD) |
|---|---|---|---|
| Global reading strategies | 2.80 (.81) | 2.64 (.81) | 2.56 (.78) |
| Male | 2.98 (.70) | 2.93 (.74) | 2.80 (.79) |
| Female | 2.66 (.87) | 2.41 (.80) | 2.38 (.74) |
| | | | |
| Problem-solving strategies | 3.22 (.74) | 2.80 (.86) | 2.65 (.87) |
| Male | 3.32 (.57) | 3.02 (.63) | 2.83 (.84) |
| Female | 3.13 (.85) | 2.63 (.98) | 2.52 (.88) |
| | | | |
| Support reading strategies | 2.43 (.72) | 2.00 (.80) | 2.19 (.87) |
| Male | 2.56 (.69) | 2.28 (.74) | 2.57 (.92) |
| Female | 2.33 (.74) | 1.78 (.78) | 1.90 (.71) |
| | | | |
| Overall reading strategies | 2.82 (.70) | 2.48 (.75) | 2.47 (.78) |
| Male | 2.96 (.60) | 2.75 (.64) | 2.73 (.80) |
| Female | 2.71 (.76) | 2.27 (.76) | 2.26 (.71) |

The repeated measures ANOVA results, presented in Table 7.2, revealed significant differences between perceived general and perceived specific use for overall strategy use ($F[2, 98] = 13.08$; $p = .001$), as well as for each of the strategy categories, namely, global reading strategies ($F[2, 98] = 4.52$; $p = .014$), problem-solving strategies ($F[2, 98] = 13.81$; $p = .001$), and support reading strategies ($F[2, 98] = 12.53$; $p = .001$). Post-hoc analyses highlighted a significant difference between the general strategy-use mean ($M = 2.81$; $SD = .81$) and each of the perceived specific strategy-use means—first perceived specific-use mean ($M = 2.64$; $SD = .81$) and second perceived specific-use mean ($M = 2.56$; $SD = .78$)—see Table 7.1 for details. These results show a significant discrepancy between the subjects' self-perceptions of their own metacognitive awareness of reading strategies when thinking of generalized academic materials and their perceived specific usage of such strategies when completing assigned reading materials (see Fig. 7.1 for details).

Table 7.2 ANOVA with Repeated Measures Analysis for Perceived Strategy Variation, Gender, and Perceived Strategy by Gender Interaction

| Effect | SS | df | MS | F | P > F |
|---|---|---|---|---|---|
| **Strategy**[**] | | | | | |
| Global reading strategies | 1.37 | 2 | .70 | 4.52 | .014 |
| Problem-solving strategies | 8.22 | 2 | 4.11 | 13.81 | .001 |
| Support reading strategies | 4.35 | 2 | 2.29 | 12.53 | .001 |
| Overall reading strategies | 3.60 | 2 | 1.80 | 13.08 | .001 |
| | | | | | |
| **Gender**[**] | | | | | |
| Global reading strategies | 6.71 | 1 | 6.71 | 4.37 | .042 |
| Problem-solving strategies | 3.36 | 1 | 3.36 | 2.34 | .133 |
| Support reading strategies | 8.11 | 1 | 8.11 | 5.67 | .021 |
| Overall reading strategies | 5.87 | 1 | 5.87 | 4.50 | .039 |
| | | | | | |
| **Strategy by gender**[**] | | | | | |
| Global reading strategies | .25 | 2 | .13 | .81 | .447 |
| Problem-solving strategies | .26 | 2 | .13 | .44 | .645 |
| Support reading strategies | 1.24 | 2 | .65 | 3.56 | .035 |
| Overall reading strategies | .41 | 2 | .21 | 1.50 | .229 |

ANOVA, analysis of variance.

[**] Values corrected for sphericity using the Huynt-Feldt multiplier.

Figure 7.1. Perceived general and specific strategy use

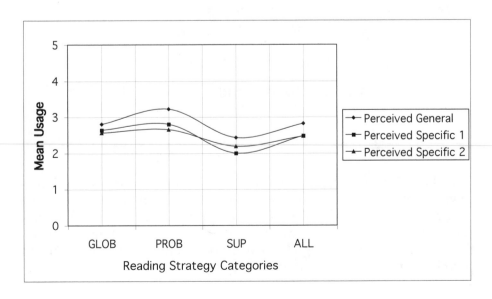

The repeated measures ANOVA results, presented in Table 7.2, revealed significant differences between male and female students in their perceived general and perceived specific use of reading strategies. These differences were found for overall reading strategies ($F[1, 49] = 4.50$; $p = .039$), global reading strategies ($F[1, 49] = 4.37$; $p = .042$), and support reading strategies ($F[1, 49] = 5.67$; $p = .021$). No significant gender differences were found for the problem-solving strategies category ($F[1, 49] = 2.34$; $p = .133$). However, a significant interaction was found between perceived strategy use and gender for the support reading strategies category ($F[2, 98] = 3.56$; $p = .035$). Figure 7.2 shows that for support reading strategies, males showed an anomalous pattern of strategy use: Their perceived general and second perceived specific strategy uses were similar while their first perceived specific use was lower. In all other cases, first perceived specific and second perceived specific uses were both lower than perceived general strategy use.

Figure 7.2. Perceived general versus perceived specific strategy use by gender.

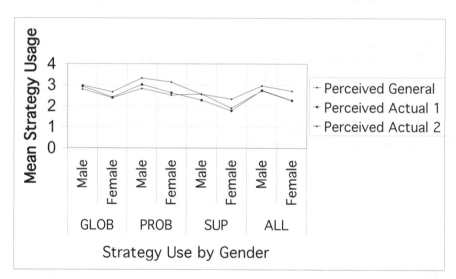

Table 7.3 shows correlations between perceived general and perceived specific strategy use by subscale. Most correlations were between .6 and .8. Thus, though subjects' thinking in general terms did significantly overestimate their perceived specific use of reading strategies, there is was a relatively high correlation between perceived general and perceived specific use of reading strategies.

Table 7.3 Correlations among Strategy Use Categories

| | 1 | 2 | 3 | 4 | 5 | 6 | 7 | 8 | 9 | 10 | 11 | 12 |
|---|---|---|---|---|---|---|---|---|---|---|---|---|
| | | | | | Strategy use categories | | | | | | | |
| **Perceived general strategy use** | | | | | | | | | | | | |
| 1. Global | | .826** | .809** | .950** | .771** | .450** | .593** | .666** | .705** | .636** | .616** | .699** |
| 2. Problem solving | | | .746** | .922** | .709** | .508** | .501** | .633** | .654** | .623** | .510** | .638** |
| 3. Support | | | | .914** | .727** | .470** | .734** | .708** | .648** | .570** | .619** | .657** |
| 4. All | | | | | .793** | .511** | .654** | .719** | .721** | .657** | .627** | .716** |
| **Perceived specific strategy use (1)** | | | | | | | | | | | | |
| 5. Global | | | | | | .711** | .786** | .919** | .822** | .728** | .789** | .836** |
| 6. Problem solving | | | | | | | .677** | .887** | .554** | .598** | .587** | .624** |
| 7. Support | | | | | | | | .905** | .700** | .630** | .804** | .765** |
| 8. All | | | | | | | | | .763** | .721** | .801** | .818** |
| **Perceived specific strategy use (2)** | | | | | | | | | | | | |
| 9. Global | | | | | | | | | | .860** | .800** | .949** |
| 10. Problem solving | | | | | | | | | | | .743** | .932** |
| 11. Support | | | | | | | | | | | | .912** |
| 12. All | | | | | | | | | | | | |

** Correlations significant at the .01 level.

## Discussion

This study examined students' general and perceived use of reading strategies while reading academic materials and whether such differences varied by gender. The results obtained (see Figs. 7.1 and 7.2) revealed two important findings that have important implications for research and teaching. First, students did not report using as many reading strategies when reading two specific textbook chapters as they professed to use when thinking about reading for academic or school-related purposes in general. Second, we found significant differences between male and female students in their perceived general and specific use of reading strategies. These findings are noteworthy in light of what we know about students' perceptions of their own cognitive abilities and skills and the role of such perceptions in text understanding.

There are few plausible reasons for the difference between perceived general and specific use of metacognitive strategies among our students. A specific textbook chapter is unlikely to feature every characteristic of academic texts that might be a factor in the strategies used for reading comprehension. For example, when responding to the strategy "When text becomes difficult, I reread to increase understanding" and thinking about academic texts in general, students may recall a difficult text and could potentially report that they "often" or "always" use the strategy when reading. However, when thinking about a textbook chapter that they may not find as hard to read, the same students may report they "never" or "seldom" use the strategy when reading.

In general, the findings are consistent with prior research studies, which have found that people are generally poor at accurately estimating how able they are at specific cognitive tasks such as reading (Kruger & Dunning, 1999; Phiffer & Glover, 1982; Schmeck, 2000). For example, Phiffer and Glover (1982) found that college students "did not consistently apply the metacognitive strategies they professed to use or they were not proficient in applying them" (p. 194). Schmeck (2000) and his colleagues, who investigated perceptions of students with different levels of reflectivity, found that "reflective students were consistently more accurate in estimates of their cognitive skills" (p. 87) than less reflective students. Finally, Kruger and Dunning (1999) found that unlike academically competent individuals, less skilled learners are not quite adept at making good judgments about their own cognitive processes. Because they are unskilled, they tend to hold overly favorable views of themselves, often without realizing they are making such errors in judgment. In the present study, we addressed the difference between perceived general and perceived subject-specific use of strategies, which is not quite the same as the difference between perceived use and actual use of reading strategies when reading texts for various purposes.

An intriguing aspect of the findings of the present study is that although the subjects' self-reports of their metacognitive awareness showed differences between perceived general and specific strategy use, there is a relatively high correlation between the two, as shown in Table 7.3. These findings would seem to indicate that a certain degree of variation in per-ceived strategy use is to be expected, depending on the circumstances under which the reading task occurs. In addition, students' perceived use of reading strategies while reading represent complex processes that are influenced by a variety of factors, including, but not limited to, the type of materials read (textbook chapter vs. lab report), the reading ability of the reader (skilled vs. less skilled), the purpose for reading (studying for a test vs. researching a topic), and the impact of classroom instruction. In addition, as some researchers have pointed out, because reading is of a highly individual nature, no two readers are likely to approach a given reading task in exactly the same way (Anderson, 1991; Sarig, 1987).

These findings have important implications for teaching and research. Practicing teachers and researchers have known for some time that stu-dents do bring a wealth of prior knowledge in the form of "theories" or ideas, and goals about learning, in general, and about cognitive process-es, such reading in particular. Nichols (1992) believes that students have theories or beliefs about academic success that generalize across different domains. Schunk (1992) agrees that students have ideas not just about the nature and value of knowledge, but also about the ways it should be ac-quired. These theoretical ideas and motivational orientations are related to a variety of factors that have diverse effects in school. Whatever ideas students have about school learning, they are often not taken into consid-eration when planning curriculum and instruction. Researchers concur that educators would benefit a great deal by determining student per-ceptions of their cognitive and metacognitive processes and goal orienta-tions toward learning in the classroom. Student perceptions, according to Schunk (1992), "can mediate the relationship of teacher behaviors to student achievement: Teaching can influence student perceptions, which in turn can affect achievement" (p. 5).

Research on the influence in classrooms of student achievement per-ceptions, teacher beliefs about student abilities, expectations of achieve-ment, cognitive and metacognitive processes, and learning and reading strategies has shown that student perceptions represent fairly complex processes that are influenced by a variety of factors and that have di-verse effects in school. Such research has contributed a great deal to our understanding of student perceptions about themselves as learners and about how those perceptions influence academic achievement, especially in domains such as mathematics and sports. However, further research is needed to better understand the discrepancies between student percep-tions and their actual performance, especially in cognitive tasks, such as reading comprehension. Research is particularly needed to determine whether such discrepancies are influenced by a variety of factors, includ-ing, but not limited to, factors such as purposes for reading (e.g., reading for academic vs. recreational purposes), type of reading materials (lab manual vs. textbook or a news story), levels of reading ability (high vs. low ability), developmental reading levels (perception of competence across grade levels), and instructional intervention (direct vs. indirect teaching of metacognitive awareness and use of reading strategies). Finding answers to these and other related questions should help us a great deal in determining students' perceptions of their own reading processes, documenting the actual usage of reading strategies while reading, refining measures for assessing such processes, and developing practical strategies for enhancing students' metacognitive awareness and use of reading strategies while reading for academic or recreational purposes. In short, reading purpose plays an important role in students' awareness and perceived use of reading strategies while reading. When reading for study purposes, students were more likely to use reading strategies more frequently than when reading for fun or recreational purposes. In addition, these differences did not appear to be impacted by gender. While female students had a tendency to invoke a greater volume of reading strategies when reading for either purpose than did their male counterparts, no significant differences were found in the ways they modulated their strategy use across reading purposes. Finally, reading ability did not have any influence on their tendency to adjust their strategy use depending on reading purpose. Both skilled and less skilled readers reported modulating their strategy use when reading for study and for entertainment purposes. It appears that readers, regardless of reading ability differences, are able to distinguish between reading for study, which is required and often more cognitively demanding, and reading for recreational purposes, which is often voluntary and, therefore, perceived as less demanding. These findings are consistent with prior research (e.g., Narvaez, van den Broek, & Ruiz, 1999) indicating that while reading purpose may not influence students' reading comprehension performance, it does influence the strategic reading processes used when reading for study or entertainment purposes.

# 8 | Rethinking Cognitive Strategy Instruction and Multilingual Students: A Review and Critique

**Robert T. Jiménez**
*Vanderbilt University*

**Lara J. Handsfield and Helen Fisher**
*Illinois State University*

## Introduction

"We read to think. We seek the experience again and again because it takes us out of the everyday world, activates our emotions, creates sensory images, satisfies curiosity, or tells us what we need and want to know" (Fountas & Pinnell, 2001, p. 328).

The view that "reading is thinking," as articulated by Fountas and Pinnell (2001), and similar perspectives on reading as a thinking process, is echoed throughout instructional texts geared toward both practicing and preservice teachers (Cunningham & Allington, 2006; Harvey & Goudvis, 2000; Tompkins, 2006). This assertion accompanies descriptions of specific instructional strategies or tools for helping students comprehend texts, typically referred to as cognitive strategy instruction (CSI). CSI, however, is drawn out of a very particular theoretical framework regarding human cognition and its relationship to literacy. Reading and literacy, for instance, could just as easily be described as "literacy is feeling or desire," identified by a recognizable set of emotive responses to text (Rosenblatt, 1985). Other views include "literacy is interacting with others" or "performing certain identities." In the latter view, reading is an outward display of a specific set of observable behaviors that involve certain postures and uses of language that occur in a circumscribed set of places (Luke, 1992), such as religious recitation or the bedtime story routine. Each of these practices or behaviors results in particular identities, carries with it a particular sociopolitical history, and can occur in a range of ways that are recognized and deemed acceptable by a potentially unlimited number of groups and communities (Barton & Hamilton, 2000; Cope & Kalantzis, 2000). All of these perspectives have both strengths and weaknesses for informing literacy instruction, as well as the potential for regulating individuals' behavior. We raise these points to emphasize that each conceptualization of reading and literacy is one among many, each of which carries different implications for literacy instruction in multilingual settings. Here, we focus on the former, namely, cognitive approaches. More specifically, we take a critical look at theory, research, and instructionally oriented recommendations (most notably, CSI) that have employed cognitive approaches to understand the comprehension processes of *bilingual* and *biliterate* readers. We ground this critique in the latter view of literacy as performing identities.

Because we were involved with some of the research that we report here, we have a fondness and appreciation for cognitivist views as well as CSI. Even so, we believe that cognitivist perspectives fail to account for the totality of what happens when bilingual and biliterate readers encounter, interact with, and make sense of print texts and other semiotic material. Further, we argue that the universalist assumptions embedded within cognitive frameworks (as well as reductionist views characteristic of sociocognitive and socioculturalist theories) may disadvantage students from diverse backgrounds. In this chapter, we begin with a historical overview of what a cognitive approach to literacy consists of, including a review of recent research on second-language (L2) literacy conducted within cognitive frameworks. We use the principles derived from our reading of the literature on cognitive approaches, data from some of our research, as well as some analytical tools recommended by New Literacies writers, to consider both the benefits and drawbacks of cognitivist frameworks for helping English language learning (ELL) students become literate.

## Historical Overview of Cognitive Approaches to Literacy

A casual perusal of either curriculum materials designed for students, such as those produced by McDougal Littell or Harcourt, or textbooks designed for prospective and practicing teachers (Alvermann, Phelps, & Ridgeway, 2007; Barr & Johnson, 1996; Fountas & Pinnell, 2001; Harvey & Goudvis, 2000), quickly reveals the pervasive influence and enthusiastic embrace of cognitive perspectives, especially as these are translated into CSI. These cognitive perspectives on literacy are rooted in cognitive science, a branch of psychology concerned with human intelligence and knowledge (Von Eckerdt, 1995). Accordingly, cognitive perspectives on literacy are concerned with how knowledge is represented and how that representation facilitates the use of that knowledge (Rumelhart, 1980). Cognitive strategy instruction takes the understanding of how representation facilitates the use of knowledge and applies it directly to investigation of the mentalistic tools or mechanisms that make textual processing possible (Brown, 1985; Baker & Brown, 1984). These tools are the component parts of the cognitive faculties, which enable the capacity to use language (i.e., perceive it, comprehend it, produce it, translate it, communicate with it, etc.), to perceive visually, to apprehend music, to learn, to solve problems (i.e., to reason and draw inferences), to plan action, to act intentionally, to remember, and to imagine (Von Eckerdt, 1995).

Those working within the framework of cognitive science share the purpose of learning how normal human beings function intellectually. The descriptor *normal* is key here. The goal is to create models of how human intelligence and intellectual functioning, as well as general cognitive processing, occur as an abstract, universally shared human activity. Von Eckerdt (1995) in her book *What Is Cognitive Science?* describes the central focus of her field as follows:

> Although there is considerable variation in how adult human beings exercise their cognitive capacities, adults are sufficiently alike when they cognize that it is meaningful to talk about a "typical" adult cognizer and it is possible to arrive at generalizations about cognition that hold (at least approximately) for all normal adults. (p. 55)

As we will show, this goal is grounded in assumptions regarding what constitutes "normalcy," and these assumptions guide cognitive approaches such as CSI.

Although cognitive researchers of reading focus their attention on the thinking of "normal" adults, we were surprised, during our review of the early literature in this field (1975–1985), by how seldom actual readers are mentioned or included in descriptions of textual processing. In other words, the individuals who served as the models for "the typical adult cognizer" or, in this case, the reader, are not identified. Instead, the process of how comprehension occurs is theorized based on cognitive models of intelligence and the few empirical results that were available at that time. When the reader is present at all, he or she is presented as an agglomeration of neurons reacting to stimuli. This agglomeration of neurons is described as a sort of biological computer, a kind of purpose-built machine that, at its best, is highly efficient and productive in extracting information from written language. The stimuli referred to in these early descriptions are typically alphabetic texts, but there is no principled reason to exclude texts written in other scripts or even other forms of semiotic representation. Rumelhart (1980) captures this idea of a "readerless" act of comprehension best in the following description:

> ...graphemic information enters the system and is registered in a visual information store (VIS). A feature extraction device is then assumed to operate on this information extracting the critical features from the VIS. These features serve as the sensory input to a pattern synthesizer. In addition to this sensory information, the pattern synthesizer has available nonsensory information about the orthographic structure of the language (including information about the probability of various strings of characters), information about lexical items in the language, information about the syntactic possibilities (and probabilities), information about the semantics of the language and information about the current contextual situation (pragmatic information). The pattern synthesizer then uses all of this information to produce a "most probable interpretation" of the graphemic input. Thus, all of the various sources of knowledge, both sensory and nonsensory, come together at one place and the reading process is the product of the simultaneous joint application of all the knowledge sources. (Rumelhart, 1980, p. 735)

In this quote, the reader is presented as if he or she were a machine, and the teacher becomes the technician, providing input in order to maximize output or output quality. Because machines are not social, there is no need for social interaction here. Rather, the only interaction is a sharing of output, not a mutual construction of output or ideas. While some cognitive strategies are taught and acted out in social settings (i.e., small groups), often these social interactions seem to be considered valid only to the extent that they enhance individual comprehension that can be measured in an individualized assessment. In other words, social interaction simply becomes a means to a more desired end, namely, individual cognition. We return to this point later, when we discuss instructional examples.

In addition to a mechanized approach to interaction, by employing the metaphor of a machine or computer, attention is diverted away from the fact that the models for thinking were, in fact, derived from a set of the population with a particular ethnic, linguistic, socioeconomic, and historical background. This normal, or ideal, machine is reminiscent of Chomsky's theory of a universal language acquisition device—a view of language as an "organ of the mind" (Chomsky, 1959, 1965). Organs are components of the body that rely on the central nervous system, to some extent, but they autonomously complete their functions without much intentional direction. Such a move, whether intended or not, contributed to claims to universality, to a kind of "obviousness" and taken-for-granted sense of necessity. As we show later in this chapter, these claims to universality have implications for the regulation and control of how students are taught to respond to, and think about, texts. Because the early models were predominantly adults in mainstream institutions, such as universities and children from mainstream backgrounds, bilingual individuals and those from racially/ethnically socioeconomically diverse backgrounds were rarely, if ever, mentioned or considered when these models were described and specified in the early literature.

To be fair to cognitive perspectives, Rumelhart (1980) provided something of an extreme example of a machine-like understanding of reading and its product, comprehension. There are hints in his work, however, of the tension between cognitive faculties that seemingly operate without intentionality and the view that a human being is purposefully directing the process. He points out that "perception is goal-directed" and that "if perception is goal-directed, then remembering is even more so" (Rumelhart, 1980, p. 51).

Of course, Rumelhart was most concerned with describing the components of schema theory. But in the following description, one wonders whether schemata are envisioned as tools that one employs to accomplish desired ends or as organs, such as the stomach, digesting food when conditions are appropriate. Both interpretations seem possible from the following description:

> ...schemata are the building blocks of cognition. They are the fundamental elements upon which all information processing depends. Schemata are employed in the process of interpreting sensory data (both linguistic and nonlinguistic), in retrieving information from memory, in organizing actions, in determining goals and subgoals, in allocating resources

> and, generally, in guiding the flow of processing in the system. Clearly, any *device* capable of all these wondrous things must be powerful indeed. (Rumelhart, 1980, pp. 33–34) [italics ours]

Other writers from this era seemed to agree with Rumelhart's views on the mechanistic nature of reading and comprehension. For example, Spiro (1980) concluded from a review of the literature that comprehension "entail[ed] some transformation of linguistic stimuli" (p. 247), and that these transformations relied upon inferential processes. Curiously, making inferences is once again described in terms that could be either the result of a subconscious process or a desired and goal-directed outcome. His description of this process seems to allow for either interpretation. Try, for example, to identify the subject in the following statement: "In the process of comprehending discourse, what is understood and stored frequently includes not only what is directly stated, but also what seems to follow from that information (probabalistically or necessarily)" (p. 255). Who exactly is comprehending and storing information? In our opinion, the cognitive processes described by these theorists are now taken for granted in literacy instruction, and they were embedded in the early thinking that conceptualized cognitive models of reading comprehension. It appears, then, that cognitive perspectives have always straddled the very permeable and indeterminate separation between conscious awareness and subconscious cognitive activity, particularly as that activity involves strategic processing, such as making inferences.

In addition, some of the early empirical work on comprehension did not make the distinction between drawing conclusions that were purposeful and those that were beyond the power of the individual to alter. For example, Steffenson, Joag-dev, and Anderson (1979) found that when reading texts that described weddings in India and in the United States, subjects from each of these two countries produced more "culturally based distortions" or inferences, depending upon their background. In another related study (Reynolds, Taylor, Steffenson, Shirey, & Anderson, 1982), the researchers found that differences in "intrusions" or, again, what is commonly viewed as the making of inferences, depended on whether the subjects were from a white agricultural region of Illinois versus a black working class neighborhood in Tennessee. In these studies, no distinction was made between conscious and subconscious processing. In fact, both leave the distinct impression that such activity is beyond the capacity of the individual to alter. In our opinion, this line of reasoning can be traced directly to the ambiguities inherent within early theoretical formulations of schema theory.

At other times, early theorists seemed to imply that strategy use is entirely conscious and within the reach of readers in terms of active deployment and manipulation. Collins, Brown, and Larkin (1980) argued that readers must learn the strategies employed by skilled readers, and that the use of these strategies is critical for understanding. They propose that "one of the most critical skills may be to choose the right questions upon which to focus one's problem-solving skills" (p. 405). Spiro (1980) felt that the ability to access relevant background knowledge was key to comprehension. He contended that "various difficulties could result from problems of schema acquisition" (p. 260). He asked whether problems with comprehension might be the result of students generating too many hypotheses, too few, or none at all while reading. The process of hypothesizing suggests active involvement of the reader but leaves some room for subconscious activity.

Although this tension between conscious decision making and subconscious thought has never been satisfactorily resolved, it continues to manifest itself in instructional recommendations that try to guarantee successful comprehension given a set of particular conditions (reading strategies) and students' use of these strategies. We contend that it perpetuates universalist assumptions regarding literacy, assumptions that are problematic when working with multilingual students. First, we worry that the metaphor of the computer hides the fact that mainstream monolingual human beings were indeed the models used to identify preferred or "normal" modes of thinking and their concomitant strategic processing. Second, a purely purposeful view of comprehension implies an agency in governing the contents and access to schemata grounded in individualist discourses of literacy that supposedly transcend social and linguistic influences on practice. This reflects what Lemke (1995) refers to as the problem of the subject: "…the classical modernist concept of the human individual conflates a physical, biological notion of the individual human organism with a social, cultural notion of the individual human person, the social actor, agent, or persona" (p. 81). This view makes differences (including linguistic and cultural differences) both easy and desirable to work around and "overcome" and removes political and ideological interestedness from the equation of literacy engagement, which we view as highly problematic. Each of these possibilities, as well as the unresolved lack of specificity between them provided by cognitivist perspectives, leaves ample room for potentially manipulating others. What we have in mind here are the possibilities for powerful interests to mobilize, intervene, and pursue their own goals while remaining unidentified, unseen, and, far too often, unresisted by students from communities with different interests. Such may be the case with respect to the relationship between CSI (and other literacy practices) and the testing industry. Nevertheless, continued and lingering traces of this tension appear to be present in contemporary recommendations and approaches to literacy instruction. We provide examples from our own research to illustrate these concerns. But first, we discuss briefly how sociocognitivists have attempted to mediate some of these issues.

## Sociocognitive Reformulations and Refinements of Cognitive Perspectives on Literacy

In more contemporary thinking, many working within a cognitive paradigm acknowledge social and cultural factors influencing literacy development. Nevertheless, as Dressman, Wilder, and Connor (2005) pointed out, these factors are typically considered as variables affecting how literacy is cognitively processed, rather than how literacy is practiced in different contexts. While sociocognitive theories, based, in large part, on Vygotsky's work (1978), blend assumptions about text processing and social interaction, they continue to construct literacy practices as social activities only insofar as they impact cognition. In this sense, literacy is still construed as a property of the individual, rather than as a dynamic, social, and ideological practice, which does little, if anything, to resolve Lemke's "problem of the subject." Other sociocognitivists' work has more adequately responded to these concerns.

The early work of Moll and his colleagues (Moll, Estrada, Díaz, & Lopes, 1980) provided evidence that Spanish-English bilingual readers were able to perform at higher levels of cognitive complexity when, and if, they were encouraged to make use of both of their languages while processing texts written in English. In other words, when Latino bilingual students read texts in English but discussed them in Spanish, they moved beyond the low-level focus on decoding texts and answering questions at the factual and literal level to deeper, more sophisticated kinds of responses to text. The focus in this research was on making changes to the social context to facilitate these students' ability to think about and process texts written in English. In essence, students were encouraged to use a cognitive and linguistic resource that was made available as a result of a change to the social organization of the classroom.

Although sociocognitivists moved cognitivist views of literacy away from "in your head" approaches to literacy processes, we feel that sociocognitive and socioculturalist theories did not go far enough in recognizing both the political and ideological conditions under which bilinguals in the United States have become literate, or the dynamic nature of culture and identity. These conditions have historically involved a constant effort to remake bilinguals as "monolinguals" while pushing them to "voluntarily" divest themselves of their cultural backgrounds. Dorothy Holland et al. (1998) critique both universalist psychological positions (e.g., cognitivist perspectives) and culturalist positions as reductionist. Taking a feminist perspective, they argue that cultural discourses operate as "impositions, pushing women and men to behavior compatible with the structures and institutions that favor members of one social category over another" (p. 25). Such a stance indicts sociocognitivist and socioculturalist frameworks as well as cognitivist ones. They argue that more current approaches to anthropology (as well as sociological work and the New Literacy Studies) should foreground issues, such as "contest, struggle, and power" (p. 26). They state: "...more recent perspectives certainly consider [culturally specific] discourses relevant, but they do not take them to be indicators of an underlying, pervasive culture. Rather they conceive them as what we will call living artifacts or living tools" (p. 23). In fact, Luis Moll's perspective on all of this seems to have shifted from a more traditional sociocultural or sociocognitive framework to a native language framework (Gonzales, Moll, & Amanti, 2005). We agree and believe that instructional strategies, such as CSI, can and should be conceived of as living artifacts or tools. When thought of in that way, rather than as mechanistic procedures, CSI is more likely to be used in ways that respond to the performative nature of literacy as enacted in classrooms and communities and indeed to the changing and dynamic nature of literacy itself.

A view of CSI as "obvious" and necessary for all readers, regardless of gendered, socioeconomic, linguistic, cultural, racial-ethnic background, could easily become a subterfuge for explicitly shaping consciousness in ways that benefit dominant interests. Awareness of how such powerful tools either reinforce the status quo or might serve to disrupt it is a necessary and important first step toward behavior and thought that does not support inequitable structures and institutions. Although Holland et al. (1998) were concerned with how universalist psychological positions are drafted to push everyone toward dominant modes of thought and behavior, we are concerned here with their effect on linguistically diverse and bilingual populations.

We are concerned because the bilingual and the biliterate have always been viewed with suspicion, or at the least, with bewilderment by those concerned with designing theories of learning and instructional approaches that can be "scaled up" for large populations. For example, Weber (1991) states: "In the view of American education, knowledge of a mother tongue other than English has been perceived until recently as a liability to learning, a factor in low intelligence, and an indicator of poverty and questionable academic potential" (p. 98). C. Baker (2001) raises the issue that for many, monolingualism is viewed as normative behavior. He goes on to make clear, however, that bilingualism is at least as prevalent on planet Earth as monolingualism and that only provincial thinking, as well as the entrenched interests of specific groups, marginalize and set aside as unthinkable the notion that schooling should equip all students with knowledge of more than one language. Still others point to the damaging and corrosive view that sees bilingualism as cognitively confusing or as a kind of linguistic schizophrenia (Crawford, 1995; E. García, 2005). These misconceptions of bilingualism and those who are bilingual set these populations apart from that of the "normal cognizing adult" and all that such a designation entails. In a sense, they set up those from bilingual communities as in need of "cognitive regulation" and repair.

Of special concern to us is what happens when cognitivist perspectives merge and blend with the neocolonialist project of remaking subjectivities through assimilation and acculturation (Collins & Blott, 2003; Macedo, 2000; Pennycook, 2001). Since many, if not most, ELL students are placed in schools and classrooms that see it as their mission to "acculturate" and "assimilate" these students, a good deal of what passes for literacy instruction is focused on this goal. New Literacies researchers, on the other hand, explicitly claim to be interested in differences and in finding ways to help students cross linguistic and cultural boundaries. The New London Group (2000), for example, make the following statement:

> ...*the most important skill* students need to learn is to negotiate regional, ethnic, or class-based dialects; variations in register that occur according to social context; hybrid cross-cultural discourses; the code switching often to be found within a text among different languages, dialects, or registers; different visual or iconic meanings; and variations in the gestural relationships among people, language and material objects. (p. 14)

The goals and objectives, both explicit and inherent, within the above statement are the universalist assumptions regarding what constitutes desired outcomes that we have determined are embedded within cognitivist approaches. More important within a native language approach are the performative aspects of literacy, that is, the ways that subjectivities and cognition are produced in the doing or performance. These conceptualizations of cognition view individuals as speaking and acting—reading included—in ways that represent static physical (neurological) processes or social (linguistic and cultural) affiliations. As can be seen in the discussion that follows, these same issues permeate how cognitive strategies are often taken up in the classroom.

## Classroom Application of Cognitive Strategy Instruction with Multilingual Students

In this section of the chapter, we present and critique examples of how cognitive strategies have been implemented in the classroom with multilingual students. We focus on two strategies geared toward both monolingual and multilingual readers, namely, accessing prior knowledge and generating questions. We draw links between how implementing these strategies in restrictive ways may inadvertently reinforce universalizing tendencies, that is, individualistic (as opposed to social) and mechanistic or "readerless" conceptualizations of reading. We then turn our attention toward two strategies that are grounded in the flexible linguistic abilities and potentials of bilingual children. As we present and critique these strategies, we remain cognizant of the value of encouraging and supporting students as they work to make meaning of texts. Rather than "toss the baby out with the bathwater," we ask what forms these strategies might take when thoughtfully implemented within a New Literacies framework.

### Accessing Prior Knowledge and Making Connections

Accessing relevant prior knowledge has been advocated as a way to support both first- (L1) and L2 reading comprehension. In fact, accessing prior knowledge and its close relative, making connections, both have a direct relationship to schema theory (Anderson & Pearson, 1984). Dole, Duffy, Roehler, and Pearson (1991) considered making inferences to be a crucial aspect of the comprehension process. McVee, Dunsmore, and Gavelek (2005) indicated that *prior knowledge* has become synonymous with *schema* and that "schema theory is still influencing our perceptions of reading and is believed to be a viable and valuable explanation for teachers" (p. 535). The process, however, is assumed to apply to all read-ers, from whatever cultural and linguistic background. In other words, little thought is given to how students from diverse backgrounds might need to modify or adapt the process given their special linguistic and cultural faculties or abilities.

Jiménez et al. (1996) were dissatisfied with the then prevailing model of expert strategic reading, based as it was on the thinking of mainstream individuals. They believed that bilingual and biliterate Latino readers were not well represented in terms of the kinds of strategies that were then being advocated. In response, these authors investigated whether bilingual/biliterate readers were the same as, or different from, main-stream, monolingual English speaking readers. Except for the use of two languages, there were similarities, as can be seen in the example provid-ed by a seventh-grade student known as Lisa. Here, she used the think-aloud procedure to show how she connected the content of a Spanish expository text on solar energy to her relevant prior knowledge:

> Y en Chicago me acordé que ví en las noticias que hay un laundrymat, una lavandería, donde ellos no meten dinero, la energía lo obtienen del sol ...(And in Chicago I remember that I saw on the news that there is a laundrymat, where they don't insert money. They get the energy from the sun...). (Jiménez et al., 1996, p. 101)

It is important to note, though, that Lisa was not directed or taught to engage in this activity, at least not by the researcher. As a high-perform-ing bilingual reader, she verbalized the use of this strategy when asked to describe her thinking while reading a text. As Fountas and Pinnell (2001) pointed out: "In guided reading, your goal is to help readers develop more effective and efficient processing systems and to expand their read-ing power to more and more difficult texts" (p. 18), and they recommend teaching students how to make their prior knowledge explicit by making text-to-text, text-to-self, and text-to-world connections. These ideas were first presented and elaborated in the empirical work of Paris and Myers (1981), Raphael (1982), and Raphael and Pearson (1985).

Making connections holds potential for struggling students who may not attempt to make such connections implicitly. But while the purpose of making connections is often articulated as creating an explicit structure for students to access specific experiences or cultural understandings, we have found that this strategy is often implemented in ways that may restrict students' access to those funds of knowledge. In the following example from Lara's research, as represented in her field notes, a read-ing specialist (Christine) and a classroom teacher (Joyce) team-taught a lesson to a group of multilingual third graders. Christine read Jacqueline Woodson's *The Other Side* (2001) aloud to the students while Joyce jotted down students' connections on chart paper:

> Christine...instructs the students to think of text-text, text-self, and text-world connections. As she reads, Danny and Patrick share connections. David makes a self-text connection between the picture of a fence on the cover of the book and a baby in a crib. Christopher then explains how he

used to climb out of his crib as a baby. Christine responds to Christopher by saying that he made a "self to David connection" and that "we need a self-to-text connection."

The teacher's insistence that the students connect the text to their own selves or understandings, as opposed to connecting with others, reflects a view of reading and textual processing as an individualistic, "in the head" experience. This may be problematic if students' relevant prior knowledge is based on social (interpersonal) connections, and if social interaction is how that knowledge is both accessed and developed. This could be limiting in two ways. First, it may limit *how* students can access prior knowledge and experiences, and second, for students whose cultural backgrounds may privilege less individualistic ways of learning and constructing knowledge, it may limit the *kinds* of prior knowledge that are deemed acceptable in school literacies. In other words, students' thinking is placed within parameters that are recognizable and familiar to mainstream teachers and researchers. Students are being taught to think in specific ways and they are being taught to interact with texts in specific ways.

Another potential pitfall with the "making connections" strategy is the ultimate purpose of the strategy itself. This relates to the notion that such comprehension strategies should be made explicit in order to support less successful readers in processing texts. In the same third-grade classroom described above, Joyce modeled the making-connections strategy to her class. As she read a story aloud, she wrote what the story "reminded her of" on yellow sticky notes. She then asked to students to use sticky notes to record their own connections during silent reading. Joyce explained that her purpose was to get them "to think about the book" and "to make connections with the book." In other words, students were to jot down their connections as a way of making their "thinking" explicit or visible. In a sense, whereas before the advent of CSI, only students' bodily and physical behaviors were available for inspection and regulation, now their innermost thoughts are also exposed to similar display and, ultimately, correction.

The strategy of making connections is both widely used and widely advocated (Allington, 2005; Cunningham & Allington, 2006; Tompkins, 2006; Fountas & Pinnell, 2001) as a strategy for helping students think about what they read, with the ultimate goal being enhanced text comprehension. However, the goal, in this instance, became not necessarily comprehending the text, but rather the process itself: making connections. In addition, the above example, like the previous one, illustrates an emphasis on text processing at the individual level, as opposed to at an interpersonal level, in which connections and meaning are socially constructed and mediated.

*Generating Questions*

These same issues surface in examples of questioning strategies in reading instruction. In *Literacy for the 21st Century*, Gail Tompkins (2006) draws from Duke and Pearson (2002) to describe generating questions as a goal-oriented comprehension strategy: "[Readers] ask self-questions out of curiosity, and as they use this strategy, they become engaged with the text and want to keep reading to find answers to their questions" (p. 230). Fountas and Pinnell (2001) take a similar perspective:

> All the time you are reading, you are actively responding and thinking. These thoughts are fleeting, elusive and largely unstated. You are not wholly conscious of your thinking while reading, although when talking with someone afterward, you may suddenly express something you thought about or an emotion you felt while reading. You feel shadows of questions arising in your mind as you anticipate what might happen next or find something puzzling. (p. 328)

While this quote eloquently describes multiple, complex processes that may occur during reading, it also implies that reading and questioning are internal cognitive activities, not typically available to inspection and regulation. Even "when talking with someone afterward," the assumption is that the interaction consists of sharing internal questions and thoughts (internal processing), rather than actually answering questions and socially constructing meaning—what, we would argue, successful readers outside of school typically do. In addition, Fountas and Pinnell (2001) reiterated the unresolved tension in earlier theoretical work between the consciously recognized and the subconsciously derived processes that comprise thought. But there is a sense here in which previously very intimate processes, some of which are barely even accessible to the reader him or herself, are now also available to outside regulation. One wonders, for example, how a child socialized into a topic-associative style of verbal interaction described by Michaels (1981) as familiar to many African-American children, would fare when revealing thoughts that, to a mainstream teacher, appear to be off-topic, irrelevant, and not related to the text. Will such a child be corrected and told that her thinking is not welcome in a think-aloud activity? Our hunch, based on Lara's research, is that these forms of participation will, indeed, be rejected or at least viewed with concern.

Nevertheless, generating questions, like making connections, is widely considered an effective self-monitoring strategy to enhance text comprehension (Allington, 2005; Fountas & Pinnell, 2001; Tompkins, 2006; Lenski & Nierstheimer, 2004; Cunningham & Allington, 2006; Palincsar & Brown, 1984) and was also recognized very early as an important, necessary cognitive strategy. In the following example from Robert's (1996) research, Gilda, a Grade 7 bilingual and biliterate student asked a series of questions about the key elements taken from the science fiction story, *The King of the Beasts*, written by Phillip José Farmer: "Well, why are they making a man? Aren't they people? They're biologists, aren't they? Why would they be scared if it was a man?" Gilda's questions allowed her to determine that "they" (the main characters) were not human beings, but rather extraterrestrials, information that was not explicitly stated in the text. In another example, Marcos asked a question while reading a Spanish text:

> Él está trabajando mientras que todos están con abrigos, y dice que va a buscar una tienda, un abrigo. ¿Pero cómo lo va a hacer así con el frío que había, sin abrigo él? (He is working while everyone else has on coats, and it says that he is going to look for a store, a coat. But how is he going to do it when it is so cold outside without a coat?)

Asking these questions helped him understand the problem faced by the protagonist. In this sense, generating questions can be a very effective strategy for self-monitoring and, ultimately, comprehension.

However, as with making connections, generating questions is often encouraged and enacted in classrooms at an individual level, as implied by Fountas and Pinnell (2001). That is, questions are generated, but asked of no one in particular. This is evident in the two examples we just presented, as well as in Joyce's teaching of the strategy, which mirrors her modeling of how to make connections while reading:

> Joyce tells her students they're going to do some reading again and that she wanted to show them how she asks questions while she reads. She models with a read aloud of *Darkness of the Butterfly*. ...She stops reading every once in a while to ask a question, or to say, "So I wonder...."
> ...After she finished reading, she asked, "Did you notice how some of my questions got answered?" and "Did all of them get answered?" Students say no, and she says that's okay. She calls out, "Reading is..." and the students all say, " ...thinking!" She then has them go in groups to the side table so she can give them books to read...and she tells them to write questions on stickies as they read independently.

The assumption that questions are to be generated solely for the generator's benefit is reminiscent of Heath's (1982, 1983) finding that mainstream styles of questioning in U.S. classrooms privileged questioning for the purpose of displaying knowledge to the teacher rather than authentic questioning to glean new information. This expectation for questioning may lie in contrast to students' expectations regarding the purpose of questioning, as evidenced in David's response to Joyce's instruction in the following example from Lara's field notes. In this lesson, Joyce wrote a sentence that articulates the main idea of a passage, and students were supposed to generate questions that would be answered by that sentence:

> Joyce writes a sentence for the main idea of the second paragraph and asks students to come up with a question that can be answered in the sentence. The students are coming up with questions, but not ones already answered by the main idea sentence Joyce wrote. Instead, they are asking questions they want to know the answers to—more authentic questions. David asks, "What did they eat?" Joyce says, "Does it say anything here about what they ate?" wanting them to come up with questions that are already answered in the text. David responds, "No, but I'm just asking." Joyce seems a bit frustrated that they can't seem to focus on asking questions that are answered in the paragraph.

Clearly, David saw the purpose of asking questions as informational and intentional—as a way of learning more about the topic discussed in the text—and grounded in social interaction for knowledge construction.

This was not Joyce's purpose, however, and the incident led to frustration for both David and Joyce.

This lesson was taught within the context of a larger focus on question-answer relationships, in which Joyce focused students' attention on two types of questions that students may ask while they read: "in the book" questions and "in your head" questions. As with other examples we've presented, questions are generated, but not used between individual students. That is, questions are asked and answered in the text or in the individual. Such a framing of how questions are to be generated and answered implies that reading is more about understanding the text as a solid, static thing, rather than as something that is open for interpretation. The goal of questioning becomes incorporating the words on the page into the brain—a mechanistic procedure that loses intentionality with respect to text comprehension and meaning making.

Joyce's classroom, cognitive strategy instruction was clearly situated within the explicit context of preparing students for standardized tests. In the lesson described above on question-answer relationships, Joyce used passages from a test-preparation booklet, attempting to enhance students' test-taking skills. Her rationale was that her students needed to perform well for her school to make adequate yearly progress, as stipulated by the No Child Left Behind Act of 2001, but that such strategies would also advance students' reading development. This rationale is also made clear in the following conversation between Joyce, Jennifer (another third-grade teacher), and Christine at one of their instructional planning meetings:

Jennifer:    What if they break into a story [while thinking out loud on the test]?

Christine:   Well, then they may make a connection, but on the state test they need to focus.

Jennifer:    'Cause my kids will do that.

Joyce:       [unintelligible]

Christine:   Yeah, if it helps them understand what they're reading, then yeah. But if it doesn't, then they need to focus on understanding the text.

There appears to be a contradiction between the literacy practice of using cognitive strategies and what really matters, test performance. High-stakes accountability is a very real issue impacting teachers' implementation of strategy instruction, and one could argue that CSI fits quite neatly within test taking as a very domesticated, circumscribed way of engaging with texts. Do cognitive strategies, along with standardized assessments, support a kind of domestication of thought in which difference is negated and intentionality is nonexistent or obscured?

*Cognate Strategy and Translation*

The issue of intentionality, or goal-driven activities in relation to cognition and reading, also frames our discussion of cognate strategy and translation. Much of the earlier research on bilingual reading strategies found that successful bilingual students brought up their cultural and linguistic resources, or funds of knowledge, in the process of reading in order to enhance text comprehension (Jiménez, et al., 1996; Jiménez, 1997; García, G. 2000). Consider the following example from Robert's research, in which Gilda demonstrated that she knew the value of English-Spanish cognate relationships:

> Gilda:  Yo sé que hay unas palabras que se parecen pero no sé que quiere decir. Proportional, hmm. Estoy buscando que quiere decir, no sé. (I know that there are some words that look alike but I don't know what it means. Proportional, hmm. I'm looking for what it means, I don't know.)

While this research brought to the forefront the notion that bilingual readers may draw upon resources not accessible to the "normal" functioning adult, what it did not adequately address was how cultural brokering is developed and practiced out of social necessity within a larger sociopolitical milieu that affords such practices very little capital in school. This research, then, tacitly accepted monolingualism as the norm and then compared it to bilingualism. However, these readers gained their abilities under very adverse conditions in which the thrust of their experiences pushed them away from developing their dual-language abilities. In essence, they were positioned to engage in the high-stakes task of becoming literate under conditions that handicapped their efforts.

Brandt (2001) reported in great detail how a bilingual Mexican-American woman from Texas but living in Wisconsin developed her dual-language literacy under social conditions that were anything but supportive. Brandt argued that because this person's Spanish-English biliteracy was not valued or recognized by members of mainstream society, she was unable to convert it into other forms of capital, either social, academic, or symbolic (Bourdieu, 1991). Under such conditions, the development of biliteracy can be considered quite an accomplishment that depends on one's willingness to invest time and effort in an enterprise that may result in few returns. For the bilingual and biliterate individual, the intention or goal of engaging with print and other meaningful representations is not simply to comprehend a text, let alone an isolated passage from a literary text, but to mediate the daily structures and challenges of living in a society that has historically been outright hostile toward bilingualism. We suggest that this political and ideological context plays into how cognate strategy and translation have been, and should be, practiced in the classroom. The point is that the documentation of an alternative set of strategies—in this case, searching for cognates, translating, and finding support from one's first-language literacy while reading in a second language—is not to prescribe a finite, closed set of ways to be literate but to understand that there are potentially many, many more ways of interacting with text than what is included in the typical "canon" of CSI.

## Summary

We began this chapter with a historical view of what a cognitive approach to literacy consists of and a brief review of significant research on L2 literacy conducted within cognitive frameworks. We then critiqued cognitive frameworks for their universalist assumptions regarding cognition and literacy, and view of literacy, including CSI, as an individualistic "in your head" experience. We also critiqued sociocognitivist frameworks that consider culturalist understandings of literacy in ways that situate language, culture, and literacy as static. Such a view assumes literate practice to be merely a representation of culture, rather than a product of individuals' subjectivities in social and cultural worlds. We then provided examples of how these issues surfaced within our research as multilingual students and teachers used cognitive strategies in school literacy practice.

To conclude, we use the terms of cognition, recognition, and misrecognition, and the connections between these terms to identify those aspects of CSI that we believe need theoretical work and further consideration. The ways that cognitivist theorists (as well as sociocognitivists) have conceptualized cognition more closely speaks to recognition—the notion that individuals speak and act (and read) in ways that simply represent static physical (neurological) or social (linguistic and cultural affiliations) processes. The "canonization" of particular reading strategies, such as questioning, making inferences, and making connections, betrays a rather fixed, unchanging notion of what constitutes thought.

The poststructuralist criticism of modernist thinking as representation and repetition is key here. Such a view does not speak to the ways in which subjectivities and cognition, and indeed structures such as language and culture, are produced in the doing, in the performance. In a sense, research that identified readers as successful and less successful or as good and poor created conditions under which particular identities could be enacted. Instructional practices, such as CSI, that required certain types of responses and rejected others provided students with a kind of "dress rehearsal" for being this or that type of reader. These instructional performances then first suggested, and later encouraged, students to accept and adopt dispositions that were capable of fitting into larger school discourses. A performative view, in concert with views set forth by New Literacies theorists, is more attuned to cognition (and literacy) as something dynamic—as a becoming, to insert a Deleuzian term.

Bourdieu's term "misrecognition" comes to play when we talk about how those imbued with authority within a given field recognize particular literate behaviors as legitimate (or not). We cite Bourdieu, Fairbanks, and Ariail (2006) on misrecognition with respect to their own research of Latina adolescents' literacy practices:

> When the value of one's economic, social, and cultural capital is deemed
> legitimate, these resources take on symbolic value. This value accrues as
> a form of misrecognition, a process whereby the arbitrariness of capital

(why some capital is more valuable than others) is presumed to be natural, even tacit. (p. 314)

They continue: "These means are legitimate, according to Bourdieu, by virtue of the fact they are 'dominant and misrecognised as such'" (p. 314). Fairbanks and Ariail (2006) also suggested that schools imposed specific ways of learning and being literate by authorizing and legitimizing particular literate dispositions, behaviors, and attitudes. These processes were on full display in the data taken from Lara's project, as evidenced by regulating moves by Joyce, Christine, and the curricular materials they used (in particular, Fountas & Pinnell, 2001) as they instructed their students very specifically on how to engage with texts.

We argue that CSI is more recognition (i.e., repetition or mimesis) than cognition, and that specific ways of cognizing are (mis)recognized within the apparatus of schooling. Having students chant the mantra of "reading is thinking" and asking questions for the purpose of asking questions, or making connections whether or not those connections are valid, illustrate this notion. What would a performative view of cognition look like? According to Deleuze and Guattari (1987):

> Thought is not arborescent, and the brain is not a rooted or ramified matter. What are wrongly called "dendrites" do not assure the connection of neurons in a continuous fabric. The discontinuity between cells, the role of the axons, the functioning of the synapses, the existence of synaptic microfissures, the leap each message makes across these fissures, make the brain a multiplicity immersed in its plan of consistency or neuroglia, a whole uncertain, probabilistic system ("the uncertain nervous system"). (p. 15)

Here, Deleuze and Guattari (1987) are talking about a performative cognition, which can never hold still, let alone be placed into a neat package, such as CSI. Some of our data show precisely how students and teachers will (and perhaps should) break apart that package in the "doing."

## Suggestions for Practice and Research

So where does this leave CSI? Although we have highlighted a number of concerns that we have regarding CSI and cognitivist frameworks of literacy learning and teaching, we feel it would be counterproductive to abandon efforts to have students recognize and tap into their cognitive resources during reading. In our opinion, cognitive strategies can be valuable tools for helping students to make meaning of texts, but we do not want to only redefine these strategies in new ways only to reimpose them in static, cookie-cutter approaches in classrooms.

Rather, we suggest new approaches to cognitive strategies that recognize the dynamic nature of both instructional strategies and language and literacy. Our hope is to push the field to consider both literacy and instructional strategies as "living artifacts or living tools" (Holland et al., 1998, p. 23) rather than as mechanistic procedures, as in the following example from Lara's research, in which Joyce asks her student, Garibaldi, to use cognate strategy to understand an unfamiliar word in English:

> To help Garibaldi figure out what "luminary" means, Joyce says, "Habla
> de la palabra 'luminar.'" (Talk about the word 'luminar.') Garibaldi asks,
> "Like una luz (like a light)?"

Joyce's and Garibaldi's use of cognate strategy fits nicely within Luke
and Freebody (1997), who suggest a model for literacy instruction that
we feel acknowledges and works from such a perspective while including strategies to access prior knowledge while "participating in texts." In
addition to "participating in text," this framework includes the areas of
"code breaking," "using text," and "analyzing text," and teaches not only
the method and meaning of texts, but also the pragmatics of language
use in context, acknowledging that texts are not neutral. We believe that
utilizing CSI within this kind of framework responds more adequately to
the literacies practiced by many language minority students and which
developed within, from, or in relation to a hostile sociopolitical context.

# 9 | Differing Perceptions of Reading Strategy Use Between Native and Non-Native College Students

**Ravi Sheorey**
*Oklahoma State University*

**Kouider Mokhtari**
*Miami University, Oxford, Ohio*

## Introduction

Even a cursory review of the literature on the processes involved in reading suggests that research on native language reading had made huge strides long before second-language (L2) researchers began to pay attention to research in the reading processes of non-native readers.[1] In fact, early research in L2 reading relied, to some extent, on native-language (in most cases, English) reading research and was considered by some (e.g., Bernhardt, 2000; Weber, 1991) as simply extensions of research trends in first-language (L1) reading. Indeed, during the 1970s and 1980s, when teachers of English as a second language (ESL) in the United States began to emphasize reading and writing skills in their classes to prepare an increasing number of international students on their campuses to deal with academic tasks, much of the early research in ESL reading utilized the theoretical framework of the researchers who had investigated reading in the native language, such as Goodman (1967) and Smith (1979). Like reading researchers in native-language reading, researchers in L2 reading proposed that reading is not a linear process, but one in which readers constantly form hypotheses, test predictions, and use their knowledge of the world and of the language to construct meaning. For example, Clarke and Silberstein (1977) and Coady (1979) proposed models of L2 reading that were clearly based on native-language models of reading (e.g., Goodman, 1967), suggesting that reading is as an active interplay among the three aspects, namely, text comprehension, background knowledge, and utilization of appropriate reading strategies. More recent models have extended that conceptualization of L2 reading as an interactive cognitive process in which readers interact with the text using their prior knowledge (Carrell, 1985; Carrell & Eisterhold, 1983) *and* their cultural background (Pritchard, 1990; Steffenson & Joag-Dev,

---

1. Parts of this paper have been reprinted from *System: Journal of Applied Linguistics and Educational Technology*, Vol. 29, R. Sheorey and K. Mokhtari, "Differences in the Meta-cognitive Awareness of Reading Strategies Between Native and Non-Native Readers," pp. 431–449, copyright (2001), with permission from Elsevier.

1984). One aspect of L2 reading, which has also been researched extensively, is that of understanding what skilled readers typically do while reading, including identifying the metacognitive awareness they have about the specific strategies they use and how, and under what conditions, they use those strategies to improve text comprehension (see, e.g., Block, 1992; Devine, 1993; Jiménez, Garcia, & Pearson, 1996; Kern, 1989; Song, 1998; Zhicheng, 1992).

Indeed, the consensus view is that monitoring of the comprehension process and the use of appropriate reading strategies are critically important aspects of skilled reading for both native and non-native readers. Pressley and Afflerbach (1995) considered proficient readers to be the ones who are "constructively responsive" and take conscious steps (i.e., are aware of and use appropriate strategies) to ensure maximum comprehension. In other words, the current view of reading strongly favors metacognitive awareness as an essential component and includes an awareness not only of whether the text is being understood, but also a conscious deployment of strategies to enhance comprehension. According to this conceptualization of reading, proficient L1 and L2 readers extract meaning from the text by using appropriate strategies, which may range from simply slowing down or rereading to more sophisticated strategies, such as figuring out relationships among the various parts of the text or guessing the meaning of unfamiliar words from the context. The research literature on metacognitive awareness of reading strategies—broadly defined here as the deliberate, conscious procedures used by readers to enhance text comprehension—indicates the need to increase our understanding of readers' metacognitive knowledge or perceptions of reading and reading strategies to mould them into active, constructively responsive readers. Literature on identifying the perceived reading strategies of L2 learners, or that comparing the strategies of such learners with those of native speakers, is somewhat limited, partly because, as Alderson (1984) put it, "proficiency in a foreign language may be more closely associated with foreign-language reading ability [than reading ability in the native language]" (p. 20). Cziko (1978) and Clarke (1979) have also reported that once L2 learners reach higher levels of overall competence in the target language, there is concurrent improvement in their reading ability in that language. However, Carrell's research (1991), which examined the relative influence of native-language reading ability and L2 proficiency on L2 reading, suggested that both native-language reading ability *and* L2 proficiency play a significant role in L2 reading. Similarly, researchers in bilingual education, such as Rigg (1977), have argued that reading ability in the native language transfers to, and is closely associated with, that in the second language. Missing from these and other studies is an examination of the similarities and/or differences between the perceived use, or awareness of, reading strategies by non-native and native-speaking readers. We consider such an examination important because reading comprehension, whether in the first or second language, involves, among other things, the use of reading strategies. Moreover, as Carrell (1998) pointed out, understanding readers' metacognitive awareness in their reading processes is important because it can help teachers to help their students recognize when there are comprehension breakdowns and suggest appropriate strategies to overcome such breakdowns.

In this chapter, we compare the metacognitive awareness or perceptions of the reading strategies of ESL college students studying in the United States with those of native-English-speaking American college students. Our underlying hypothesis in undertaking this comparative study was that although these two groups of students could be considered to have the requisite language proficiency for college-level academic reading in English, they are unlikely to have similar strategic awareness in handling their academic reading tasks because they come from different sociocultural and educational backgrounds. To explore our hypothesis, we conducted the study reported here to find answers to the following three primary questions in the context of native and non-native-English-speaking students' perceptions of reading strategies while reading texts related to their academic tasks (such as reading textbooks, journal articles, study guides, class handouts, etc.):

- Are there any statistically significant differences between ESL and U.S. students in their perceived use of reading strategies while reading academic texts?
- Are there any differences by gender (male vs. female) between ESL and U.S. students in their perceived use of reading strategies while reading academic materials? This question was considered, partly, to examine what Oxford, Ehrman, and Nyikos (1988) called "the language learning folklore that women learn languages 'better' than men" (p. 321).
- Is there a relationship between perceived or reported strategy use and self-rated reading ability?

## Method

*Subjects*

The participants in this study were 152 non-native-English-speaking international students ("ESL students" from hereon) and 150 native-English-speaking American students ("U.S. students" from hereon) who were studying at two midwestern universities in the United States. The ESL students were admitted to the respective universities for full-time academic study and were enrolled in the ESL Composition course sections (the equivalent of one of the required English Composition classes for U.S. students). The ESL students, as part of their application for admission to the university, had to submit a score of 500 or better on the Test of English as a Foreign Language (TOEFL), a score level considered by the respective universities to be indicative of their proficiency in English sufficient enough to pursue university-level course work without any language-related restrictions. The mean age of the students was 21.75 years, and there were 92 male (60.5%) and 60 (39.5%) female students in the sample. A little over 68% of the students reported that they had studied English for at least 7 years, with a mean of 8.36 years. Their self-reported scores on the TOEFL ranged from 503 to 643, with an average of 544.94. The 21 native languages that were represented in the ESL sample belonged to five broad language groups: Far East Asian (57.2%); South Asian (9.2%); Middle Eastern (5.9%); Latin American (3.9%); and Other (20.9%). On a scale of 1 ("far below average") to 6 ("excellent") to rate their reading ability in English, the participants gave themselves an average rating of 3.48 (between "average" and "above average").

The U.S. students ($N = 150$) were enrolled in the various sections of the required Freshman English Composition course. These sections of the course were randomly chosen from among the ones offered at different times and days of the week (e.g., some met 3 days a week for 50 minutes, while others met twice a week for 75 minutes). The mean age of the group was 19.14 years, and the sample included 73 males (48.7%) and 77 females (51.3%) participants. On the reading ability scale mentioned above, the U.S. students gave themselves an average rating of 4.30 (i.e., between "above average" and "very good").

*Instrument*

The data for this study were collected with an earlier version of the Survey of Reading Strategies (SORS; see chapter 4, this volume, for details), which was adapted to make sure that it would be suitable for postsecondary students, whether they are native or non-native speakers of English. The SORS, as we have mentioned elsewhere in this volume, is intended to measure the perceived use of reading strategies by college students while reading academic materials in English typically encountered in college. The SORS version used for this study consists of 28 items, each of which uses a 5-point Likert scale ranging from 1 ("I never or almost never do this") to 5 ("I always or almost always do this"). Students are asked to read each statement and circle the number that applies to them, indicating the frequency with which they use the reading strategy implied in the statement. A background questionnaire, which was administered along with the SORS statements, asked students to provide information about their age, gender, and self-rated ability in reading English; in addition, ESL students were asked to self-rate their proficiency in English as well as to report the overall score they obtained on the TOEFL. The SORS measures three broad categories of reading strategies, namely, global strategies, problem-solving strategies, and support strategies. A brief description of each SORS category and the number of items within each category are given below:

- *Global strategies* are those intentional, carefully planned techniques by which learners monitor or manage their reading. Such strategies include having a purpose in mind, previewing the text as to its length and organization, or using typographical aids and tables and figures (10 items).

- *Problem-solving strategies* are the actions and procedures readers use while working directly with the text. These are localized, focused techniques used when problems develop in understanding textual information. Examples of cognitive strategies include adjusting one's speed of reading when the material becomes difficult or easy, guessing the meaning of unknown words, and re-reading the text for improved comprehension (12 items).
- *Support strategies* are intended to aid the reader in comprehending the text, such as using a dictionary, taking notes, or underlining or highlighting the text to better comprehend it (6 items).

*Data Collection and Analysis*

The SORS was administered at the beginning of individual class periods with the help of the classroom instructor. The students were informed of the purpose of the survey and of the fact that there were no right or wrong answers, and were asked to express their honest opinion by circling the appropriate number printed on the right side of each SORS statement. Typically, the participants were able to complete the survey in 8–10 minutes, with some of the ESL students taking a slightly longer time. Each completed survey was manually examined, and, after discarding the incomplete ones, the 302 (152 ESL and 150 U.S.) usable questionnaires were coded for statistical analysis.

We analyzed the data obtained using descriptive statistical procedures as well as *t*-tests and analyses of variance (ANOVAs) to examine whether significant differences existed between the two groups of subjects with respect to reported strategy awareness while reading. Similar procedures were used to ascertain the extent to which the subjects' strategy awareness varied by gender (male vs. female) and self-reported reading ability (high vs. low). Reading ability was determined by having the study participants rate themselves on their self-perceived reading ability in English on a scale of 1 ("poor") to 6 ("excellent"). Based on their responses, the participants were divided into two groups: the "high reading ability" group consisted of those who considered their ability to be "very good" (5 on the scale) or "excellent" (6 on the scale), while the "low reading ability" group consisted of those who rated themselves "average" (3) or "below average" (2). In examining reading strategy use among these students on the SORS scale, which ranges from 1 to 5, we identified three types of usage, as suggested by Oxford and Burry-Stock (1995, p. 12) for general language-learning strategy usage: high (mean = 3.5 or higher), medium (mean = 2.5–3.4), and low (mean = 2.4 or lower). These usage levels provided a convenient benchmark, which enabled us to make comparisons between the two groups of subjects with respect to their awareness of reading strategies while reading academic texts.

## Results

To answer the first research question, "Are there any differences be-tween ESL and U.S. students in their perceived strategy use while reading academic materials?", we examined the students' responses in terms of the individual strategies as well as the three categories or subscales iden-tified (i.e. global, problem-solving, and support strategies). The means of individual strategy items ranged from a high of 3.98 to a low of 2.67 for ESL students (overall $M = 3.36$) and 4.05–2.03 for U.S. students (overall $M = 3.08$), indicating a moderate overall use of reading strategies, according to established strategy usage criteria as described above; the observed difference in the overall means of the two groups was statistically signifi-cant ($t[298] = -3.08; p < .05$). Among the strategies U.S. students reported using most frequently were "trying to stay focused on reading" ($M = 4.05; SD = .89$), "paying close attention to the content" ($M = 4.01; SD = .98$), and using "typographical aids while reading" ($M = 3.99; SD = 1.01$). ESL students' top preferences, in terms of frequency of reported individ-ual strategy usage, were as follows: "rereading for better understanding" ($M = 3.98; SD = .99$); "paying close attention to the content" ($M = 3.97; SD = 1.06$), and "trying to stay focused on reading" ($M = 3.85; SD = .96$). The two strategies perceived to be used the least by both groups were "asking oneself questions about the text" (U.S. $M = 2.37, SD = .99$; ESL $M = 2.81$; 1.12) and "taking notes while reading" (U.S. $M = 2.03, SD = 1.09$; ESL $M = 1.24; SD = 1.24$). For ESL students, 10 of the 28 strategies (35%) fell in the high usage group (mean = 3.5 or above), while the remaining 18 strate-gies (64%) had means between 2.50 and 3.49, indicating a medium usage of these strategies. None of the strategies in the survey was reported to be used with low frequency (mean values below 2.4). For U.S. students, 8 strategies (29%) fell in the high-usage category (mean = 3.50 or higher); 18 strategies (64%) fell in the medium-usage group; and the remaining 2 strategies (7%) had means below 2.50.

We further analyzed the data according to the three SORS subscales or categories. The averages for these categories revealed a moderate to high strategy usage. Both groups showed a clear preference for prob-lem-solving strategies (U.S. $M = 3.48, SD = .61$; ESL $M = 3.57, SD = .64$) followed by global strategies (U.S. $M = 3.24, SD = .62$; ESL $M = 3.32, SD = .66$) and support strategies (U.S. $M = 2.53, SD = .75$; ESL $M = 3.18, SD = .73$). The differences between the two groups were statistically significant ($t[298] = -7.52; p < .001$) only in the reported use of support strategies. In addition, we examined the correlations among the means of these three categories and found that although all the category means were positive-ly correlated with one another ($p < .01$), most correlations were moderate, ranging from .56 to .66 for ESL students and .57 to .68 for U.S. students. These correlations among these categories suggest, in our opinion, that the strategies included in each category are different yet valuable for ef-fective reading on the part of both student groups.

The second research question we wanted to explore with this study was as follows: "Are there any differences between male and female ESL and U.S. students, respectively, in their perceived strategy use while reading academic materials?" As far as individual strategies or strategy categories are concerned, no statistically significant differences were found between the male and female ESL students ($p > .05$) except in the means of one support reading strategy ("underline or circle information in the text"), nor were any significant differences found in the overall means for male and female students (ESL male $M = 3.33$ vs. ESL female $M = 3.34$; $p > .05$). However, we should note that for 16 of the 28 strategy statements as well as for the support strategy category, the female ESL students' means were higher than those for male ESL students. In the case of U.S. students, the results were somewhat different. U.S. female students had higher mean scores (indicative of their more frequent reported use of strategies or strategy categories) for 21 of the 28 strategy statements; the means of eight strategies were significantly different ($p < .05$) from the reported usage of the same strategies by male students. The overall male and female means were also significantly different (male $M = 2.97$ vs. female $M = 3.19$; $p < .05$); the female means for all the strategy categories was higher than that for males, although only the mean for support strategy category was significantly different ($p < .05$).

To answer the third research question, "Is there a relationship between reported strategy use and self-rated reading ability?", we analyzed the students' responses using ANOVA, which enabled us to compare the "high" reading ability students to the "low" ability students within ESL and U.S. student groups. The results obtained revealed statistically significant differences for a number of individual reading strategies between the high- and low-reading-ability groups. Among ESL students, significant differences ($p < .05$) were found between the means of the problem-solving strategy category ($F[1, 110] = 7.79$; $p = .006$) and the global strategy category ($F[1,110] = 6.44$; $p = .013$) as well as the overall strategy usage means ($F[1,110] = 8.56$; $p = .004$). Furthermore, the high, self-rated reading ability group had higher means for 25 of the 28 strategies. As for U.S. students, the means for the high-reading-ability group were higher for each of the 28 strategies as well as for all the three strategy categories. However, these differences were statistically significant for only seven strategy statements. When the data were analyzed for the awareness of overall strategy use, the results were statistically significant ($F[1, 110] = 10.02$; $p = .002$), and for each of the three subscales: global strategies ($F[1, 110] = 6.38$; $p = .013$), problem-solving strategies ($F[1, 110] = 8.04$; $p = .005$), and support strategies ($F[1, 110] = 8.63$; $p = .004$). In our opinion, these differences suggest that the reading strategies identified in this survey are generally perceived to be deployed more frequently by the students in our sample who self-rated their reading ability as being "high" as compared to those who self-rated themselves as having a "low" reading ability.

## Discussion

In this study, we wanted to explore whether there were any significant differences in the metacognitive awareness and perceived use of reading strategies between ESL and U.S. college students while reading academic materials. The results of this study, the likes of which have not been conducted to our knowledge, revealed five major noteworthy findings. These findings, which are illustrated in graphic form in Figure 9.1, are summarized below:

Figure 9.1 Mean reported strategy use: U.S. versus ESL students.

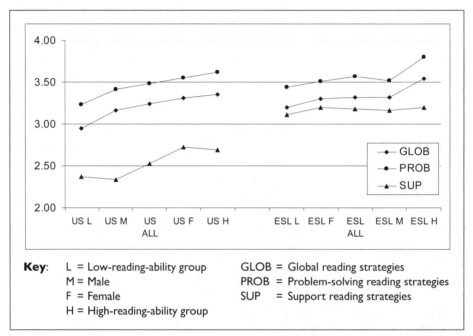

Key:    L = Low-reading-ability group          GLOB = Global reading strategies
        M = Male                               PROB = Problem-solving reading strategies
        F = Female                             SUP  = Support reading strategies
        H = High-reading-ability group

- The major [statistically significant] distinction between U.S. and ESL students' reported use of reading strategies is in the category of support reading strategies (SRS), in that the ESL group mean for SRS was considerably higher than the U.S. group mean for the same category ($p < .002$).
- Both U.S. and ESL learners attribute the same order of importance, irrespective of their reading ability or gender, to problem-solving, global, and support strategies when reading academic texts.
- Both U.S. and ESL high-reading-ability students show comparable degrees of higher reported usage for metacognitive and cognitive reading strategies than lower reading ability students in the respective groups.
- However, while the high-reading-ability U.S. students seem to consider support reading strategies to be relatively more valuable than low-reading-ability U.S. students, ESL students attribute high value to support reading strategies, regardless of their reading ability level.
- In the U.S. group, which included comparable numbers of male

and female students, the females show greater awareness of reading strategies (i.e., report higher frequency of usage), mirroring the differentiation between higher and lower reading ability students in this sample of U.S. learners. This gender effect is not reflected in the ESL sample, perhaps because in this group, the males outnumbered females by 50% (male $N = 92$ vs. female $N = 60$).

Three of the findings mentioned above are worthy of further discussion. First, an examination of the relationship between reported strategy use and reading ability for both native and non-native readers reveals an interesting interaction between these two variables. As the results discussed above show, non-native readers report using support mechanisms (e.g., using a dictionary, taking notes, or underlining textual information) significantly more than native readers. These results suggest, at the outset, that the differences in reported strategy usage may be due to differences in the reading ability between good and poor readers. However, a closer inspection of the data shows that [self-rated] high-reading-ability native speakers, like their high-ability non-native counterparts, report using support strategies significantly more than low-achieving native readers. Apparently, there are two possible factors driving the reported usage of reading strategies, namely, non-nativeness and reading ability. The interaction between these two forces in the present study is quite predictable, especially in light of prior research in L2 reading, which has shown that reading proficiency is closely associated with L2 readers' level of proficiency in the target language. Researchers generally agree that the relationship between language proficiency and reading ability is reciprocal; for example, Alderson (1984) and Cziko (1978) have suggested that high levels of overall competence in the target language often lead to improvement in reading ability in that language. On the other hand, other researchers (e.g., Carrell, Pharis, & Liberto 1989) have provided evidence that proficient L2 readers can compensate for a lack of native-like English proficiency by increasing awareness and use of reading strategies to enhance comprehension. Research in L1 literacy has established a similar interface between reading ability and strategy use among native speakers of English; for example, Baker and Brown (1984) and Kletzien (1991) found that poor readers are generally deficient in reading skills and using strategies. Skilled readers, on the other hand, are more able to reflect on and monitor their cognitive processes while reading. They are aware not only of which particular strategies to use, but they also tend to be better at regulating the use of such strategies while reading. In other words, they seem to be aware of which strategies to use and how to use them, and are cognizant of the conditions under which they ought to be used. In the same vein, Alexander and Jetton (2000) and Pressley (2000) have also suggested that the awareness and use of reading strategies is a characteristic of superior reading comprehension and successful learning.

Second, our analysis of the differences in strategy use by gender showed that female students in general reported using certain strategies more frequently than did their male counterparts. Female ESL students reported using 16 of the 28 strategies more frequently than male ESL students, but these differences were statistically significant for only 1 of the 28 strategies in the case of female ESL students. Similarly, U.S. females reported higher mean scores than for U.S. males for 21 of the 28 reading strategy statements; the means of eight of the strategies were significantly different from those of males. Additionally, the means observed for the three strategy categories were higher for U.S. female participants, with statistically significant differences ($p < .001$) noted in the support-strategy category means for male and female students. In the case of ESL students in this study, our results seem inconsistent with a number of studies on the general language-learning strategies of L2 learners, which have found that, in general, females use language-learning strategies (not specifically reading strategies) more frequently than males (e.g., Green & Oxford, 1995; Kaylani, 1996; Oxford et al., 1988; Oxford, 1993; Sheorey, 1999). We suspect that one reason for the lack of gender effect for ESL readers in the present study may be due to the uneven distribution between male ($N = 92$) and female ($N = 60$) subjects in our sample of ESL students. The interaction between reported reading strategy use and gender should be subjected to further research.

Third, our analysis of the differences between ESL and U.S. students with regard to their self-perceived reading ability showed that reading ability was related to the students' reported usage of those strategies. Students who gave themselves a high rating on reading ability, regardless of their language background, reported a more frequent use of all of the reading strategies in the survey than did those students who gave themselves a low-reading-ability rating. These differences were statistically significant for overall mean use as well as for the three strategy categories identified, namely, global, problem-solving, and support reading strategies. These findings, while not entirely unexpected, provide additional support for prior research on the positive relationship between reading ability and reading strategy awareness and (perceived) use among native and non-native readers.

## Conclusion

The findings reported in this study pertain to the metacognitive awareness of reading strategies among native and non-native college readers. We believe it is important for all readers, whether native and non-native, to be aware of the significant strategies proficient reading requires. Teachers can play a key role in increasing students' awareness of such strategies and in helping them become "constructively responsive" readers (Pressley & Afflerbach, 1995). We realize, of course, that an awareness of strategic reading does not necessarily translate into an actual use of the strategies concerned. Nonetheless, we believe that it is important for metacognitive reading strategies instruction to be integrated within the overall reading curriculum so as to enhance students' metacognition about reading. Such instruction can help promote an increased awareness of the mental processes involved in reading and the development of thoughtful and constructively responsive reading. Teaching students to become constructively responsive readers can be a powerful way to promote skillful academic reading, which will, in turn, enhance academic achievement.

# 10 Perceived and Real-Time Use of Reading Strategies by Three Proficient Triliterate Readers: A Case Study

**Kouider Mokhtari**
*Miami University, Ohio*

## Introduction

Recent research addressing metacognitive awareness and use of reading strategies by first- (L1) and second-language (L2) readers of English indicates that the use of reading strategies for planning, regulating, and evaluating text understanding has been found to be effective in promoting thoughtful, constructively responsive reading by L1 and L2 readers (Anderson, 1991; Baker & Brown, 1984; Block, 1992; Garner, 1987; Jiménez, Garcia, & Pearson, 1995, 1996; Sheorey & Mokhtari, 2001; Mokhtari & Reichard, 2004; Pressley, 2000; Pressley, El-Dinary, & Brown, 1992; Paris, Lipson, & Wixon, 1994; Song, 1998). Available research suggests that proficient L1 and L2 readers use a wide range of reading strategies that reveal careful planning, monitoring, and evaluation of text understanding. Examples of such strategies include setting a purpose for reading, making predictions, paraphrasing, summarizing, resolving conflicts, and evaluating self-understanding. In addition, L2 reading research indicates that the supply of strategies used by proficient bilingual and biliterate readers often includes supporting strategies (e.g., code mixing, translation, and use of cognates) that are unique and particularly useful to reading in a second or a third language (Jiménez et al., 1995, 1996). For instance, in a study which examined the reading strategies used by 20 proficient Chinese college students when reading easy and difficult texts in English and Chinese, Feng and Mokhtari (1998) found that biliterate English and Chinese readers invoked a wide-ranging supply of strategies while reading academic texts in English and in Chinese; however, a majority of the strategies presumably used while reading appeared to be invoked more frequently when reading in English than in Chinese. In addition, the subjects used more strategies when they read difficult texts than when they read easy texts.

In a study aimed at examining differences in the metacognitive awareness and perceived use of reading strategies among college-level native and non-native speakers of English, Sheorey and Mokhtari (this volume, chapter 9) found that both native (U.S. college students) and non-native speakers of English (international college students) demonstrated a high level of awareness of diverse reading strategies when reading in English. They also found that U.S. female students reported using a significantly higher amount of reading strategies than did their male counterparts, and that the use of reading strategies was associated with higher levels of reading ability for both U.S. and international students. In a more recent study, Mokhtari and Reichard (2004) investigated the strategic reading processes of L1 and L2 readers in two different cultural contexts. Specifically, they measured the metacognitive awareness and perceived use of specific reading strategies of 141 U.S. university students and 209 Moroccan university students. The data, which were collected in the cultural contexts of the two groups involved (e.g., the United States and Morocco), revealed that despite the fact that the two student groups had been schooled in significantly different sociocultural environments, they reported remarkably similar patterns of perceived strategy awareness and use when reading college-level materials in English. Where differences were found, Moroccan students reported using certain types of reading strategies (e.g., pausing and thinking while reading and rereading for better understanding) significantly more often than American students. The findings have helped unveil sophisticated metacognitive processing strategies by readers of English as a second language (ESL), who have, by and large, been seen in terms of deficiencies but not in other, presumably more beneficial or even neutral ways.

The above findings are consistent with earlier studies (e.g., Garcia, Jiménez, & Pearson, 1998; Jiménez, 1997; Jiménez et al., 1995, 1996) whose research has focused on the metacognitive reading processes of bilingual English and Spanish readers. In one study, Garcia et al. (1998) examined the reading strategies of eight bilingual Latina/o sixth- and seventh-grade students in the United States. They focused on these students' views of reading, the strategies they used when reading in two languages, and the conditions under which they invoked such reading strategies. For comparative purposes, they included a smaller sample of three native English-speaking students, all of whom were considered to be successful English readers, and three bilingual English-Spanish students considered to be marginally successful English readers. Using mixed methodologies (e.g., think alouds, interviews, a measure of prior knowledge, and passage recalls), they examined the type of strategies both successful and less successful readers used in their English reading. The study revealed that successful bilingual readers (i) perceived reading in Spanish and English as being fairly similar, (ii) that they demonstrated awareness of several reading strategies, with some limited actual use of supporting strategies (e.g., use of cognates, code-switching, and translation), which are typically used by biliterate readers, and (iii) that they did show evidence of reading strategy transfer across languages. In other words, successful biliterate English and Spanish readers "knew that information and strategies learned or acquired in one language could be used to comprehend text written in another language" (Garcia et al., 1998, p. 204).

On the other hand, the less successful bilingual readers did not appear to hold different views about reading in two languages; rather, they "believed that the two languages were more different than similar and that knowledge of one was not useful for reading the others" (p. 211). Additionally, because they viewed reading in one language as unrelated to reading in the other languages, they did not believe it was worthwhile to invoke strategies such as searching for cognates, code mixing, and translation as supporting strategies for reading in the target language. Garcia and her colleagues concluded that "heightened metacognitive awareness as applied to reading is not an automatic outcome of children's bilingualism or bilingual education" (p. 213). In other words, less successful readers must be helped in developing an awareness of the reading used by successful readers and in using these strategies when reading across languages.

Clearly, the L2 reading research, which has investigated the reading processes among good and poor bilingual readers, has contributed a great deal to our understanding of how bilingualism and biliteracy influence metacognitive processing and reading development. The research work that serves as the focus of the present study is informed by these research efforts, but focuses more specifically on documenting the type of metacognitive awareness and real-time or actual use of reading strategies by proficient non-native speakers of English while reading across multiple languages. Despite the overwhelming number of studies on various aspects of L2 and foreign-language reading, little research has been carried out on the metacognitive knowledge and reading strategies of multilingual and multiliterate readers. At present, there are no published studies that have investigated the metacognitive knowledge and reading strategies of successful readers who are proficient in multiple languages, particularly those languages that have significantly contrasting orthographies, such as Arabic and English or French. The present study is intended to contribute to the existing knowledge base regarding the reading strategies and behaviors of 3 college students who are native speakers of Arabic and French and who have near native speaker ability in English.

## The Present Study

In the study reported here, I sought to explore the perceived and actual use of reading strategies by three proficient readers when reading in three different languages. This case study is part of a series of investigations aimed at contributing to the current knowledge base regarding the potential impact of multiple literacies in languages (in the present case, Arabic, English, and French), which differ markedly in terms of direction, orthography, lexicon, and syntax, on the strategic reading processes of successful college readers. Unlike Roman alphabets used in English and French, written Arabic differs in terms of script and direction (e.g., Arabic is read from right to left; English and French are read from left to right), orthography (e.g., Arabic has 28 letters; English has 26), lexicon, and syntax. However, despite such differences, research has shown that the literacy skills and strategies acquired in the native language do transfer to second or third literacies across language systems with similar orthographies, such as Spanish and English (e.g., Jiménez et al., 1995, 1996; Padron, Knight, & Waxman, 1986; Calero-Breckheimer & Goetz, 1993), as well as across languages with radically different orthographies, such as Arabic or Berber and French (e.g., Wagner, 1993) or Chinese and English (e.g., Feng & Mokhtari, 1998).

This study focuses on the unique capabilities of trilingual and triliterate readers when reading across multiple languages. The underlying hypothesis in undertaking this cross-cultural study is that the reading potential of multilingual and multiliterate readers is often underestimated and mistakenly perceived as a problem among some educators (e.g., Carson, 1992; Field & Aebersold, 1990), and that careful study of the reading potential of these readers should reveal that mature, strategic, and constructively responsive reading can be associated with all readers, including those often labeled as disadvantaged, marginalized, and at-risk. The specific research questions of interest in the study are as follows:

1.  What strategies do multiliterate readers report using when reading across three languages (i.e., Arabic, English, and French)?
2.  What strategies do they actually use when reading texts in these three languages?
3.  Under what conditions does reading strategy use vary across the three languages?

## Participants

The participants for this study consisted of 3 college students who were literate in three or more languages. At the time of the study, all 3 participants were college students pursuing graduate degrees at a comprehensive research university in the midwestern United States. The following description provides a profile of each of the students.

- *BJ*: BJ is a 39-year-old male from Morocco. At the time of the study, he was a graduate student pursuing a master's degree in engineering. He had been in the United States for nearly 1.5 years and had studied English for 4 years prior to study. He is a fluent bilingual and speaks Arabic and French as native languages and learned English as a foreign language in Morocco. He describes himself as most proficient in French and least proficient in English.

- **MC:** MC is a 33-year-old male from Morocco. At the time of the study, he was a graduate student pursuing a master's degree in chemistry. He had been in the United States for nearly a year and a half, and had studied English for 4 years prior to coming to the United States for study. He speaks Arabic and French as native languages and learned English and German as foreign languages in Morocco and Germany. He considers himself as most proficient in French but least proficient in Arabic and English.

- *HE*: HE is a 38-year-old female from Sudan. At the time of the study, she was a graduate student pursuing a doctoral degree in special education. She had been in the United States for nearly 6 years, and had studied English as a foreign language in Sudan for 6 years prior to relocating to the United States. She speaks Arabic and French as native languages, and learned English as a foreign language in Sudan. She describes herself as most proficient in Arabic and English but least proficient in French.

*Data Collection*

The data collected for purposes of the study consisted of demographic information collected via a background questionnaire, an assessment of metacognitive reading strategies collected through the use of a survey of reading strategies, and a corpus of reading strategies collected through the use of think-aloud techniques. A brief description of these data collection sources and procedures follows.

Each participant completed a background questionnaire (see Appendix) aimed at gathering information about their age, gender, academic major, educational background, and a rating of their perceived reading ability. The students' metacognitive awareness of reading strategies was assessed through the use of the Survey of Reading Strategies (SORS), details of which can be found in Mokhtari, Sheorey, and Reichard (this volume, chapter 4). Following an overview of the study's main tasks (see Table 10.1), each participant completed the SORS instrument in Arabic, English, and French. Following a brief overview of the purpose of the study and an explanation of the various tasks in the study (see Table 10.1), each of the participants was instructed to complete the SORS instrument, which required their circling the number that best described their perceived use of strategies, using a 5-point Likert scale ranging from 1 ("I never or almost never use this strategy when reading academic texts") to 5 ("I always or almost always use this strategy"). They were advised to work at their own pace and to keep in mind reading academic or school-related materials (such as textbooks) while responding to the strategy statements. Finally, they were told that there were no "right" or "wrong" responses to the statements, and that they could take as much time as they needed to complete the inventory. On average, it took each participant roughly 12 minutes to complete the instrument.

The next step in the data collection consisted of each participant being asked to read three reading passages, one in each language. The readings (750–1,000 words) were selected from popular Arabic, French, and English magazines, which were read fairly regularly by each of the participants. The topics addressed in each of the readings were of general (academic) interest and were familiar to the participants. The reading selections had readability indices ratings ranging from 45 to 55 using the Flesch Reading Ease formula, indicating moderate difficulty but appropriate for college-level students. The following is a brief description of each reading selection.

The Arabic reading selection was entitled "Al-kiimiaa inda al arab wa al muslimin" (Chemistry among Arabs and Muslims) and written by Abd Erahman Allabun and published in the August issue of the *Saudi Chemical Society* magazine (1999). The article discussed the contributions of Arabs and Muslims in the area of science in general and chemistry in particular. The article was printed in color on a single page accompanied by a colorful picture of a chemical lab in Saudi Arabia on the opposite page. The English reading selection was entitled "Couscous: Past and Present" by Kitty Morse and was published in the November/December 1998 issue of the *ARAMCO* magazine. The reading selection described couscous, which has been a staple diet and a presence in the culture of North Africa for more than 100 years. The article was printed in color on a single page accompanied by a colorful picture of a type of couscous called *sfuf* in Moroccan Arabic. The dish featured a sugar-topped mountain of sfuf, decorated with spokes of cinnamon and served at the Palais Jamai Hotel in Fez, Morocco. The French reading selection was entitled "Obesite: la piste virale" (Obesity: AD 36 Virus) and written by Emilie Tran Phong. The article was published in the March 2000 issue of *L'Express* and presented recent research on the various causes of obesity, with particular focus on AD 36, the first human virus known to cause obesity among humans and animals. The article was printed in color on a single page accompanied by a colorful picture of an obese man standing by a tree.

Following established methodological recommendations for increasing the likelihood of obtaining reasonably complete and accurate self-reports (see Afflerbach & Johnson, 1984; Ericsson & Simon, 1993; Pressley & Afflerbach, 1995), each passage was marked with intermittent red dots, placed after one to two sentences. The markings served as a steady reminder for the participants to verbalize their thoughts while reading across languages. To gain insights into the readers' strategic reading processes while reading, the think-aloud procedure was used as a means of eliciting accounts of participants' thinking while reading. The subjects were asked to read each of the reading selections at designated times during the study and to verbally report their thinking while reading the text in each language. The resulting protocols were audiotaped to ensure completeness and accuracy in data transcription and analysis.

Because of the inherent challenges of thinking aloud while engaged in complex cognitive tasks such as reading, researchers (e.g., Van Someren, Barnard, & Sandberg, 1994) recommend exposing the subjects to the procedure and providing ample practice in verbalizing their thoughts while reading silently. Prior to conducting the think alouds, the subjects were first briefed about the nature of the study. During this briefing, they listened to an explanation and a description of the think-aloud procedure. They were then provided with an example of how thoughts can be verbalized while reading and were given an opportunity to practice thinking aloud using practice passages similar to the ones used in the actual study.

After the think-aloud procedure had been explained and modeled, the subjects practiced verbalizing their thoughts while reading practice passages until they felt comfortable with the process involved in thinking aloud. The practice sessions, which lasted approximately 1 hour, were audiotaped so as to give each participant a sense of their think-aloud performance and to help them gain confidence in using the procedure. The tape recordings provided useful feedback to the subjects concerning the completeness and accuracy of their verbal reports. During the practice sessions, they were given feedback about their performance while conducting the practice think alouds until they felt thoroughly comfortable with the procedure. Finally, they were encouraged to ask questions regarding any aspect of the study, including the think-aloud process.

The data for the study were collected case by case in several phases, spread over approximately 4 weeks. As indicated earlier, the data set included demographic information collected via a background questionnaire, an assessment of metacognitive reading strategies collected through the use of a survey of reading strategies, and a corpus of reading strategies collected through the use of the think-aloud technique. Table 10.1 provides an outline of the main phases of the data collection for this study.

Table 10.1 Overview of the Study's Main Tasks

| | Study Tasks | | | | | |
|---|---|---|---|---|---|---|
| Main phases | Orientation | Think-aloud training | Think-aloud study | | | Debriefing and exit interview |
| | | | Arabic | English | French | |
| Week 1 | • Study overview<br>• Complete questionnaire<br>• Complete SORS | | | | | |
| Week 2 | | • Complete think-aloud training | | | | |
| Week 3 | | | • Complete think-aloud study | | | |
| Week 4 | | | | | | • Complete debriefing and informal exit interview |

SORS, Survey of Reading Strategies.

With the exception of the initial phase of the study, all data-collection sessions were individually scheduled and all were conducted within a few days immediately following the think-aloud training sessions so that participants would remember how to perform the think alouds. In addition, at the beginning of each think-aloud session, participants were reminded of the basic steps for completing the think-aloud procedure. While the sessions were in process, the researcher was available to answer questions and provide assistance if needed. The participants were allowed to select the language (i.e., Arabic, English, or French) in whichever order they chose. Because the sessions were conducted one-on-one, the duration of the entire think aloud varied from 60 to 90 minutes per participant.

*Data Analyses*

The data obtained from the background questionnaire and the SORS instrument were analyzed using basic descriptive statistics. These data were helpful in developing a profile of the participants with respect to age, gender, self-evaluated reading proficiency, and related information. The data obtained from the think-aloud protocols were analyzed using established qualitative research techniques. The think-aloud framework, developed by Van Someren et al. (1994), was applied to analyze the think-aloud data in order to identify the reading strategies and extract instances of reading strategy usage. The framework consists of three main steps: (i) data transcription (verbalized thoughts along with the actual text reading are written down verbatim on a word processor with the thoughts italicized to distinguish between text selection and verbalized thoughts); (ii) data segmentation (the think-aloud data corpus is marked or dissected into segments consisting of strategy segments or divisions; and (iii) data coding (the reading strategies identified are coded and labeled appropriately).

These three steps of the proposed framework were helpful in identifying the strategies used by the participants while reading, and in finding specific examples to support the actual use of such strategies. For this study, a strategy is defined as any overt purposeful effort or action used on the part of the reader to make sense of the material with which he or she interacts (Pressley, 2000). Examples of reading strategies and their labels include "setting purpose of reading," "using prior knowledge," "pausing and thinking about what one reads," "solving reading problems," "summarizing what one reads," "translating from one language to another," and "asking questions." In an attempt to increase the accuracy and validity of the strategies identified, the strategies identified were examined by two additional independent judges who were well versed in the think-aloud procedure. These two individuals essentially conducted the same analyses following the three steps outlined above, and their findings were then compared to the researcher's findings with the goal of reaching a reasonable level of concurrence or consistency with respect to the type, number, and labeling of strategies extracted from the participants' verbal reports. Throughout this process, disagreements among the judges were scrutinized and discussed until consensus was reached.

# Results and Discussion

The results obtained are presented in Tables 10.2 and 10.3. Table 10.2 presents data pertaining to each student's perceived use of reading strategies when reading academic materials (Research Question #1: What strategies do the participants report using when reading across three languages (i.e., Arabic, English, and French)?

Table 10.2 Subjects' Awareness (Perceived Use) of Reading Strategies

| | BJ | | | MC | | | HE | | |
|---|---|---|---|---|---|---|---|---|---|
| | Ara | Eng | Fre | Ara | Eng | Fre | Ara | Eng | Fre |
| **Global Reading Strategies** | **3.31** | **3.30** | **3.15** | **4.15** | **3.53** | **4.0** | **3.70** | **3.61** | **3.58** |
| Setting purpose for reading | 5 | 5 | 5 | 5 | 4 | 4 | 5 | 4 | 3 |
| Using prior knowledge | 4 | 3 | 3 | 5 | 4 | 4 | 5 | 5 | 4 |
| Previewing text before reading | 4 | 4 | 4 | 3 | 4 | 4 | 5 | 2 | 5 |
| Checking how text content fits purpose | 4 | 4 | 3 | 4 | 3 | 3 | 2 | 4 | 5 |
| Noting text characteristics | 4 | 4 | 4 | 4 | 4 | 3 | 5 | 3 | 3 |
| Determining what to read | 4 | 4 | 3 | 4 | 3 | 4 | 4 | 4 | 3 |
| Using text features (e.g., graphs) | 3 | 3 | 3 | 4 | 4 | 3 | 4 | 5 | 4 |
| Using context clues | 3 | 3 | 3 | 4 | 3 | 4 | 4 | 5 | 4 |
| Using typographical aids (e.g., italics) | I | I | I | 2 | 2 | 2 | 2 | 5 | 4 |
| Critically evaluating what is read | 2 | 2 | 2 | 3 | 4 | 4 | 4 | 4 | 3 |
| Checking one's understanding | 2 | 3 | 3 | 5 | 5 | 5 | 5 | 4 | 4 |
| Predicting or guessing text meaning | 3 | 4 | 4 | 5 | 4 | 4 | 5 | 3 | 5 |
| Confirming predictions | 4 | 3 | 3 | 4 | 2 | 3 | I | 3 | 3 |
| | | | | | | | | | |
| **Problem-Solving Strategies** | **3.87** | **3.57** | **3.57** | **4.0** | **3.44** | **3.75** | **4.87** | **4.57** | **4.0** |
| Getting back on track while reading | 4 | 3 | 3 | 4 | 4 | 4 | 3 | 5 | 3 |
| Reading slowly but carefully | 5 | 4 | 4 | 4 | 2 | 3 | 5 | 5 | 5 |
| Adjusting reading rate | 3 | 3 | 3 | 4 | 2 | 2 | 5 | 4 | 5 |
| Paying close attention to my reading | 3 | 4 | 4 | 5 | 4 | 4 | 3 | 5 | 4 |
| Pausing and thinking about reading | 3 | 3 | 3 | 5 | 4 | 4 | 3 | 5 | 4 |
| Visualizing information read | 3 | 5 | 5 | 4 | 2 | 3 | 4 | 4 | 3 |
| Rereading for better understanding | 4 | 3 | 4 | 5 | 5 | 5 | 4 | 5 | 5 |
| Guessing meaning of unknown words | 3 | 3 | 3 | 5 | 4 | 4 | 4 | 3 | 3 |
| | | | | | | | | | |
| **Support Reading Strategies** | **2.89** | **2.55** | **2.70** | **3.77** | **3.40** | **3.44** | **3.67** | **4.30** | **4.0** |
| Taking notes while reading | 2 | 2 | 2 | 2 | 2 | 2 | 5 | 4 | 3 |
| Reading aloud when text becomes hard | 3 | 3 | 3 | 5 | I | I | 5 | 5 | 5 |
| Underlining information in text | 4 | 4 | 4 | 3 | 4 | 4 | 5 | 5 | 4 |
| Using reference materials | 3 | 4 | 4 | 3 | 4 | 4 | 2 | 4 | 5 |
| Paraphrasing for better understanding | 2 | 2 | 2 | 4 | 3 | 4 | 5 | 4 | 5 |

*(cont.)*

*Table 10.2 (cont.)*

| | | | | | | | | | |
|---|---|---|---|---|---|---|---|---|---|
| Going back and forth in text | I | I | I | 4 | 5 | 5 | 4 | 4 | 4 |
| Asking oneself questions | 2 | 2 | 2 | 3 | 2 | 2 | 3 | 2 | 2 |
| Translating from one language to another | 3 | 3 | 3 | 3 | 3 | 3 | 4 | 3 | 5 |
| Thinking in multiple languages | 2 | 2 | 2 | 5 | 5 | 4 | 4 | 4 | 5 |
| **Overall Reading Strategies** | 3.35 | 3.14 | 3.14 | 3.97 | 3.45 | 3.73 | 4.08 | 4.16 | 3.86 |

Note. Numbers 1, 2, 3, 4, and 5 indicate how often subjects reported using specific strategies when reading academic materials. A rating scale from 1 ("low perceived use") to 5 ("high perceived use") was used.

The data presented in Table 10.2 indicate that each of the participants reported using all of the 30 strategies outlined in the SORS instrument in each of the three languages to varying degrees. The overall reported mean strategy use varied from a mean of 3.14 for BJ when reading in English to a mean of 4.16 for HE when reading in English on a 5-point scale ranging from 1 ("low perceived usage") to 5 ("high perceived usage"). In addition, the overall average use of reading strategies did not appear to be much different across the three languages for any of the participants. In other words, the average perceived strategy use was fairly consistent across the three languages for each participant. In addition, a close examination of the data in Table 10.2 indicates that each of the participants reported using certain types of strategies more than others. For instance, support reading strategies (means ranged from 2.55 to 4.3) were used far less than global reading strategies (means ranged from 3.15 to 4.15) or problem-solving strategies (means ranged from 3.44 to 4.87). These data seem to indicate that despite the peculiarities and challenges of reading texts in quite different languages, the participants reported invoking a fairly similar pattern of strategy use when reading across the three languages.

These findings corroborate the work of prior researchers (e.g., Garcia et al., 1998; Jiménez et al., 1995, 1996; Sheorey & Mokhtari, 2001; Mokhtari & Reichard, 2004) who have found that biliterate and multiliterate readers, like native speakers of English, report invoking a wide range of strategies while reading academic or school-related materials. These findings are consistent with Garcia et al.'s (1998) findings that proficient readers appear to have a unitary view of reading, in that they see that the cognitive processes involved in one language are similar to those required when reading in another language, even when reading in languages such as Arabic, which is quite different from English or French in terms of direction, sound system, word formation, and syntax.

Table 10.3 presents data pertaining to the real-time or actual use of reading strategies while reading texts in three languages (Research Question #2: What strategies did the participants actually use when reading texts in these three languages?). The data obtained revealed three interesting findings relative to the actual use of strategies when reading across three languages. First, there was a discrepancy between reported (or perceived) strategy use and real-time or actual strategy use among all three participants. In general, the data indicate that several of the strategies that the participants reported using when reading academic materials in general were either not used at all (e.g., "previewing text before reading" or "getting back on track while reading") or used quite infrequently (e.g., "underlining information in text" or "asking oneself questions"). These data seem to indicate that while the three participants, who viewed themselves as proficient readers, may be aware of and use a rich supply of reading strategies when reading for academic purposes, which strategies they end up using and how intensely they end up using them depends, to some extent, on the type of reading they're faced with. In other words, it is conceivable that the pattern of actual strategy usage may be quite different had these readers been asked to read a book chapter or a computer manual. These questions ought to be explored in greater detail with greater numbers of readers while engaged in multiple academic tasks.

Table 10.3 Subjects' Reported Use of Real-Time Reading Strategies

| | BJ | | | MC | | | HE | | |
|---|---|---|---|---|---|---|---|---|---|
| | *Ara* | *Eng* | *Fre* | *Ara* | *Eng* | *Fre* | *Ara* | *Eng* | *Fre* |
| **Global Reading Strategies** | | | | | | | | | |
| Setting purpose for reading | --- | --- | --- | 1 | 1 | 2 | --- | 1 | 1 |
| **Using prior knowledge** | 3 | 4 | 5 | 4 | 4 | 3 | 3 | 4 | 1 |
| Previewing text before reading | --- | 1 | --- | --- | 1 | --- | --- | 1 | --- |
| Checking how text content fits purpose | --- | --- | --- | --- | --- | --- | --- | --- | --- |
| Noting text characteristics | --- | --- | --- | --- | --- | --- | --- | --- | --- |
| Determining what to read | --- | --- | --- | --- | --- | --- | --- | --- | --- |
| Using text features (e.g., graphs) | --- | --- | --- | --- | --- | --- | --- | --- | --- |
| Using context clues | --- | 1 | --- | --- | --- | --- | 3 | 6 | 2 |
| **Using typographical aids (e.g., italics)** | --- | 2 | 1 | 1 | 3 | 3 | 3 | 3 | 3 |
| Critically evaluating what is read | --- | 2 | 1 | 1 | 3 | 3 | 3 | 3 | 5 |
| Checking one's understanding | --- | 2 | 4 | 3 | 4 | 2 | 9 | 1 | 5 |
| **Predicting or guessing text meaning** | --- | --- | 2 | 4 | --- | 3 | 9 | 2 | 14 |
| **Confirming predictions** | --- | --- | --- | 3 | --- | 2 | 9 | 1 | 13 |
| | | | | | | | | | |
| **Problem-Solving Strategies** | | | | | | | | | |
| Getting back on track while reading | --- | --- | --- | --- | --- | --- | 3 | --- | --- |
| Reading slowly and carefully | --- | --- | --- | --- | --- | --- | 4 | --- | 1 |
| Adjusting reading rate | --- | --- | --- | --- | --- | --- | --- | --- | --- |
| Paying close attention to reading | --- | --- | --- | --- | --- | --- | --- | 1 | 1 |
| **Pausing and thinking about reading** | --- | 6 | 2 | 6 | 4 | 2 | 11 | --- | 5 |
| Visualizing information read | --- | 1 | --- | --- | --- | --- | --- | 2 | --- |

*(cont.)*

*Table 10.2 (cont.)*

| | | | | | | | | | |
|---|---|---|---|---|---|---|---|---|---|
| Rereading for better understanding | --- | --- | 2 | --- | --- | 2 | 4 | 2 | 6 |
| Guessing meaning of unknown words | --- | 2 | --- | 5 | --- | --- | 5 | 11 | 10 |
| **Support Reading Strategies** | | | | | | | | | |
| Taking notes while reading | --- | --- | --- | --- | --- | --- | --- | --- | --- |
| Reading aloud when text becomes hard | --- | 2 | --- | --- | --- | --- | --- | --- | 1 |
| Underlining information in text | --- | --- | 1 | --- | 1 | 2 | --- | 2 | 2 |
| Using reference materials | --- | --- | --- | --- | --- | --- | --- | 2 | 2 |
| **Paraphrasing for better understanding** | 5 | 5 | 7 | 3 | 2 | 3 | 12 | 10 | 17 |
| Going back and forth in text | --- | --- | --- | 1 | --- | --- | 5 | 5 | 7 |
| Asking oneself questions | --- | --- | 2 | 1 | --- | 2 | 2 | 2 | 5 |
| **Translating from one language to another** | 21 | 3 | 3 | 5 | 3 | 2 | 3 | 1 | 11 |
| **Thinking in multiple languages** | 11 | 12 | 3 | 6 | 3 | 2 | 1 | 2 | 12 |
| **Type of Strategies Used** | 4 | 13 | 12 | 14 | 11 | 14 | 17 | 20 | 21 |
| **Volume of Strategies Used** | 40 | 43 | 33 | 44 | 29 | 33 | 89 | 62 | 124 |

*Note.* Numbers indicate how many times subjects actually used the specific strategies when reading. Thus, the number "4" indicates the strategy was used 7 times while reading the assigned passages.

Second, all the three participants appear to have a preferred stack of strategies that each invoked most often when reading the assigned readings in each of the three languages. As Table 10.2 shows, each participant relied on a certain type of strategies when reading across the three languages. The number of strategies relied on ranged from a low of 4 strategies for BJ when reading in Arabic to a high of 21 for HE when reading in French (see Fig. 10.1). In addition, all three participants had a tendency to invoke their respective preferred strategies in all three languages but with greater frequency when reading in the language in which they felt least proficient. On the other hand, they had a tendency to invoke those strategies with less frequency when reading in the language in which they felt most skilled (see Fig. 10.2). For instance, BJ used 4 strategies a total of 40 times when reading in French, his strongest language, while he used 13 strategies a total of 43 times in English, his weakest language. The two strategies he relied on most of the time were "translating from one language to another" and "thinking in multiple languages." HE, on the other hand, used 17 strategies for a total of 89 times in Arabic, her strongest language, while she used 21 strategies for a total of 124 times in French, her weakest language. Finally, MC used 14 strategies a total of 44 times in Arabic and French, two of his weakest languages, for a total of 44 and 33 times, respectively. In general, it seems that the level of perceived language proficiency was important for each participant in determining not only the type, but also the volume of strategies used.

Figure 10.1 Type of strategies used by language

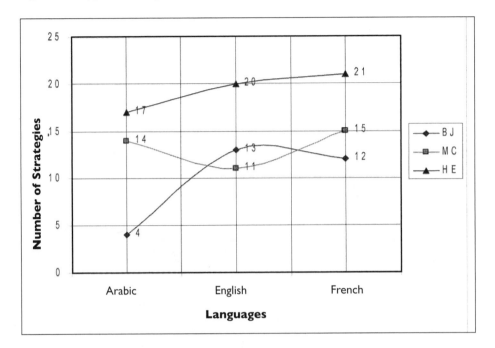

Figure 10.2 Number of strategies used by language

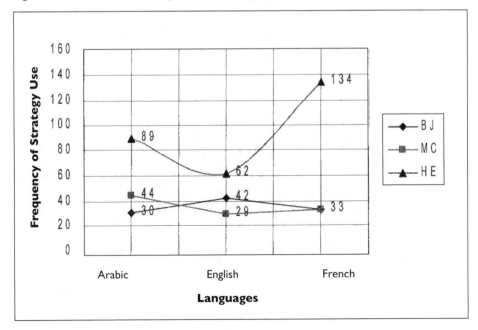

**Figure 10.3** Number of strategies used by category

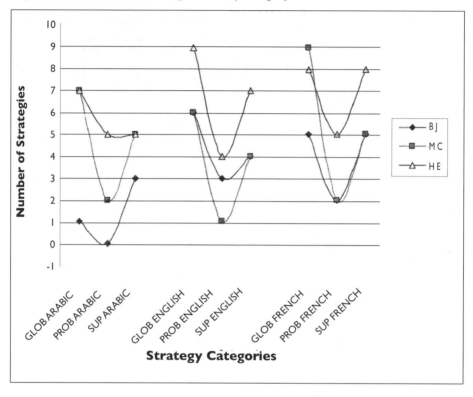

A closer examination of the real-time or actual strategy-use data pre-sented in Table 10.3 (and, as illustrated in Figs. 10.1–10.3, reveals some important information regarding variation in strategy use across the three languages; Research Question #3: Under what conditions does reading strategy use vary across the three languages? These data presented pro-vide some evidence for strategy transfer across the three languages for each of the participants. In most cases, and especially for certain strategies, each of the participants used similar strategies across the three languages used. This transfer can be seen not just in the type of strategies used (see Fig. 10.1), but also in the intensity or volume of strategies invoked while reading (see Figs. 10.2 and 10.3). It seems as though these three proficient readers, like the successful readers described in prior bilingual reading research (e.g., Feng & Mokhtari, 1998; Jiménez et al., 1995, 1996), seem to be aware of the fact that good reading strategies learned or acquired in one language could be used to comprehend texts written in another lan-guage. Note, for instance, that the strategies of "translating from one lan-guage to another" and "thinking in multiple languages" are used with the same level of intensity and uniformity across the three languages.

However, while there is some evidence of strategy transfer across languages among the three participants, it is unclear which language or languages are influencing the use of strategies in the other language(s). In other words, it is difficult to determine from the data in this study which of the languages (i.e., Arabic, English, or French) is the principal source of transfer. It is conceivable that the participants would resort to French as a source of transfer when reading English, since English and French are much closer typographically than French and Arabic or English and Arabic. These questions cannot be answered by the data examined in this study and must, therefore, be subjected to further investigations with multiliterate speakers.

## Conclusion

The overall purpose of this case study was to find out the perceived and real-time or actual use of reading strategies of three proficient triliterate adult readers when reading across three languages, namely, Arabic, English, and French. The main findings of the study seem to indicate that while there were some differences for each participant in their perceived and actual strategy use across the three languages, the patterns of perceived and real-time strategy use were quite similar across the three languages, despite the differences among these languages in terms of direction, sound system, lexicon, and syntax.

As indicated earlier, the findings reported above are consistent with prior research on reading strategy awareness and use among bi- and multiliterate readers. However, a series of questions need to be addressed by future research investigating metacognitive awareness and use of reading strategies across multiple languages by poor and good readers. For instance, one might ask: Why did the three participants use or not use some of the strategies during real-time reading across the three languages? Does the type of text read make a difference in whether or not certain categories of strategies get used? Does passage length, difficulty level of the material, and/or topic familiarity make a difference in perceived and/or actual strategy use?

Finally, taking into account differences in metacognitive awareness and use of reading strategies among readers varying in reading ability, is it conceivable that possible differences in metacognitive awareness and real-time use of reading strategies across languages simply wash out with increased levels of language proficiency. Although some prior research has established a link between the development of metacognitive beliefs and reading development (see, especially, Wagner, 1993), further research is needed to determine whether major differences in metacognitive reading strategy awareness and actual use weaken out at higher levels of overall reading ability and/or language proficiency.

# Appendix

## Background Questionnaire

1.  Age: _____     2. Gender:   Male_____   Female_____
3.  Birthplace:_____
4.  Length of stay in U.S.: _____     5. Years studying English: _____
6.  Current major in college:_____
7.  Rank in college:  Graduate _____     Undergraduate____
    (1st Year ____     2nd Year ____     3rd Year ____     4th Year ___)
8.  Grade point average (optional) _____
9.  TOEFL Score in English (if known):_____
10. List all the languages you can speak, read, and write: _____

11. Which language(s) is (are) *your first or native language(s)?* _____
    11.1. How often do you use your first or native languages?
          Every day___ Often ___ Occasionally ___ Never_____
    11.2. For what purposes do you use your first or native language(s)?

    11.3. Where did you learn your first or native language?
          Home country_____          Another country_____
    11.4. On a scale from 1 to 10, rate your proficiency in your first or
          native language. Please provide a rating for each of the
          language skills listed. Circle your proficiency ratings.

| *Language Skill* | *Low Proficiency* | | | | | *High Proficiency* | | | | |
|---|---|---|---|---|---|---|---|---|---|---|
| • Listening | 1 | 2 | 3 | 4 | 5 | 6 | 7 | 8 | 9 | 10 |
| • Speaking | 1 | 2 | 3 | 4 | 5 | 6 | 7 | 8 | 9 | 10 |
| • Reading | 1 | 2 | 3 | 4 | 5 | 6 | 7 | 8 | 9 | 10 |
| • Writing | 1 | 2 | 3 | 4 | 5 | 6 | 7 | 8 | 9 | 10 |

12. Which language(s) is (are) your *second language(s)*? _____

    12.1. How often do you use your second language(s)?
          Every day___ Often ___ Occasionally ___ Never_____
    12.2. For what purposes do you use your second language(s)?

    12.3. Where did you learn your second language(s)?
          Home country_____          Another country_____

12.4. Approximately how old were you when you began learning your second language? _____

12.5. Approximately how many years did you spend learning your second language? _____

12.6. On a scale from 1 to 10, rate your proficiency in your second language. Please provide a rating for each of the language skills listed. Circle your proficiency ratings.

| *Language Skill* | *Low Proficiency* | | | | | *High Proficiency* | | | | |
|---|---|---|---|---|---|---|---|---|---|---|
| • Listening | 1 | 2 | 3 | 4 | 5 | 6 | 7 | 8 | 9 | 10 |
| • Speaking | 1 | 2 | 3 | 4 | 5 | 6 | 7 | 8 | 9 | 10 |
| • Reading | 1 | 2 | 3 | 4 | 5 | 6 | 7 | 8 | 9 | 10 |
| • Writing | 1 | 2 | 3 | 4 | 5 | 6 | 7 | 8 | 9 | 10 |

13. Which language(s) is (are) your *third language(s)*? _____

_____

13.1. How often do you use your third language(s)?
Every day___ Often ___ Occasionally ___ Never____

13.2. For what purposes do you use your third language(s)?
_____

13.3. Where did you learn your third language(s)?
Home Country____     Another Country_____

13.4. Approximately how old were you when you started learning your third language? _____

13.5. Approximately how many years did you spend learning your third language? _____

13.6. On a scale from 1 to 10, rate your proficiency in your third language. Please provide a rating for each of the language skills listed. Circle your proficiency ratings.

| *Language Skill* | *Low Proficiency* | | | | | *High Proficiency* | | | | |
|---|---|---|---|---|---|---|---|---|---|---|
| • Listening | 1 | 2 | 3 | 4 | 5 | 6 | 7 | 8 | 9 | 10 |
| • Speaking | 1 | 2 | 3 | 4 | 5 | 6 | 7 | 8 | 9 | 10 |
| • Reading | 1 | 2 | 3 | 4 | 5 | 6 | 7 | 8 | 9 | 10 |
| • Writing | 1 | 2 | 3 | 4 | 5 | 6 | 7 | 8 | 9 | 10 |

14. Overall, in which of the languages above are you *most proficient*? _____ and *least proficient*?_____

15. What particular difficulties, if any, do you face when you read in your first, second, or third languages?

# 11 | Metacognitive Awareness of Reading Strategies among Hungarian College Students

**Ravi Sheorey**
*Oklahoma State University*

**Edit Szoke Baboczky**
*Pecs University, Hungary*

## Introduction

There can be little disagreement that for students who have opted to specialize in English language and literature at a college or university in a non-native-English country, the skill of reading academic materials in English with adequate comprehension is perhaps the most important and useful one. Hungarian college students majoring in English are no exception to this assumption on our part. Not that other language skills, such as the much-valued speaking ability, are any less important; rather, as Cheng (1995) pointed out, "reading is one of the most pervasive and important skills…[and] without good reading proficiency, learners are unable to carry out their academic studies" (p. 2). In this chapter, we examine the perceptions of Hungarian college English majors about the types of reading strategies they report using and the frequencies with which they use those strategies. We define reading strategies here—along the same lines we have defined them in other chapters—as those intentional, deliberate, or conscious actions that readers take in order to comprehend what they are reading. "For example," as Kern (1989) illustrated

> a reader may skim a text in order to get a gist, use context or morphological analysis to decode unfamiliar words, or review mentally the content of the text in order to monitor comprehension. If the text has not been understood, the reader may need to reread all or parts of the text (p. 145)

In this sense, the strategic readers, among Hungarian college students majoring in English, would be those who perceive themselves to be deploying a variety of strategies to construct meaning from a given text.

Reading researchers who have examined second-language (L2) reading have given considerable attention to understanding metacognitive awareness as a condition for thoughtful, constructively responsive reading by L2 learners. This research has shown that important reading strategies that deal with planning, controlling, and consciously thinking about one's understanding while reading, such as checking the title before beginning to read the rest of the text, using prior knowledge to understand what is read, or using typographical features such as bold or italic fonts, are widely used by first- (L1) and L2 readers. For example, in a study of the reading strategies of native and non-native college readers, Sheorey and Mokhtari (2001) found that metacognitive awareness of reading strategies varies significantly according to reading ability levels, that high-ability readers tend to exhibit higher levels of metacognitive awareness about reading processes than low-ability readers, and that they report using appropriate strategies to make sure they understand what they read. As has been suggested elsewhere in this volume (see chapter 3), the reader's metacognitive knowledge about reading includes an awareness or a perceived use of reading strategies, and that it is the combination of this awareness and the actual utilization of appropriate reading strategies that distinguish the skilled from unskilled readers. Metcognitive knowledge, in the context of reading, may include an awareness of one's thinking processes as well as such mental activities as monitoring one's understanding of the text during text processing and remembering and/or learning from it. The reader's metacognitive knowledge about reading may be influenced by a number of factors, including previous experiences, beliefs, culture-specific instructional practices, and, in the case of non-native readers, proficiency in the target language. Additionally, one or more strategies may be triggered, consciously or subconsciously, when the reader has to deal with a specific reading task.

Research in the reading strategies of L2 learners has revealed that readers' cultural and educational backgrounds affect their choice of strategies, as reported by Pritchard (1990), Knight, Padron, and Waxman (1985), and in a series of articles by Parry (1987, 1993, 1996). However, few studies have dealt with the specific reading strategies of Hungarian college students. The only study we know of was reported by Monos (2005) with a small sample ($N = 86$) of English majors at a single university in Hungary. As Monos pointed out, "…we know virtually nothing about how Hungarians read, worse still, how they read in academic contexts" (p. 53). The present chapter is our attempt to fill that gap in the research by adding information on the *perceived* or *reported* reading strategies of Hungarian students, majoring in English at the college level and studying in the English as a foreign language (EFL) environment of Hungary. In the study reported here, we set out to explore two specific research questions in the context of Hungarian students' perceived use of reading strategies while reading texts related to their academic tasks (e.g., English textbooks, journal articles, study guides, or class handouts):

1. What kind of reading strategies do Hungarian college students perceive they use (and with what frequency) when reading academic materials in English?
2. Is there any relationship between Hungarian students' reported reading strategy use and (i) gender, (ii) self-reported English proficiency, (iii) self-rated reading ability in English, and (iv) time spent on reading?

## English Language Situation in Hungary

Until 1989, when the Soviet occupation ended, Russian was the compulsory foreign language in Hungarian primary schools, although students were able to choose a second foreign language from English, German, French, and also Latin. Since 1990, however, the Hungarian government has allowed a free choice of foreign languages in the curriculum and, subsequently and especially, after Hungary's joining the European Union in 2004, English has increasingly become the dominant foreign language learned and taught in Hungary. English is not a required subject of study, but Hungarian students have figured out that competence in English, the language of global communication, opens up employment opportunities both in and outside the country. According to Csizér and Dörnyei (2005), "people increasingly study English not necessarily because they are motivated to do so but because it is seen as part of general education, similar to reading, writing, and arithmetic" (p. 649). There are other reasons for the current dominance of English, especially among the young. As Petzold and Berns (2000) point out, in the Hungarian middle and upper class social circles, "knowledge of a foreign language has long been considered a mark of cultivation and decent upbringing" (p. 115), and proficiency in English is almost a requirement to remain part of the elite club. Another reason for learning English among young Hungarians in general is the same as that commonly observed among the youth all over the world, namely, an interest in western popular culture, including music, movies, and fashion, all of which are expressed through English. In fact, during the 1990s, watching English-language television programs was fashionable among even those Hungarian families who knew no English. And today, MTV remains one of the most popular English-language channels among Hungarian youth (Petzold & Berns, 2000). In recent years, the spread of the Internet has also resulted in an increased interest in studying and using English.

The rapid rise in the interest in studying English during the 1990s was not, however, accompanied by an increase in the availability of well-trained and competent EFL teachers. Back then, the Hungarian government decided to solve the problem by training the large pool of teachers of Russian to teach English (and German, the second most popular foreign language). The solution was only partially appropriate, particularly because the teachers of Russian and other subjects were not necessarily proficient in English. According to Nikolov (2002): "In 1991–1992, less than half of the teachers of English had a teaching degree [but] schools were so much in need of [English] teaching staff that they allowed people of other professions or teachers of other subject areas to teach a foreign language with an intermediate-level language certificate" (p. 12). Nonetheless, nearly 5,000 teachers of Russian and other subjects completed teacher-training degree programs, which attempted to wean them away from grammar-translation and audiolingual methods of teaching English and encouraged them to use more communicative approaches.

A concurrent occurrence in Hungary during the last decade has been the increasing presence of foreign, mainly western, businesses and Hungarian companies forming joint ventures with western companies. These businesses typically employ people who are English proficient and have higher paying jobs than comparable jobs with local businesses. The multinational companies even hire English teachers to teach EFL to their Hungarian employees, and an increase in private English tutoring is also a reflection of the increasing demand for English. All these circumstances led to high enrollments of students majoring in English language and literature at Hungarian institutions of higher education, resulting in a saturation of English major graduates. In any case, these college English majors are the ones who are supposedly more proficient in English than other college students, and they are the ones who have to read more academic materials in English than any other group of students in Hungary.

## Method

### Subjects

The participants in this study were 545 Hungarian students, including 134 males (24%) and 411 females (75%) who were enrolled as English majors at five institutions of higher education in various parts of Hungary. They ranged in age from 18 to 38 years, with a mean age of 22.48, and they reported having studied English an average of a little over 7 years. On a scale of 1 (low) to 6 (high), they gave themselves an average rating of 3.97 for their overall proficiency in English and a self-rating of 4.06 for their reading ability in English. The participants reported that, on average, they spent just a little under 7 hours per week on reading academic materials in English during the academic year. Some other interesting facts about the participants emerged from the background questionnaire. For example, only 21% of the students admitted to reading in English for pleasure; nearly 79% agreed or strongly agreed that an ability to read in English is a key to a good education; and 82% agreed or strongly agreed that the ability to read English well can lead to obtaining a good job after graduation. Asked what their reasons for reading English were, more than two thirds of the participants (68%) indicated that they read in English to obtain new information or learn new things, and that much of their reading was related to their academic requirements.

### Instrument

The data for this study were collected through a slightly modified version of the Survey of Reading Strategies (SORS; Mokhtari & Sheorey, 2002). The major modification we made to SORS, other than minor changes in wording to suit the Hungarian context, was that of using a 6-point Likert scale ranging from 1 ("I never or almost never do this") to 6 ("I always or almost always do this"). The 6-point scale was used in place of the traditional 5-point scale when it was discovered during the pilot-testing of the survey that the subjects tended to choose "3" as the option far too often; some of the students' instructors also suggested that a 6-point scale would yield more reliable information. Such a scale was also used in the study by Monos (2005), although she did not indicate any rationale for the modified scale.

The SORS measures three broad categories of reading strategies, detailed descriptions of which can be found in chapter 3. Briefly, global reading strategies are typically deployed to get an overall analysis or overview of the text (13 items); problem-solving strategies are the procedures by which readers decode meaning while working directly with the text when problems develop in understanding textual information (9 items); and support strategies refer to the use of support materials or tactics intended to aid the reader in improving text comprehension (8 items).

The reliability alpha for SORS for this population of Hungarian college students turned out to be .83, indicating an acceptable degree of internal consistency in measuring the reading strategy perceptions of the subjects. The alpha values for the three subscales of SORS were as follows: .69 for global strategies; .72 for problem-solving strategies; and .61 for support strategies.

# Results

In examining reading-strategy use among these students on the SORS scale, which ranges from 1 to 6, we identified three types of usage as follows: *high* (mean = 4.50 or higher), *medium* or *moderate* (mean = 3.00–4.49), and *low* (mean = 2.99 or lower). These usage levels, similar to the ones used in other studies in this volume, provided a reasonable benchmark to identify characteristics of subjects with respect to their perceived use of reading strategies while reading academic texts in English.

*Reading Strategy Use by Individual Items and Categories*

Responses given by the students to SORS statements were examined in terms of the individual items as well as the three strategy categories mentioned above, namely, global strategies, problem-solving strategies, and support strategies. The mean of individual strategy items ranged from a high of 4.75 ("I look at tables, figures, and pictures in the text to understand the text better") to a low of 2.76 ("I check with myself to see if my guesses about the content are right or wrong"); the overall mean for the sample was 3.95, indicating a medium overall perceived use of reading strategies according to the criteria stated above. Table 11.1 summarizes the five most favored or most often used and the five least favored or least often used individual reading-strategy preferences of Hungarian students.

The data were further analyzed according to the three groupings or categories of the 30 reading strategies to examine the types of strategies and the mean frequency of their use by Hungarian college students. The averages for these categories revealed a moderate usage according to the criteria described above. Hungarian students appeared to show a preference for support and problem-solving strategies (means = 4.03 and 4.00, respectively), followed by global strategies ($M$ = 3.83), all in the medium category of perceived usage. These results are shown in greater detail in Table 11.2.

Table 11.1 Most- and Least-Favored Reading Strategies of Hungarian Students

| Strategy | Most favored strategies | M | SD |
|---|---|---|---|
| PROB8 | While reading, if I don't understand something, I read it again. | 4.84 | 1.15 |
| GLOB7 | I look at tables, figures, and pictures in the text to understand the text better. | 4.75 | 1.13 |
| GLOB13 | I look at the title before reading the text to get a hint about its content. | 4.70 | 1.19 |
| SUP7 | I go back and forth in the text to see if the ideas/ information go together. | 4.63 | 1.09 |
| SUP4 | I underline or circle important information in the text when I read. | 4.55 | 1.24 |
| *Strategy* | *Least favored strategies* | *M* | *SD* |
| SUP6 | I paraphrase (say the ideas in my own words) to better understand what I read. | 3.24 | 1.37 |
| SUP5 | I use reference materials (e.g., a dictionary) to better understand what I read. | 3.14 | 1.45 |
| GLOB5 | I look through what I have to read to see how long it is and how it is organized. | 3.01 | 1.56 |
| GLOB1 | When I read academic texts, I have a purpose in mind. | 2.79 | 1.55 |
| GLOB12 | I check with myself to see if my guesses about the content are right or wrong. | 2.76 | 1.34 |

PROB, problem-solving strategies; GLOB, global reading strategies; SUP, supporting strategies.

Table 11.2 Reported Strategy Use by Categories and Overall

| Strategy category (N) | N (respondents) | Minimum | Maximum | M | SD |
|---|---|---|---|---|---|
| Support strategies (8) | 545 | 1.63 | 5.75 | 4.03 | .70 |
| Problem-solving strategies (9) | 545 | 1.33 | 5.89 | 4.00 | .77 |
| Global strategies (13) | 545 | 2.08 | 5.46 | 3.83 | .62 |
| Overall (30) | 545 | 2.13 | 5.40 | 3.95 | .57 |

*Variables Affecting Reading-Strategy Use*

We also examined whether any individual characteristics of the subjects (specifically, gender, self-rated English proficiency, self-rated reading ability in English, and reported weekly amount of time spent in reading academic materials) had any significant influence on the choice or frequency of use of reading strategies. These differences were examined by using the independent-samples *t*-test.

*Variation by gender.* Information available from the background questionnaire indicated fairly similar background profiles (i.e., in terms of age, self-reported proficiency in English, and self-perceived reading ability) of the males and females in the sample. A total of 132 males and 407 females were included in this analysis. As far as individual strategies and strategy categories are concerned, significant differences were found between the male and female students ($p < .05$) in the means of 13 of the 30 reading strategies, The overall mean value for all the strategies taken together was also higher for females, and the difference was statistically significant (male $M = 3.75$ vs. female $M = 4.00$; $p < .05$). Additionally, for all the three strategy categories—that is, problem-solving, global, and support strategies—the female students had higher mean values than that for male students ($p < .05$). Table 11.3 shows the results of the differences mentioned above.

Table 11.3 Impact of Gender on Reported Strategy Use

| Variable | Gender | N | Mean | SD | Significance |
|---|---|---|---|---|---|
| Global strategies | Male | 134 | 3.65 | 0.59 | .01 |
| | Female | 411 | 3.90 | 0.62 | |
| Problem-solving strategies | Male | 134 | 3.77 | 0.74 | .01 |
| | Female | 411 | 4.08 | 0.78 | |
| Support strategies | Male | 134 | 3.90 | 0.77 | .01 |
| | Female | 411 | 4.07 | 0.68 | |
| Overall | Male | 134 | 3.75 | 0.55 | .01 |
| | Female | 411 | 4.00 | 0.56 | |

*Variation by self-reported English proficiency.* Subjects were asked to self-rate their overall proficiency in English on a scale of 1 ("low") to 6 ("high"). For purposes of statistical analysis, we divided the students into high proficiency (self-rating of 4–6; $N = 114$) and low proficiency (self-rating of 3 or lower; $N = 127$) groups, respectively. We found that the high-proficiency group had statistically higher means for 6 of the 30 strategy items than their low-proficiency counterparts. There were no significant differences between these two groups in the global, problem-solving, and support strategy categories ($p > .05$), and the same was true for overall strategy usage for all the strategy statements taken together ($p > .05$). These results are presented in Table 11.4 below.

Table 11.4 Differences in Reported Strategy Use by Self-Rated English Proficiency

| Variable | Proficiency level | N | Mean | SD | Significance |
|---|---|---|---|---|---|
| Global strategies | High | 114 | 3.90 | 0.64 | .26 |
| | Low | 127 | 3.81 | 0.57 | |
| Problem-solving strategies | High | 134 | 4.00 | 0.87 | .49 |
| | Low | 411 | 3.98 | 0.71 | |
| Support strategies | High | 134 | 4.13 | 0.77 | .41 |
| | Low | 411 | 4.05 | 0.67 | |
| Overall | High | 134 | 4.01 | 0.55 | .29 |
| | Low | 411 | 3.93 | 0.60 | |

*Variation by self-reported reading ability.* Participants were divided into two groups: the "high reading ability" group consisted of those who rated themselves 5 or 6 on the scale ($N = 153$) while the "low reading ability" group consisted of those who rated themselves 3 or lower ($N = 127$). The means of the high-ability group were significantly higher in 8 of the 30 strategy statements ($p < .05$). Moreover, there were no significant differences between the overall means of the high- and low-reading-ability groups (high group $M = 4.04$ vs. low group $M = 3.91$; $p > .05$) or the means for problem-solving and support strategy categories ($p > .05$). Only in the case of the global strategies category were the differences in the means significant ($p < .05$). Table 11.5 reports the results described above.

Table 11.5 Differences in Reported Strategy Use by Self-Rated Reading Proficiency in English

| Variable | Proficiency level | N | Mean | SD | Significance |
|---|---|---|---|---|---|
| Global strategies | High | 153 | 3.96 | 0.62 | .01 |
| | Low | 127 | 3.79 | 0.58 | |
| Problem-solving strategies | High | 153 | 4.08 | 0.87 | .30 |
| | Low | 127 | 3.97 | 0.74 | |
| Support strategies | High | 153 | 4.14 | 0.75 | .28 |
| | Low | 127 | 4.05 | 0.70 | |
| Overall | High | 153 | 4.04 | 0.61 | .06 |
| | Low | 127 | 3.91 | 0.55 | |

*Variation by time spent in reading academic materials in English.* We also examined whether there was any variation in the perceived use of reading strategies by the average amount of time the subjects reported spending on reading academic materials in English during the academic year. On the background questionnaire, students were asked to estimate the number of hours they spent per week in reading study-related materials. For purposes of statistical analysis, we divided the students into two groups ("high" and "low") according to the average number of hours spent in reading per week. The "high group" ($N = 204$) included those who reported spending 8 or more hours per week, while the low group ($N = 199$) included those who estimated that they spent 1–5 hours per week in reading academic materials for their classes. We found significant differences in the reading strategy usage between these two groups. As Table 11.6 shows, subjects who reported spending more time in reading academic materials in English (the "high" group) had higher mean values for each of the three strategy categories, namely, problem-solving, global, and support strategies, as well as for all except 1 of the 30 individual strategy statements. Additionally, we found statistically significant differences in the frequency of use of 23 of the 30 strategies ($p < .05$) and each of the three strategy categories ($p < .01$), the means for the high-group readers being significantly higher than those for the low-group readers in individual strategy items and categories.

Table 11.6 Differences in Reported Strategy Use by Self-Reported Time (Number of Hours) Spent on Reading Academic Materials in English

| Variable | Reading per week (hours) | N | Mean | SD | Significance |
|---|---|---|---|---|---|
| Global strategies | 8 or more | 204 | 4.01 | 0.61 | .01 |
| | 1–5 | 199 | 3.67 | 0.59 | |
| Problem-solving strategies | 8 or more | 204 | 4.21 | 0.78 | .01 |
| | 1–5 | 199 | 3.82 | 0.71 | |
| Support strategies | 8 or more | 204 | 4.18 | 0.69 | .01 |
| | 1–5 | 199 | 3.90 | 0.71 | |
| Overall | 8 or more | 204 | 4.11 | 0.55 | .01 |
| | 1–5 | 199 | 3,78 | 0.55 | |

## Discussion

In this study, we wanted to explore the awareness and perceived use of reading strategies of Hungarian college-level students majoring in English when they read academic materials such as textbooks and other types of study-related texts. We chose college English majors as our subjects because, given the non-native context of learning and using English in Hungary, they were thought to be the more likely candidates to read academic materials in English on a regular basis than other students. Overall, the results of this study show that Hungarian college students report using reading strategies with moderate frequency (overall SORS mean = 3.95) and that they particularly favor support and problem solving strategies ($M$ = 4.03 and 4.00, respectively). The strategy that Hungarian students perceived to be using most frequently was the support strategy of "rereading if something is not understood" ($M$ = 4.84). However, two global strategies ("looking at tables, figures, etc.," and "getting a hint of the content from the title") were the next two most favored strategies, with means of 4.75 and 4.70, respectively. Two support strategies were also perceived to be used with high frequency, namely, "going back and forth in the text to check if the ideas/information go together" ($M$ = 4.63) and "underlining or circling important information in the text" ($M$ = 4.55). Another strategy perceived to be used with high frequency was the global strategy of "trying to decide what is really important to better understand the text" ($M$ = 4.53). Among the five least-favored strategies were two global strategies, namely, "checking to see if my guesses about the content are right" ($M$ = 2.76) and "having a purpose in mind when reading an academic text" ($M$ = 2.79). However, given the popularity of bilingual and monolingual dictionaries among Hungarian college students, we were surprised that "using reference materials such as a dictionary" ($M$ = 3.14) was reported to be among the five least favored strategies. This last finding supports Monos' (2005) observation that Hungarian students "avoid time consuming strategies" (p. 62).

In general, Hungarian English majors' reading strategy usage described above displays strategic reading behaviors that are generally associated with skilled or proficient readers, whether native or non-native, as reported by a number of previous studies (e.g., Block, 1986; 1992; Pressley & Afflerbach, 1995; Pritchard, 1990; Sheorey & Mokhtari, 2001). Whether or not they read English slowly or rapidly, Hungarian students, overall, appear to prefer strategies similar to those used by skilled readers. In other words, they *perceive* themselves to be *strategic readers* when they read academic materials in English. Putting these patterns together, one can say that when reading academic texts, Hungarian students like to take an overall or global view of what they have to read (e.g., looking at the title and at the tables or pictures) and then, with the use of support mechanisms (such as reading the text back and forth or noting the important information by highlighting or underlining it) or the problem-solving strategy of rereading, they manage and monitor the comprehension of their academic reading tasks. These results are somewhat different from those reported by Monos (2005), whose subjects ($N$ = 86)—English majors at the beginning of their college careers—reported using problem-solving strategies more than any other category of strategies.

Our analysis of the results revealed some other key findings that deserve to be noted here. First, our analysis of the differences in strategy use by gender showed that female students in general reported using most of the strategies (13 of 30) included in SORS significantly more frequently than did their male counterparts (male $M$ = 3.75 vs. female $M$ = 4.0; $p$ < .01). Additionally, the means for each of the three strategy categories were significantly higher for female students ($p$ < .01) than for male students. These results are consistent with a number of studies on the general learning strategies of L2 learners, which have found that, in general, females use language-learning strategies (not specifically reading strategies) more frequently than males (see, e.g., Oxford, Ehrman, & Nyikos, 1988; Oxford, 1993; Green & Oxford, 1995; Kaylani, 1996; Sheorey, 1999). This study confirms once again, as Green and Oxford (1995) have said, that "gender difference trends in strategy use are quite pronounced within and across cultures, and this means that women and men are using different approaches to language learning" (p. 291).

Unlike some other studies, we did not find a significant linear relationship between reported reading strategies and English proficiency. In other words, although students who rated themselves to have higher English proficiency reported using the reading strategies in our survey with higher mean frequency than those who self-rated their proficiency to be low, the differences in strategy usage for each of the categories and overall were not significantly different ($p$ > .05). These results are not consistent with several studies of general learning strategies of L2 learners have shown a "linear relationship...between strategy use and language proficiency" (Oxford & Burry-Stock, 1995, p. 9) and reading strategies of L2 learners (Monos, 2005; Sheorey & Mokhtari, 2001). According one of the Hungarian instructors, these results may have to do with the general tendency among Hungarian students to rate themselves somewhat modestly with regard to English proficiency.

The analysis of self-rated reading proficiency level (i.e., "high" vs. "low") yielded similar results: Statistically significant differences ($p$ < .05) were found only in the case of eight statements; for the three strategy groups, significant differences were found only in the case of global strategies ($p$ < .05). This finding was rather surprising because prior research has indicated just the opposite: a positive relationship between reading ability and reading strategy awareness and reported use among both native and non-native readers (Carrell, Pharis, & Liberto, 1989; Monos, 2005; Sheorey & Mokhtari, 2001).

Our most significant finding is related to the number of hours students reported spending on academic reading in English. The results showed that there is a significant linear relationship between the time spent on reading and the perceived use or awareness of reading strategies: Students who spent more time reading academic texts per week (8 or more hours per week, on average) reported using reading strategies (both in each category and overall) with significantly more mean frequency ($p$ < .01) than those who reported reading relatively less per week (5 or fewer hours, on average). The analysis of our data also revealed that although both groups (high = 8 hours or more; low = 1–5 hours) reported using the same four strategies most often—namely, "looking at tables, figures, or pictures," "looking at the title," "rereading the text," and "going back and forth to better understand the text"—the mean values for the high group were significantly higher ($p < .01$) than those for the low group. This finding suggests, perhaps, that the more time Hungarians students spend in reading academic materials in English—and presumably, a larger amount of reading materials—the more frequently they appear to use reading strategies. So we concur with Monos (2005), whose findings were similar to ours, that "skilled reading can be developed through a lot of reading; that is to say, the more one reads, the more strategic, consequently, a better reader he/she becomes" (p. 63).

With regard to reading strategies of this group of non-native readers studying English in the non-native context of Hungary, our results seem to provide further evidence that, broadly speaking, gender differences in the use of reading strategies may be independent of cultural or educational background. In other words, whatever their cultural or educational background, female learners (as opposed to males) tend to use general learning strategies as well as reading strategies with higher frequency. Additionally, at least in the case of Hungarian students, more time spent in reading academic texts is associated with a higher frequency of reading-strategy use. On the other hand, a higher self-rating of English proficiency or reading ability does not seem to have any significant impact on the perceived use of reading strategies.

So what kind of an image or profile of the Hungarian college student-reader does one get from this study? We would say that the typical Hungarian college student is a careful, strategic reader who reads his or her academic materials in English carefully, previews the text by examining its title before reading it, who looks for the main point of the text, adjusts his or her reading speed according to the nature of the text, all the time making sure he or she comprehends what he or she reads even if he or she has to reread it or read it slowly and carefully. Clearly, Hungarian students make conscious decisions about how and what to do when it comes to reading academic texts, and their most frequently used reading strategies reflect the kinds of behaviors that are characteristic of good or experienced readers, as described by Pressley and Afflerbach (1995) in a summary of the results of 38 studies of native-English-speaking readers at various levels. The results discussed above are not entirely surprising, given the fact that as a group these students can be considered "academically successful," having done very well in secondary school examinations and selected for admission to a university in a competitive process that rewards high academic achievement in admission decisions. It is reasonable to assume that among the characteristics of academically successful students is an ability to read skillfully and comprehend academic materials in a second language.

## Limitations and Concluding Remarks

We must add a note of caution here: The findings reported in this study pertain only to awareness or *perceived use* of reading strategies among Hungarian college readers majoring in English. Nonetheless, the study has some important implications for reading instruction in Hungary or in the larger EFL context. We believe it is important for L2 readers to be aware of the significant strategies proficient reading requires. Hungarian EFL teachers can play a key role in increasing students' awareness of such strategies and in helping them become what Pressley and Afflerbach (1995) called "constructively responsive" readers. Classroom teachers can and should do at least the following: They should assess students' awareness of reading strategies by using instruments such as the SORS, which is easy to administer and does not take a lot of time and effort on the part of the teacher. Additionally, English teachers should try to create the conditions under which their students can learn to become constructively responsive and strategic readers. English teachers could offer direct explanation of the processes and steps involved in reading strategically and constructively. To teach a reading strategy, for example, the following steps can be taken: (i) describing what the strategy is, (ii) explaining why the strategy should be learned and used, and (iii) providing examples of the circumstances under which the strategy should be used. In turn, such instruction will be a useful way of increasing students' metacognition and strategic reading. Finally, based on our finding that those who read more often tend to have a higher awareness of reading strategies, we would recommend that giving students regular reading assignments, along with follow-up quizzes to check their comprehension of what they are assigned to read, would lead to enhanced reading competence.

We realize, of course, that awareness or even direct teaching of strategic reading may not necessarily translate into actual use of the strategies concerned. Nonetheless, we believe that if reading strategies instruction is integrated within the overall English language curriculum, it can help promote an increased awareness of the mental processes involved in reading and the development of thoughtful, strategic readers. Teaching students to become constructively responsive readers can be a powerful way to promote skillful academic reading in English.

# 12 | Reading Strategies of the Users of English as a Library Language: The Case of Japanese ESP Students

**Ravi Sheorey**
*Oklahoma State University*

**Yumi Kamimura**
*Ibaraki Christian University, Japan*

**Mark R. Freiermuth**
*Gunma Prefectural Women's University*, *Japan*

## Introduction

Scientists of the world would readily acknowledge that a significant body of scientific and technical literature in today's world is available primarily in English and that, therefore, the ability to read that literature—that is, technical, academic texts—efficiently would be considered highly desirable by students who choose to major in scientific and technical fields of study, whether it is computer science or engineering, and for whom English is a foreign language (EFL). In this paper, we examine how a group of Japanese college students, majoring in computer science, go about accomplishing the task of comprehending the academic texts they are called upon to read as part of their college education. Specifically, we explore these "technical" students' English-reading strategies when they read academic materials, such as textbooks and other study materials in English. A major reason for our investigating the reading strategies of this particular group of students is that literature on the reading strategies of these Japanese college students who are expected to read English for specific purposes (ESP)—in this case, computer science–related English textual materials—is almost nonexistent. Additionally, we believe that reading and comprehending technical English is a crucially important skill for students majoring in a technical field in any country, especially in a technologically advanced country such as Japan.

Another observation we have come across in the literature is that Japanese students studying English are said to be better at reading than speaking, listening, or writing. However, Kitano (1994), after years of teaching English at the college level, believes that this is a myth. Foreign researchers who have taught English in Japan seem to agree with him (e.g., Christensen, 1990; Dadour & Robbins, 1996). They observe that students enter Japanese universities with extremely limited reading strategies, regardless of their previous English instruction. We wanted to find out whether these observations were empirically supportable.

Moreover, as we have discussed in several chapters in this volume, reading strategies research with second-language (L2) learners has revealed that readers' cultural and educational background affects their choice of strategies. Some of the previous studies on the reading skills of Japanese students (e.g., Christensen, 1990; Kitano, 1994) mostly describe particular methods for developing reading skills in university courses, while others (e.g., Harrington, 1987; Koda, 1993) have examined whether language learners' native languages (including Japanese) have a significant effect on their choice of strategies in responding to L2 language tasks. If that is the case, strategies introduced to the Japanese subjects in earlier studies may not necessarily have been the most effective or culturally appropriate ones for their particular linguistic and cultural background. We think, therefore, that it is important to identify the academic reading strategies routinely employed by Japanese students when reading their academic materials in English. Identifying such strategies can be useful in designing programs to teach culturally appropriate reading strategies for Japanese students; such instruction can ultimately help them to become better readers of English academic texts. The present study is our attempt to add additional information on the reading strategies of this specific group of EFL learners who use English as a "library language" (i.e., they use it mainly for reading to obtain information). In other words, the present study supports and extends previous research in the metacognitive awareness of reading strategies of students for whom English is a foreign language. We consider these students as EFL readers of ESP; that is, they are expected to read textual materials in English as part of their course work in the specific field of computer science in an environment where the primary language of instruction is Japanese. We wanted to explore two specific research questions in the context of Japanese students' awareness of reading strategies (or what we have termed elsewhere in this volume as these readers' "perceived use" of reading strategies) while reading texts related to their academic tasks, such as reading textbooks, journal articles, class handouts, and so on:

1.  What are some of the most commonly used reading strategies among Japanese college students majoring in computer science?
2.  Is there any relationship between reported reading strategy use and (i) self-rated English proficiency and (ii) self-rated reading ability in English? (The relationship between strategy use and gender was not examined in this study because of the small number of females in the sample [female $N = 33$]).

## Method

*Subjects*

The participants in this study were 237 Japanese university students (204 males and 33 females) who were enrolled in technical (i.e., English) reading courses at a university in northern Japan. The aforesaid university is a specialized institution inasmuch as all students are majoring in computer science. Consequently, English courses are geared toward pro-

viding students with learning tools to help them to develop their proficiency in technical English as it relates to computer science. Nearly 92%
of the participants were between the ages of 18 and 21 years, with an average age of 19.4. On the background part of the survey, the participants
indicated that they had studied English a little over 7 years, on average,
and on a scale of 1 ("low") to 6 ("high"), they gave themselves an average
rating of 2.75 for their overall proficiency in English. As for their ability in
reading English, the participants gave themselves an average self-rating
of 3.03 on a scale of 1 ("low") to 6 ("high").

*Instrument*

The data for this study were collected through a modified version of
the Survey of Reading Strategies (SORS), details of which can be found
in Mokhtari, Sheorey, & Reichard, chapter 4, this volume. The modifica-
tions were warranted after we pilot-tested SORS with a small group of
Japanese students ($N = 40$) and after 3 of these participants, with various
English proficiency levels and mean overall use of strategies, later participated in the think-aloud procedure and in-depth interviews concerning their reading-strategy use. The pilot-testing and think aloud resulted
not only in modifying the wording of some of the statements, but also in
the dropping of two statements, namely, "I have a purpose in mind when
I read a text in English" and "I think about what I read to determine if
it fits my purpose" and adding seven items to the survey as follows: (i)
"I use grammar and punctuation to understand English text"; (ii) "I first
skim (read over quickly) a text, then go back and read it carefully"; (iii)
"I silently pronounce each word when reading in English"; (iv) "I make
an outline in my mind while I read"; (v) "I summarize the English text
in Japanese to understand it better"; (vi) "I use an English-Japanese dictionary"; and (vii) "I revise my reading techniques when I know that a
technique is not working."

The modified SORS was presented to the students in Japanese, as
translated by the second author, a native speaker of Japanese and fluent in
English, having completed her doctoral course work in the United States.
This Japanese version of 35 SORS statements consisted of 14 global reading strategies (i.e., strategies typically deployed to get an overview of the
text); 13 problem-solving strategies (i.e., procedures by which readers decode meaning while working directly with the text); and 8 support strategies (i.e., the use of support materials or tactics intended to aid the reader
in improving text comprehension). The reliability alpha for SORS for this
population of Japanese college students turned out to be .85, indicating
a reasonably high degree of internal consistency in measuring Japanese
students' perceived use of reading strategies. The alpha values for the
three subscales of SORS were as follows: global strategies .79; problem-
solving strategies .67; and support strategies .56.

*Data Collection and Analysis*

The SORS was administered either by one of the authors, with the help of the classroom instructor concerned, or a college faculty member who was briefed about how to administer it. The students completed the survey during their regular English class period, after being informed that the questionnaire was not a test, but simply a means of gaining information about how they cope with their academic reading. After discarding the incomplete ones, the 238 usable questionnaires were coded for statistical analysis. We analyzed the data obtained using descriptive statistical procedures as well as the *t* test to ascertain the extent to which the subjects' strategy use varied by self-reported English proficiency (high vs. low) and self-reported reading ability in English (high vs. low).

In examining reading strategy use among these students on the SORS scale, which employs a Likert scale ranging from 1 to 5, we identified three types of usage as suggested by Oxford and Burry-Stock (1995, p. 12) for general language learning strategy usage—that is, the same benchmarks that we have used in reporting other studies in this volume: high (mean = 3.5 or higher), moderate (mean = 2.5–3.4), and low (mean = 2.4 or lower). These usage levels provided appropriate levels of strategy use, which enabled us to identify characteristics of subjects with respect to their awareness of reading strategies while reading academic texts.

## Results

### Reading Strategy Use by Individual Items

Responses given by the students to SORS statements were examined in terms of the individual items as well as the three strategy categories mentioned above, namely, global, problem-solving, and support strategies. The mean of individual strategy items ranged from a high of 4.21 to a low of 1.54; the overall mean for the sample was 2.91, indicating a *moderate* overall (i.e., perceived) use or awareness of reading strategies according to the criteria stated above. Seven of the 35 strategies fell in the high usage, with means above 3.5; 19 strategies had means between 2.5 and 3.5, indicating moderate usage of these strategies; while six strategies had means below 2.5. Table 12.1 summarizes the five most favored (i.e., perceived to be most often used) and the five least favored (i.e., perceived to be least used) individual reading strategy preferences of Japanese students, arranged in descending (most favored) and ascending (least favored) order, respectively, by their means. Clearly, Japanese students seem to prefer global strategies, such as "looking at pictures, tables, etc. (if any) to better understand the text" and "looking at the title before reading a text to get a hint about the content." Among the least favored were support strategies, such as "using an English-English dictionary" (their preference being that of using English-Japanese dictionaries) and "taking notes while reading."

### Reading Strategy Use by Category

The data were further analyzed according to the three groupings or categories of the 35 reading strategies to examine the types of strategies and the mean frequency of their use by Japanese college students. The averages for these categories revealed a moderate usage, according to the criteria described above. The students showed a nearly equal preference for both problem-solving strategies ($M = 3.06$) and global strategies ($M = 3.04$), followed by support strategies ($M = 2.64$). An examination of the correlation among the means of these three categories revealed that although all the category means were positively correlated with one another ($p < .05$), most correlations were moderate, ranging from .38 to .71. The lack of a strong correlation among these categories suggests that the strategies included in each category are sufficiently distinct from one another as to indicate the use of different types of strategies by the students.

Table 12.1 Most- and Least-Favored Reading Strategies of Japanese Students

| Strategy | Most favored strategies | M | SD |
|---|---|---|---|
| GLOB6 | I look at pictures, tables, etc. (if any), to better understand the text. | 4.21 | 1.03 |
| GLOB10 | I look at the title before reading a text to get a hint about the content. | 4.11 | 1.07 |
| PROB8 | When the text becomes difficult, I pay close attention to it. | 3.94 | 1.06 |
| SUP5 | I use an English-Japanese dictionary to help me understand what I read. | 3.94 | 1.20 |
| GLOB5 | I think about what I know to help me understand what I read. | 3.80 | .99 |
| Strategy | Least favored strategies | M | SD |
| SUP2 | I use an English-English dictionary to help me understand what I read. | 1.54 | 1.13 |
| PROB7 | When the text becomes difficult, I rephrase what I have read in English. | 1.63 | .95 |
| SUP7 | I take notes while reading to help me understand what I read. | 1.66 | 1.01 |
| GLOB14 | I read the first and last paragraphs first because it usually helps me find the main idea. | 1.91 | 1.17 |
| SUP3 | After I read a text, I summarize it to understand it better in English or Japanese, or both. | 1.94 | 1.13 |

GLOB, global strategies; PROB, problem-solving strategies; SUP, support strategies.

We also examined whether any individual characteristics of the subjects (specifically, self-rated English proficiency, self-rated reading ability in English) had any significant influence on the choice or frequency of use of reading strategies. These differences were examined by using the independent-samples *t* test.

*Variation by Self-Reported English Proficiency*

Subjects were asked to rate their overall proficiency in English on a scale of 1 ("low") to 6 ("high"). For purposes of statistical analysis, students were divided into high proficiency (self-rating of 4, 5, or 6; $N = 54$) and low proficiency (self-rating of 3 or lower; $N = 180$). Because of the considerable disparity in the size of the two groups, we randomly selected approximately one third (34%) of the subjects from the low-proficiency group ($N = 62$) for comparison purposes. An analysis of the mean values for individual strategy items revealed that the high-proficiency group had higher means for 33 of the 35 strategy items than their low-proficiency counterparts. The overall mean for the high-proficiency group was also higher and significantly different from that of the low-proficiency group (high group $M = 3.10$ vs. low group $M = 2.81$; $p < .05$). The results of the *t* test also revealed that the mean differences were statistically significant in the case of 14 of the 35 strategies ($p < .05$ in each case). As for differences in strategy usage by categories, statistically significant differences were found between two of the three strategy categories, namely, problem-solving ($M = 3.33$ vs. $M$ 2.92; $p < .05$) and global strategies ($M = 3.30$ vs. $M = 2.95$; $p < .05$).

*Variation by Self-Reported Reading Ability*

On the background questionnaire, participants were asked to rate themselves on their self-perceived reading ability in English on a scale of 1 ("low") to 6 ("high"). Based on their responses, the participants were divided into two groups: the "high reading ability" group consisted of those who rated themselves 4, 5, or 6 ($N = 73$), while the "low reading ability" group consisted of those who rated themselves 3, 2, or 1 ($N = 160$). Once again, because of the unequal size of the groups, 50% of the participants from the low group were chosen at random for purposes of comparative analysis. Although the high-ability group means were higher in 28 of the 35 strategy statements, the results of the *t* test revealed that only in the case of nine strategies did the two groups differ significantly ($p < .05$). There were no significant differences between the high and low groups in neither the overall mean nor the means for global, problem-solving, or support strategy categories.

## Discussion

In this study, we wanted to explore the metacognitive awareness or perceived use of reading strategies of Japanese college students majoring in a technical field of study, namely, computer science. In discussing the results of this study, we refer to the results of the study dealing with another group of EFL students, namely, Hungarian students, as reported in Sheorey and Szoke-Baboczky (this volume, chapter 11). The two groups of students are somewhat similar in that they both study English in a linguistic environment where a single language is dominant (i.e., Japanese and Hungarian, respectively).

Overall, results of this study show that Japanese college students perceive their use of reading strategies (while reading academic materials such as textbooks and other types of study-related materials) as one of moderate frequency (overall SORS mean = 2.91) and that they particularly favor problem-solving strategies ($M = 3.06$)—those during-reading techniques that readers consciously use to better understand what they are reading—and global strategies ($M = 3.04$)—the generalized, intentional procedures applied by learners to get an overall sense of the text. Among the most frequently used problem-solving strategies favored by Japanese students include "paying close attention when the text becomes difficult to understand"; rereading difficult text to increase understanding"; and "guessing the meaning of unknown words or phrases." The most frequently used global strategies included the following: "looking at pictures, tables, etc. (if any), to better understand the text"; "looking at the title before reading a text to get a hint about the content"; and "thinking about what is already known to understand what is being read." Most of these strategic reading behaviors (except the use of a bilingual dictionary) are associated with skilled or proficient readers, whether native or non-native, as reported in a number of studies, which we have referred to in other chapters in this volume (e.g., Block, 1986, 1992; Pressley & Afflerbach, 1995; Pritchard, 1990; Sheorey & Mokhtari, 2001). One other finding of interest needs to be noted here. The global strategies that Japanese students employ seem to be visually oriented (e.g., "*looking* at tables or pictures," "*looking* at the title to get a hint about the content," and "*using* bold type and italics to identify key information"). This may be partly because Japanese students are, in general, visual learners (Reid, 1987). In contrast, "nonvisual" global strategies are reported to be used with much lower frequency ($M = 2.4$ or lower); among these are strategies such as "looking for the main point of the text" and "distinguishing between the main points and supporting details."

In addition, our analysis revealed at least one finding that was different from the one found among Hungarian EFL students: While there was no significant linear relationship between reported reading strategies and (self-rated) English proficiency among Hungarian EFL students, the opposite was true of Japanese EFL students. That is, we found that there was considerable differentiation in the strategy usage in terms of Japanese students who considered themselves to have higher overall proficiency in English, as opposed to those with lower proficiency ($p < .05$). An additional finding was that both groupings (namely, higher-lower English proficiency and higher-lower reading ability) accord the same order of importance when reading academic texts: the most frequently used being problem-solving strategies, followed by global, which are followed by support strategies. However, the significant differences in the reported use of strategies seen between high and low English proficiency were not mirrored when the subjects were broken down by their self-rated reading ability (high vs. low) in the overall means or means of the three categories ($p > .05$). We think that these results suggest that Japanese students' self-perceived reading ability does not seem to affect their choice of strategies as does their level of English proficiency.

As we have seen elsewhere in this volume, a closer examination of the relationship between reported strategy use and overall proficiency in English reveals an interesting interaction between these two variables. It seems that the relationship between English proficiency and strategy use is not an unexpected finding, especially in light of prior research in L2 reading, which has shown that reading proficiency is closely associated with L2 readers' level of proficiency in the target language. Researchers generally agree that target language proficiency and reading ability are closely linked; for example, Alderson (1984) and Cziko (1978) have suggested that as overall competence in the target language increases, so does an improvement in reading ability in that language. On the other hand, other researchers (e.g., Carrell, Pharis, & Liberto, 1989) provide evidence that proficient L2 readers can compensate for a lack of English proficiency by increasing awareness and use of reading strategies to enhance comprehension. The results of the present study provide additional support for prior research on the positive, linear relationship between proficiency in the target language, and a heightened awareness (and perhaps actual use) of reading strategies among both native and non-native readers (Sheorey & Mokhtari, 2001).

In the light of the discussion above, we can present a rough profile of the Japanese college student-reader majoring in computer science in terms of his (the male pronoun is used here because of the high number of male participants in this study) metacognitive awareness of reading strategies when reading academic texts in English. The typical Japanese college computer science major reads his academic materials in English carefully, using global strategies, such as examining tables or pictures, looking at the title, and utilizing his previous knowledge about the topic; then, as he reads the text, he pays close attention when the text becomes difficult to understand, rereading it if necessary. It appears that Japanese EFL students, like the Hungarian EFL students, seem to have the kind of awareness of reading strategies that is characteristic of good or experienced readers, as described by Pressley and Afflerbach (1995). The results of this study reported here also support the earlier finding (as reported by Block, 1986, 1992; Jiménez, Garcia, & Pearson, 1995; Song, 1998; Sheorey & Mokhtari, 2001), that L2 readers who have a high proficiency in the target language have a greater awareness of reading strategies in the sense that they report using them with higher frequency than those who have lower proficiency in the target language. The overall similarity of results between the Hungarian and Japanese student populations is not entirely surprising, given the fact that both these groups of students can be considered "academically superior" when compared to other students because these students had to have earned good grades in high school and been selected for admission to a university and a technical institution, respectively, in a competitive process that rewards high academic accomplishments in admission decisions. It is reasonable to assume that among the characteristics of academically accomplished students is a metacognitive awareness of reading strategies when it comes to reading academic materials in a second language.

## Conclusion

The findings of this study pertain to awareness or perceived use of reading strategies among Japanese college readers, not necessarily *actual* strategy use. The study has some important implications for reading instruction in Japan. In our opinion, Japanese students will benefit from being made aware of the important role played by strategies associated with proficient reading. As Singhal (1998) pointed out, reading is "…a meaning-making process through which readers employ strategies to facilitate their comprehension" (p. 1). Needless to say, Japanese EFL teachers can play an important role in increasing students' awareness of such strategies and in helping them become what Pressley and Afflerbach (1995) called "constructively responsive" readers. If L2 learners are to use a reading strategy, they and their teachers must, of course, know what a given strategy is, as well as how and when to apply it in the reading process with the goal being one of improving reading comprehension. The following procedure (adapted from Singhal, 1998) is one way to teach reading strategies to EFL students majoring in any field of study. The first step is for the teacher to explain what the strategy is and then model it, using a short reading passage. Next, under the careful direction from the instructor, the students are given opportunities to practice the strategy with appropriate reading materials that call for the use of the strategy concerned. The last step is for students to practice the strategy without the guidance of the teacher, but with appropriate teacher feedback as needed. Strategy instruction along these lines can increase learners' awareness of not just appropriate reading strategies, but also of the reading processes in general. In other words, we believe that when learners become more aware of reading strategies and know how to use them, they are more likely to have greater control over using reading strategies in comprehending their academic texts. Auerbach and Paxton (1997), in fact, reported that when students are taught strategies, particularly at the beginning stages of reading instruction, such as asking questions and making predictions before reading and writing summaries after reading, they become metacognitively aware of what they need to do in order to comprehend their texts and learn to overcome comprehension trouble spots. In short, when teaching reading strategies, the reading teacher needs to be a coach who explains and models the strategy, guiding the students to observe and participate and providing feedback. If Japanese EFL reading teachers can periodically engage their students in reading-strategy-awareness coaching, they can help students become *actual* users of the strategies taught. Such coaching will undoubtedly lead to enhancing Japanese students' overall ability in comprehending their academic texts.

# 13 | Reconceptualizing Reading Strategy Use in Online Environments

**Angel Kymes**
*Oklahoma State University*

## Introduction

The evolving nature of literacy, brought about by continual technological change, has left literacy researchers searching for both theories and practices which address the complexities of learning to read on and with the Internet. As texts have shifted from pages to screen, researchers have questioned the ability of preexisting models and conceptualizations of reading and writing to apply to a radically new and interactive electronic medium. Can the skill sets, strategies, and practices that have been validated and used successfully with print texts be modified for use in online environments with online texts, or does the nature of the new medium require a dramatic reconceptulization on literate activities and literate practices to define reading success? This chapter attempts to summarize relevant research related to students' awareness and use of reading strategies in print and online environments.

Although a number of skeptics continue to doubt the effectiveness or use of computer-based media, or online texts, the proliferation of the machine and schools' continued investments in technology secure their position in most educational institutions. Related to the field of literacy, and literacy research, there likewise exists conflicting evidence and justification for the use of computer-based, online, and hypertexts in reading education. Over the past decade, much of the work with online texts has either argued for the possibilities and potentials afforded by these new mediums, compared the new medium to the old (print texts), or attempted to justify a new, radical approach to teaching literacy using new texts.

Early research on computer texts was conducted in the late 1980s and early 1990s, prior to the advent of the World Wide Web, as we know it today. Screen resolution was often poor, color was not available, and processors were small and slow. With the advent of the Web, hypertext research flourished and the links and nodes that defined the "new" medium was compared to the natural ways in which the human brain connects, groups, and accesses information. Much of the research in the last 5 years has utilized the World Wide Web as a primary source of information. In this chapter, an online text is one that can be found on a computer through an Internet connection, using a search engine or bookmarked Web site. The primary purpose for reading such a text is to gain information from the site and use the information in meaningful and relevant ways to achieve the goals of education and, specifically, reading.

Researchers in many different areas, including educational technology, information communication studies, instructional design, and literacy, are all seeking to discover how the visual and verbal are working together in the forms of online texts (Chen & Rada, 1996; Bolter, 1998; Mayer & Moreno, 1998; Mayer, 1997; Kamil & Lane, 1998; Leu, Kinzer, Coiro, & Cammack, 2004; Hill & Hannafin, 1997; Shapiro & Niederhauser, 2003). All of these fields wish to understand how online texts are reshaping instructional practices and how students use new texts. Researchers from this range of disciplines are invested in knowing how technology is changing our views of written communication, the concept of text, and what it means to be a literate individual in the 21st century. What has failed to happen is a separation from the ideological base defining each field, as well as a willingness to use theories and methodologies from the others.

This chapter will attempt to synthesize relevant research that analyzes major differences between print and electronic or online texts. For each type of text, the characteristics of the text, as well as the nature of the reading experience, the skills and strategies that foster success, and the unanswered questions will be presented. What similarities exist between these types of texts? What are the differences? This chapter will conclude with thoughts on how these texts are each struggling for primacy in the classroom, as well as the implications for instruction that result from the research at present.

## Print Texts: Known and Familiar

With the average book, textbook, or print material, readers progress through the material in a linear, logical fashion. Starting at the beginning, and finishing at the end, readers follow a path predetermined by the author of the work. While we can still account or allow for the theories of reader responsiveness, it is true that most readers of a text will understand the text in much the same way—that is, the way the author intended. Arguments are laid out in a thoughtful, progressive manner in which the author draws the reader to focus on critical points of an argument or thesis, while leading the reader away from incidental facts or irrelevant material. Because of this intentionality on the part of the author, the text and the reader are placed in subordinate positions. While the text is authoritative in its own right, it is because of the author's craft and decision making that the information is revealed to the reader. The path is fixed from reading to reading for the individual; neither does it change from reader to reader. The exchange between the text and the reader allows comprehension to occur. When the text provides a familiar structure, or one that the reader can determine, readers comprehend better (Gillingham, 1996). When cohesion occurs at the syntactic, semantic, and discourse level, the reader is able to devote more attention to strategies and prior knowledge and allow these to inform the reading of the text and increase the ability to understand the information therein.

Pressley and Afflerbach (1995) summarized the research on think-aloud methodology and reading comprehension to determine which strategies good readers use with print texts. They determined that prior to reading, good readers determine a goal for their reading exercise. They skim through the text, looking for clues about the structure of the text. As they identify the structure and what is known about the type or category of text they will encounter, good readers will determine if the text at hand is relevant to meeting their reading goal, or if the text should be discarded in favor of another that may be more meaningful and informative. If they proceed with the text, good readers activate their prior knowledge of the topic or subject, summarize and remind themselves of the information they gathered in the overview of the text, and generate some ideas regarding what the text will offer them as they continue reading.

In general, as they progress through a text, good readers move in a linear fashion, from the beginning to the end of a text. They skim the text searching for relevant facts and keywords, and may skip over sections that seem unnecessary to the reading goal. Good readers rely on the automatic processing skills that have been refined with practice until a cognitive breakdown occurs. When this disconnect is recognized, good readers will reread portions of the text and read aloud or rephrase parts of the text to commit them to working memory. They may make notes, highlight sections, paraphrase the text, or simply pause and reflect upon the information they've obtained. At this point, good readers will look for new ideas and begin to reformulate initial hypotheses regarding the text and its ability to achieve the reading goals established at the beginning. They may also begin to make predictions regarding the resolution of the information and seek ways to incorporate the new information into existing mental structures, or integrate the new information with their prior knowledge.

At the end of the reading task, good readers often reread and skim back through parts of the text that was especially important or relevant to their initial reading goal. They may create lists, models, outlines, or summaries of the text to organize it into a visual representation or graphic organizer. Good readers may self-test over the new information learned. They often reflect upon the text, evaluating the information within, respond to the text, imagine new scenarios or situations where they may apply information from the text, or plan how they can use the information gained to teach others or expand their own learning goals. Many researchers have taken these skills and developed assessments that can be used by students or adults to measure their own level of strategy use and their metacognitive awareness of the reading strategies they routinely use when interacting with printed texts. One assessment, the Metacognitive Awareness of Reading Strategies Inventory (MARSI), has been especially useful in classroom settings with adolescent readers, and other versions of this instrument have been successful in addressing the reading strategies in first- (L1) and second-language (L2) reading (Mokhtari, Sheorey, & Reichard, this volume, chapter 4).

As Pressley and Afflerbach (1995) analyzed the existing research, all of the studies focused on print texts and the ways in which readers interact with print materials. Online texts were not considered, or had not been included in the studies. The majority of the studies focused on the ways that readers would construct meaning and respond to the text as they prepared to be tested over the content and attempted to commit sections of the text to memory. At present, it is critical for researchers to determine if these same sets of strategies apply to online environments, or if there are new strategies and new skill sets used by readers when they interact with an online text. Initially, it appears that many of the skills and strategies used in print environments indeed do apply to online texts. In both print and online environments, each phase of reading (i.e., before, during, and after) occurs in succession, and the majority of reader behaviors are similar. Indeed, McKnight (1996) argues that comprehension is not affected by the presentation medium, yet concedes that comprehension is difficult to assess because "there is a general lack of agreement about how comprehension can best be measured" (p. 218).

As decades of literacy research has focused on print texts, it is critical at this juncture to determine if the findings and theories can be applied to electronic texts. Yet before the transfer is made, we must analyze the research and theories of hypertext, electronic texts, online texts, and Web usability to characterize the texts themselves, the nature of the reading experience, and the skills and strategies required in a screen-based medium.

## Electronic Texts: New and Original

With the explosion of the World Wide Web, and the sudden integration of browsing or "surfing the net" into classrooms in the mid- to late 1990s, a great deal of educational research was conducted in an attempt to understand how the information online could be used by students, and how to reconcile the different medium with what teachers and researchers already knew about reading and learning with print texts. Vacca and Vacca (1999) advised that electronic texts be used to supplement the existing print texts in a classroom, extending and enriching the curriculum. They claimed that electronic texts should be used because "they added variety, generated interest and engagement, improved comprehension, allowed students to read extensively, and invited readers to think critically about topics" (p. 103).

One characteristic of electronic texts is the ability to change and manipulate the text presentation in a way that is impossible with print. Because of the malleability of the text itself, the reader is removed from a position that is submissive to both the author and the text, and is elevated to a position of authority and given the power to determine the sequence or progression of the information. While most researchers term these electronic texts as nonlinear, Bolter (1998) argues that they are instead multilinear, with "the assumption that the text will be multiple governs our relationship to the text as writers and readers" (p. 5). Regardless, the superiority of the reader allows for a level of interactivity and meaning construction that is typically not possible with print texts, and the reading experience changes with each interaction the reader has with a text, and will vary from reader to reader. Instead of the reader following the predetermined path of argument and logic set forth by the author of the text, the reader becomes a coauthor, rearranging and juxtaposing ideas. Bolter (1998) contends that the "traditional" essay may not survive as a hypertextual presentation of a logical argument, which begs the reader to identify the purposes and conclusions of the writing, as well as determine his or her own relationship to those points of view. In the electronic environment, these goals are challenged as the "methods of writing and reading are changed dramatically" (p. 7).

Much of the research with electronic texts in the past few years has focused on how readers interact with the text, and which strategies are employed by readers to be successful with these texts. McEneaney (2003) reported difficulties for readers in hypertext, although the study did not reveal why these difficulties existed. Because familiarity with technology did not significantly correlate with hypertext scores, difficulty could not be attributed to participants' frequency of using the Internet. McEneaney (2003) attributes the inconsistency to differences in reading online, which do not have parallels in print material, and he argues that hypertext reading requires a different set of skills than does reading in traditional print environments. Goldman (1996) suggests that most existing comprehension theories assume linear texts, and that these theories may prove to be insufficient for explaining the processes and skills required for success in electronic environments. Because the electronic environment requires search and retrieval skills unmatched in print texts, "the skills of monitoring and evaluating comprehension become more important than in a linear text environment" (p. 34).

Any discussion of electronic texts, and their potential to afford readers with supports for constructing meaning, improving comprehension, and affecting learning would be incomplete without an analysis of the decades of work by David Reinking (Reinking, Hayes, & McEneaney, 1988; Reinking & Rickman, 1990; Reinking & Schreiner, 1985). For decades, Reinking has attempted to determine under what conditions electronic texts can assist the reader in becoming more proficient. First, electronic texts have the ability to combine visual and verbal messages in unique ways. Second, electronic texts can create true interaction between the reader and the text. Third, electronic texts are useful in not only accomplishing traditional literacy goals, but they are beginning to advance new literacy agendas. Reinking's experimental research has also focused on the ability for computer-mediated texts to improve the skills of the reader and result in greater comprehension of a text.

The research by Reinking and his associates determined that when the computer controlled textual presentations or made mandatory assistive features available to the reader, significant gains in comprehension and vocabulary learning resulted (Reinking, Hayes, & McEneaney, 1988; Reinking & Rickman, 1990; Reinking & Schreiner, 1985). While strategy use is generally considered to be only part of comprehension and metacognitive research, Reinking's body of research with electronic texts indicates that students may need to be somewhat less proficient in their use of extraneous strategy and more reliant on the assistive features provided by the text itself. However, it is critical to realize that successful manipulation and exploitation of the assistance provided by the electronic text comprises another set of strategies, which may be similar or entirely different from the strategies used in print-based environments. Leu and Reinking (1996) suggest that strategic knowledge may be more important in electronic environments than print environments, because the "electronic environment requires more decisions about which sources of information to explore in order to accomplish a learning goal" (p. 56).

However, the learning goal itself must be clearly identified in order for the research to have much to bear on the nature of the reading experience. Some authors (Hacker, 1998; Pressley, 2000) have criticized research that presents texts which have been contrived or exaggerated for experimental purposes. Texts found on the Web are often not controlled, and are rarely assistive in the ways researchers have demonstrated foster success with students. Hacker (1998) feared that "much of what is known about self-regulated comprehension during typical reading does not generalize to the kinds of reading typically encountered in educational contexts" (p. 175). This may also mean that there is an inability to transfer our knowledge of reading behaviors with print text to electronic text.

Elshair (2002) made a distinction between browsing, navigating, and reading. Each seems to move to higher levels of cognitive ability. Elshair (2002) noted that browsing is an activity which often lacks purpose, while navigating allows the user to learn the structure of the site and maneuver through the space. Reading is a purposeful use of meaning-making strategies, where the user interacts with the text to elaborate, recall, and evaluate the information. Usability studies have often focused on the ways that individuals interact with Web sites, but fail to separate reading strategies from navigational studies (Elshair, 2002). Stimson (1998) theorized that the metacognitive skills of the reader, especially monitoring and control, determines the amount of information the reader is able to learn from the hypertext. The results of Stimson's studies show that the activation of metacognitive control can increase learning in electronic environments.

## Similarities and Differences: Which Text Is Best?

Some reading strategies seem to apply to both print and online texts, while others may depend on the medium. Elshair (2002) proposed that future research should focus on both print and Web texts concurrently, as the strategies can be integrated and teased apart from variations in strategy. Two recent studies have investigated the differences in strategy use in online environments. Poole and Mokhtari (this volume, chapter 14) compared the reading strategies college English as a second language (ESL) students used with print texts to those the same individuals used while reading online texts. These researchers found that students exhibited reliance on a small cluster of strategies, deployed multiple strategies when reading became more difficult, and used supplementary materials online, but not with print texts. In an early study of adult users with high levels of computer skill, Bland (1995) found that users transferred strategies that were successful to them in print texts to online texts. These experienced users also invented new strategies to assist them in managing and integrating information. Additionally, the users were able to read more online and understand more of what they read when they experienced greater control of the online document.

Foltz (1996) focuses on the background knowledge of the individual, and the ways that either inexperience or skill can contribute to success in online environments. Because the texts are so flexible and because the information is not presented in a traditional linear path, readers with little background knowledge may be unable to attach the new information to a conceptual frame while additionally struggling with how to navigate through the information presented. In contrast, readers with higher levels of background knowledge may be able to compensate for less order in the presentation of information because they possess the conceptual structure of the topic and can "exploit some of the less coherent links in the hypertext"(p. 128). Foltz (1996) believes that as in print environments, readers in electronic environments must draw on a number of strategies to maintain coherence throughout the text, also called for a better understanding of the constraints of the reader and the constraints of the text so that "weaknesses in each can be supported by the other" (p. 131).

Britt and Gabrys (2001) identified the skills required for success online, which they believe are inherent to multiple fields and disciplines, and which they term "advanced literacy skills." These include sourcing, corroborating, and integrating. Integration allows the reader to connect new information to existing knowledge structures, building links between the old and the new. In electronic environments, integration is more difficult because a nonlinear presentation loses the coherence usually assumed in print texts, and because the number of texts to integrate is increased, as the quality is inconsistent. Corroborating requires the reader to evaluate the quality and accuracy of the information by cross-checking it against other sources. Sourcing may be the most difficult of the skills, as it requires the reader to evaluate the credibility and trustworthiness of the information located. Because of the additional requirements of searching, navigating, following links, and situating oneself in cyberspace, many researchers have suggested that the skills traditionally associated with reading comprehension using print text become even more important when reading online texts (Goldman, 1996; Leu & Reinking, 1996; Foltz, 1996; Levonen, Dillon, & Spiro, 1996).

## Strategies and Transfer

Researchers are in disagreement over the ability of readers to transfer skills and strategies learned in one area to another area. Many authors state that the differences in the mediums and the texts are too numerous to reliably transfer the skills from print to online texts. Leu (2000) concurred with Mayer (1997) and stressed that just as transfer may not occur from print to online texts, so also must researchers refrain from forcing transfers from old technologies to new technologies. Leu (2000) stated that technological changes occur with such rapidity that traditional research is not possible, whereas Kamil, Intrator, and Kim (2000) argued that the basic underlying goals of human-computer interaction do not change so quickly so as to eradicate the need for reliable research and validated methods and practices; they suggested that the "underlying principles of obtaining meaning from text will not, and simply cannot, change as rapidly as either hardware or software" (p. 775).

## Implications for Instruction

Alexander and Jetton (2000) believed that the current knowledge of learning strategies in online environments is too limited to guide practice. What students of varying levels of knowledge, interests, and goals *actually do* while reading online or which skills and strategies they *do and should employ* are still not known (Alexander & Jetton, 2000, pp. 295–296). Manzo, Manzo, and Estes (2001) feared that the amount of information online and the speed with which it can be accessed has prevented some of the basic research that allows teachers to understand how students read, process, and critique that information.

Kamil and Lane (1998) argued that while the pace of technology accelerates, literacy researchers have been silent "on the sidelines" of this area of research (p. 328). These researchers believe that while much is known about the strategies readers employ with print texts, a systematic analysis of strategy use with online texts is missing from the knowledge base. In a document on the research Web site for the New Literacies Research team (available online at: http://www.newliteracies.uconn.edu. Retrieved April 17, 2007), reading researcher Don Leu (2000) called for the addition of online reading comprehension to the Program for International Student Assessment (PISA) studying in 2009 so that researchers will have a baseline for the future. Because the nature of reading is changing so rapidly with the use of the Internet, Leu (2000) argued that without this information, we as researchers and teachers will have an incomplete picture of the types of reading activities and the amount of reading in which students are actually engaged.

Kamil and Lane (1998) additionally stated that "until we have data about whether or not students can and do utilize hypertext in productive ways, we will have no way of grounding theory" (p. 333). Educators also have a responsibility to teach students to read the types of materials they will encounter (Kamil, Intrator, & Kim 2000). Kress (2003) recognized that the types of literacy practices and behaviors typically taught in schools have little resemblance to the kinds of literate behaviors in which students engage outside of the classroom. He stated that the new literacy skills required by students are guided by multimodal assimilation and a "near instant response" (p. 174). While educators may feel the need to teach students in a way to help them concentrate on reading (or other tasks) over an extended period of time, Kress (2003) argued that this cannot be the only form of reading that is taught, and that it should not be the only form of reading that defines the activity for future generations.

Schmar-Dobler (2003) suggested that educators must guide students to success by transferring what they already know about different types of texts and applying this knowledge to online texts or Internet reading. Wilhelm (2001) reminded researchers and teachers that students may need more direction when moving between different types of text. Some of the skills they already know can be transferred from type to type, but within each there may be "new skills [that] need to be awakened and exercised" (p. 53). His recommendation was the think-aloud protocols, which assist students in developing strategies for adapting to new texts. Although Wilhelm (2001) focused solely on print texts, online texts can be seen as an extension of this same thought. As students begin to encounter online texts with greater frequency, and as the demands to recall and application of learned material increases, there may be a greater need for readers to be given strategies and skills to use when reading from, and learning from, these online texts.

Dail (2004) found that students often need direct instruction to be able to apply reading strategies from print to online texts. Vye et al. (1998) also determined that students had little prior experience referencing and indexing materials, and should have increased opportunities to participate in activities that support the use of these strategies in Web environments. All of this research seems to concur that more explicit instruction is needed. The direct teaching of skills and strategies that will increase the potential for students to be successful in the online environment appears to be a requirement at this time. Britt and Gabrys (2001) concluded that because most high school and college students do not possess such advanced skills, "efforts must be made to explicitly train these skills in order to enable students to make sense of the vast quantities of information the Internet makes available to them" (p. 89). Hartley and Bendixen (2001) believed that it may not have as much to do with the ability of the reader as with the reader's confidence and persistence to complete the task. They believe that epistemological beliefs and self-regulatory skills (which are very similar to metacognitive skills) are individual characteristics that may have a greater impact on how learners interact with computer-based tools and texts.

A group of researchers, led by Donald Leu and David Reinking, is currently working on developing a system of reciprocal teaching strategies for students who are at risk of dropping out of school. These teaching strategies will allow teachers to focus on the new strategies for achieving comprehension and developing critical thinking and reading skills that are essential for online text. The group's Web site, available at http://www.newliteracies.uconn.edu/iesproject/index.html (retrieved April 17, 2007), stresses the importance of teaching students to recognize the unique strategies that are required in the online environment. The goals of the project appear to be in line with the recommendations made by these researchers themselves and others, such as Kamil, Intrator, and Kim (2000), who suggested that questions of engagement, self-efficacy, and cognitive strategies as they relate to electronic or online texts are the most urgent ones facing reading researchers today.

## Conclusion and Classroom Applications

Technology, as education, is often driven less by research-based best practices, and more by social and economic forces. It is no surprise to literacy educators that the legislation known as the No Child Left Behind of 2001 has generated intense focus on reading instruction and reading achievement. However, Karchmer, Mallette, Kara-Soteriou, and Leu (2005) determined that none of the "goals" or "benchmarks" for progress allow for technological literacies to be evaluated within the context of traditional literacy behaviors and capabilities. The authors fear that the focus on fundamental literacies has distracted policy makers from the realization that the skills required to be fully literate in society are changing at a rapid and accelerating pace. They fear that educators will "[raise] test scores on foundational literacies without preparing students for the new forms of reading, writing, viewing, and communicating that will be required in their adult lives" (p. 6).

Can the strategies that have been validated through decades of research with print texts be applied to online texts, or must both questions and methodologies change as readers go online? Perhaps as an interim step, those skills and strategies should be applied as researchers begin to forge new designs. Leu (2000) cautioned that literacy today is "deictic," meaning that it is ever shifting and ever changing, without a constant referent from day to day. As literacy researchers strive to hit this moving target, they must focus on the goals of comprehension and understanding, without getting lost in the technical aspects that also change daily.

Future researchers must commit to taking a broad approach to answering these questions of text affordances and capabilities, incorporating not only reading research, but also the strong base of research from the field of educational technology and information studies. As a conclusion to this chapter, teachers can find effective strategies for promoting and increasing students' awareness of reading strategies online with suggestions for how these can be modeled and taught in classrooms.

*Strategy 1: Text Authority and Validity*

Text authority is one issue that seems to trouble students. For many readers, if something is in print, it is believable. However, due to the publishing capabilities now available on the Internet, anyone can claim to be an expert. Books seemed trustworthy due to the controls set in place by editors and publishing companies, but the speed with which information can be posted online and the lack of editorial control should give educators pause. By using many of the strategies for source verification and authority, students can be taught to question the stance and credentials of the author. If students will ask such questions as, Does this site have a date? When was it updated last? Is this a commercial or educational site? Who wrote this information? How can I trust what he or she says? Can the information be independently verified by another source or another site?, they can begin to question the authority of online texts and become more strategic online readers.

### Strategy 2: Web Site Layout, Design, and Hyperlinks

Many students, when using the Internet, often begin scrolling down a page even as it is loading. It is worthwhile to preview different types of Web sites with students to show them how to dissect the page and how the parts of the page operate. By skimming and scanning through different sites, teachers can model how to locate relevant information on a page and navigate through the pages that are linked. Students should know how to find site maps, which can function similarly to a contents page or index page in books, to locate the information they need on a site. Teachers can demonstrate the effectiveness of hyperlinks and roll-over functions. They can also show students how the visual information on a page can either add to, or detract from, the overall purpose of the Web site. By previewing different types of pages, from a variety of sources, organizations and file extensions, teachers can help students learn to strategically interact with Web sites.

### Strategy 3: Setting Purpose and Conducting Effective Searches

Setting a purpose for reading may be even more relevant online than it has been with traditional texts. The sheer volume of information, combined with the distractions and competition for students' attention online, can cause many to become quickly derailed from their original intent. Teachers can help students not only set a purpose for their online reading activity, but also outline a search strategy, determine keywords and Boolean operators needed for search engines, and generate ideas about the types of information they need to accomplish their goal.

### Strategy 4: Referencing and Making Intertextual Connections

Teacher-led think-aloud protocols may be a very useful way of showing students how to make connections within an online text or between online texts. This type of referencing or corroboration may indeed be a skill that must be explicitly taught and demonstrated. By taking information from a variety of sites and weaving it together and synthesizing the information to create a more complete resolution to the information need, teachers can model the strategic processes that students must undertake as they encounter different Web sites with varied levels of complexity and authority.

# 14 | ESL Students' Use of Reading Strategies when Reading Online and in Print

**Alex Poole**
*Western Kentucky University*

**Kouider Mokhtari**
*Miami University, Ohio*

## Introduction

Since the widespread use of the Internet starting in the 1990s, reading in online environments has gone from being something that was occasional to something that college students need to be highly skilled in to succeed at both the undergraduate and graduate levels. Selber (2004), for instance, pointed out that several large state universities, such as the University of Louisville, Utah State University, and Old Dominion University, now require their students to obtain the skills necessary to complete academic work in online environments. Such a requirement seems reasonable in light of the widespread proliferation of electronic media that were nonexistent even at the beginning of the millennium. Leu, Kinzer, Coiro, and Cammack (2004) demonstrated that the increase in Web-based reading is, indeed, probably a result of an explosion in technological resources by pointing out that current high school graduates, who initially started reading and writing in almost entirely print-based environments, now have a plethora of online reading sources available to them, such as "...Web logs (blogs), word processors, video editors, World Wide Web browsers, Web editors, email, spreadsheets, presentation software, instant messaging, plug-ins for Web resources, listservs, bulletin boards, avatars, virtual worlds, and many others" (p. 5). Likewise, a plethora of research published in the past 5 years has demonstrated that college students in the United States and abroad are increasingly using these sources in order to obtain library resources (Bodomo, Lam, & Lee, 2003), take classroom and standardized exams (Korbin & Young, 2003; Sawaki, 2001), and complete course work in writing (Cook, 2002), psychology (Heffner & Cohen, 2005), education (Harlen, 2004), and foreign-language learning (Daud & Husin, 2004; Konishi, 2003; Sun, 2003), among other fields. Leu et al. (2004) noted that the development of such a wide variety of online-based reading environments has fundamentally changed the way we think about reading. Among other things, they assert that online reading is constantly changing and evolving as technology evolves, forcing readers to quickly adapt if they are to be successful readers. This contrasts with traditional print reading, which has changed relatively slowly in comparison with electronic fora. Coiro (2003) further specified that all of these newly developing online reading environments—the "new literacies" environments—differ significantly from traditional print in that they are "...typically nonlinear, interactive, and inclusive or multiple media forms" (p. 8). She claims that hypertext differs from traditional print, in that learners are allotted a high measure of choice in what they read because hypertext is multilinear, unlike the linear printed text. In addition, implanted hyperlinks give readers the option to read what they want and the order in which they want to do it.

Another feature of reading in online environments that distinguishes it from traditional print texts is that its interactive, authentic, and demanding nature have been shown to motivate low-achieving readers, leading Coiro (2003) to suggest that loss of motivation to read, that many students feel, may be a thing of the past. In fact, she foresaw an increase in reading due to the potential that online reading has to motivate students, although this does not mean they will necessarily become better readers, for recent studies have shown a decline in recent college graduates' literacy proficiency (Romano, 2005). There is, however, some evidence that has suggested that young readers who do not consider themselves good readers are very enthusiastic and adept at online reading (Ryan, 2005). Thus, reading in online environments has the potential to change students' motivation to read, but it also could change basic teacher–student roles in the literacy classroom. In the past, highly literate teachers imparted various bottom-up and top-down reading skills to their less literate students. Now, in contrast, online reading's ever-changing nature makes it plausible that many students will be more literate in certain new literacies than their instructors, which, in turn, will obligate teachers to use more skilled students to help them instruct their less knowledgeable peers (Leu et al., 2004).

The most striking feature of online reading that distinguishes it from print-based texts is its interactive nature. Coiro (2003) reported that symbols, cartoons, audio and video clips, photographs, and a variety of font and color sizes are unique to, and an integral part of, virtual environments. Such features often permit—and often, oblige—readers to interact with others, thereby jointly constructing texts, rather than just receive them from authors, which is often the case with traditional print texts. Importantly, interactive tools, such as discussion boards, photographs, and audio and visual clips, compel the reader to develop strategies to answer previously unheard of questions, such as: "How should I navigate this text? How can I expect to interact with this environment? What is my role in this activity? How can I add to this body of knowledge?" (p. 15). Not surprisingly, Coiro (2003) stated that since readers' roles in constructing text have expanded in electronic formats, their ability to develop strategies to distinguish credible sources from untrustworthy ones, do background research, and fact check must likewise improve.

While developing such strategies may seem like a lot of work for many college students, those for whom English is a second language

(ESL) may have even more difficulties developing for them because of the already demanding task of learning English grammar, vocabulary, cultural schema, and text organization (Clarke, 1980), even though research has clearly demonstrated that successful reading for college ESL learners, as for their native-speaking counterparts, demands the use of a complex array of strategies (e.g., Block, 1992; Li & Munby, 1996; Konishi, 2003; Mokhtari & Reichard, 2004; Sheorey & Mokhtari, 2001; Simpson & Nist, 2002; Song, 1998). What is certain is that ESL students will utilize certain strategies that native speakers will not utilize or will do so infrequently. The limited research done on college ESL students' use of online reading strategies has shown that the use of a bilingual dictionary, for example, is quite common (Anderson, 2003; Liou, 2000); yet, this is a strategy that obviously has little relevance for native speakers of English.

Surprisingly, however, there are few studies on the strategies ESL learners use when they read online, and those that are available—specifically, those by Anderson (2003), Liou (2000), and Konishi (2003)—do not present a consistent picture of how they use them. Anderson, for example, compared the print and online strategies used by 247 ESL students studying the United States and Costa Rica, using a quantitative survey called the Online Survey of Reading Strategies, which is an adaptation of an earlier survey for printed texts developed by Mokhtari and Sheorey (2002). Interestingly, the results showed that among the most frequently used strategies were those that could be used when reading print texts (e.g., skimming and scanning, guessing the meaning of unknown words, and adjusting reading speed), while those strategies that were rarely used often were concerned with features unique to technology (e.g., participation in live chat and the use of the online bilingual dictionary).

Using qualitative research methods, Liou (2000) examined the use of the online dictionary by 14 female Taiwanese University students, among whom low, intermediate, and high English language proficiency levels were represented. The participants read texts, during which time their use of the online bilingual texts was tracked. After having completed the reading, they completed reading comprehension questions and a questionnaire about the ways in which they dealt with unknown words. Unlike in Anderson's (2003) study, the results revealed that the use of the bilingual dictionary was quite common for all participants; however, those with higher English proficiency utilized it less frequently, read at a quicker pace, and utilized more global strategies to deal with difficulties in deciphering individual words than those with lower proficiency.

Finally, Konishi's (2003) study of six native speakers of Japanese studying English in Australia showed them using strategies pertinent only to online reading. As in Liou's (2000) study, the participants engaged in think-aloud protocols and filled out a questionnaire, but in addition, they took part in follow-up interviews. While Konishi (2003) did not report any instance of using an online bilingual dictionary, as Anderson (2003) did, she reported that they utilized other strategies not applicable to paper-based texts, such as comparing the content of one

Web site to another in order to check for accuracy; abandoning Web sites when hyperlinks did not work; reloading visual images when they failed to download them the first time; and maintaining several windows open at once and switching back and forth between them.

While the studies by Anderson (2003), Liou (2000), and Konishi (2003) shed light on the strategies that college ESL students use when reading in online formats, more research needs to be done in order to get a fuller picture on how students read online, especially if they are to be given appropriate strategy instruction. As mentioned above, the complex use of a variety of strategies is strongly linked to successful reading for ESL learners at the college level. Logically, since online reading is a relatively new phenomenon, recommendations on how to successfully impart such strategies are largely based on research studies that have taken place in traditional print environments (e.g., Anderson, 1999; Carrell, Pharis, & Liberto, 1989; de la Peña & Soler, 2001; Grabe, 1991; Kamhi-Stein, 1998). However, if the strategies that successful ESL readers use to read in on-line environments differ from those they use in print environments, as the studies by Liou (2000) and Konishi (2003) suggested, then strategy instruction will have to be specific to each environment. Thus, the fol-lowing case study seeks to discover whether or not college ESL learn-ers use different strategies while reading online and in traditional print texts, and by extension, if strategy instruction will have to be separately crafted toward each environment. In this study, we were not interested in how students responded to specific technological tools (e.g., live chat, discussion boards, or hypertext), but rather in what they brought to a specific text in order to comprehend it. In conducting this study, we have assumed that online reading is a fundamentally different activity from that of reading in print and that, therefore, at least some of the reading strategies used when reading online are likely to be different from those used when reading printed materials. The following question was used to guide the study: What reading strategies do college ESL students use when reading online and traditional print texts?

## Method

*Participants*

The participants in this study consisted of 7 college ESL students (4 males and 3 females), the majority of whom spoke Spanish ($N = 5$) as their native language, although Turkish ($N = 1$) and Arabic ($N = 1$) were also represented. All participants were fully matriculated into one me-dium-sized U.S. university that required them to have achieved a the Test of English as a Foreign Language (TOEFL) score of at least 525 (197 on the computer-based version) for admission. They were studying at the undergraduate ($N = 4$) or graduate level ($N = 3$), ranged in age from 18 to 43 years ($M = 26.7$), had studied English from 2 to 25 years ($M = 10$), and were majoring in English, biology, social work, history, hospitality man-agement, dance, and education. On average, participants read academic materials in English for 10.7 hours a week, ranging from 1 to 20 hours.

On a scale of 1 ("lowest") to 6 ("highest"), on average, students self-rated their reading ability in English at 4.8.

The participating students were chosen for this study because they were in good academic standing and expressed an interest in participating in the study; none of them had participated in a formal research project in the past. In addition, the first author had extensive interaction with the participants academically (e.g., they were his former students) or socially via participation in university- and community-based cultural events, and observed that not only were they interested in improving their English proficiency, but also had a broad knowledge of a number of different academic subjects, and thus were more likely to successfully read texts on a variety of issues. Finally, since the students had already established a good rapport with the first author, they were comfortable and eager to participate in the study; according to Van Someren, Barnard, and Sandberg (1994), such rapport is crucial for maintaining the validity of the research data, since many types of qualitative research methods require subjects to reveal their innermost thoughts and feelings, which they will not do if they feel uncomfortable in the presence of the researcher. The following is a brief description of each participant (see Table 14.1):

- Anita is a 20-year-old female undergraduate student from Panama majoring in dance. She has studied English for 10 years and reads for an average of 5 hours a week. She rates her reading proficiency in English at 6 on a scale of 1 ("low") to 6 ("high").
- Clara is an 18-year-old female undergraduate student from Colombia majoring in biology. She has studied English for 2 years and reads an average of 12 hours a week. She rates her reading proficiency in English at 4.
- Danilo is a 34-year-old male graduate student from Venezuela majoring in history. He has studied English for 25 years and reads an average of 15 hours a week. He rates his reading proficiency in English at 5.
- Manuel is an 18-year-old male undergraduate student from Puerto Rico majoring in hospitality management. He has studied English for 10 years and reads an average of 1 hour a week. He rates his reading proficiency in English at 5.
- Marwan is a 29-year-old male graduate student from Jordan majoring in social work. He has studied English for 8 years and reads an average of 20 hours a week. He rates his reading proficiency in English at 5.
- Pedro is a 43-year-old male graduate student from Mexico majoring in education. He has studied English for 10 years and reads an average of 15 hours a week. He rates his reading proficiency in English at 5.
- Selin is a 25-year-old female undergraduate English major from Turkey. She has studied English for 5 years and reads an average of 7 hours a week. She rates her reading proficiency in English at 4.

Table 14.1 Description of Participants by Age, Native Language (L1), Years of English Study, and Self-Rated Reading Proficiency in English

| Name | Age | L1 | Years of study | Read per week (hours) | Self-rated proficiency |
|------|-----|-----|------|------|------|
| Anita | 20 | Spanish | 10 | 5 | 6 |
| Clara | 18 | Spanish | 2 | 12 | 4 |
| Danilo | 34 | Spanish | 25 | 15 | 5 |
| Manuel | 18 | Spanish | 10 | 1 | 5 |
| Marwan | 29 | Arabic | 8 | 20 | 5 |
| Pedro | 43 | Spanish | 10 | 15 | 5 |
| Selin | 25 | Turkish | 5 | 7 | 4 |

*Note.* Self-rated reading proficiency ranged from 1 ("poor") to 6 ("excellent").

## Data Collection

Participants' strategies were revealed using the think-aloud protocol procedure. The think aloud requires students to verbally state what they are thinking while carrying out a task (Pressley & Afflerbach, 1995; Van Someren, Barnard, & Sandberg, 1994). Spires and Estes (2002) claimed that even though there are concerns with the validity and reliability of think-aloud protocols, their effectiveness in the fields of computer interface design, cognition and instruction, and literary response make it "…reasonable that this approach can be used to help uncover potential cognitive processes inherent in Web-based environments that have not yet been articulated" (p. 123). In addition, Ericsson and Simon (1984) have demonstrated that this research technique does not fundamentally change cognition, although Jiménez, Garcia, and Pearson (1995) reported that many researchers still worry, "…whether the need to divide attention between reading and verbalizing thinking processes interferes with subjects' thinking" (p. 71).

The participating students read two passages, one in hard copy and the other Web-based, each approximately 750 words in length. The hardcopy passage came from the *Smithsonian*, and was entitled "Chief Lobbyist" (Broache, 2005). It dealt with the life of the 19th-century Lakota leader, Chief Red Cloud. The online reading came from *National Geographic Magazine* and was entitled "A Vote for Democracy" (Lange, 2004). It addressed the issue of the growth of democracy in developing nations. These particular texts were chosen because we felt that they were academic in nature, yet neither overly technical nor excessively long. While the texts were similar in length and difficulty of reading, they differed in that the paper-based copy included pictures, while the online copy did not.

All students read the paper-based text first, then approximately 1 week later, read the online text. Each reading session took approximately 45 minutes to 1 hour. All students were tape-recorded while reading texts in order to obtain a record of the strategies that they were using.

However, Jiménez, Garcia, and Pearson (1996), among others, asserted that since the think-aloud procedure can be cognitively demanding for ESL learners, the process should be fully explained and exemplified prior to engaging in it; therefore, all students were individually trained by the first author during 1-hour sessions, which involved three phases. In the first phrase, the purpose of the study was explained to them, as were the procedures involved in the think-aloud procedure, and the estimated time they would be involved in the study. Students were told that the purpose of the study was to see what they did while they were reading in order to successfully understand and complete a text in print and online. More specifically, instead of simply being told "Tell me what you think," which Van Someren, Barnard, and Sandberg (1994, p. 43) claimed is so vague that it often causes the learner to feel confused, they were told to verbally state their thoughts about the content of the reading, the physical features of the text, and what they were doing in order to overcome difficult parts. During this time, students also established the times and dates on which they would complete the think-aloud protocols.

In the second phase, the think-aloud procedure was modeled to the participants in both print and online formats by using sample texts from various periodicals similar to those chosen for the study. In order to model strategy use, he selected specific strategies outlined by Mokhtari and Sheorey (2002) in the Survey of Reading Strategies (SORS), a 30-item self-report instrument aimed at determining students' awareness of reading strategies while reading (see Mokhtari, Sheorey, & Reichard, chapter 4, this volume for the strategies outlined in the SORS instrument). Using two to three sample strategies, the researcher would read an excerpt from a sample text while thinking aloud. He would then explain to them what he was doing, and then answer their questions about any part of the procedure.

In the third and final phase, students were given the opportunity to practice the procedure, to ask any questions, and get accustomed to recording equipment. Although Van Somoren, Barnard, and Sandberg (1994) recommended that each participant practice the think aloud for approximately 15 minutes, some of the students practiced for almost twice that amount of time, as they were reading in two different formats; during this time, not only did they ask questions about aspects of the procedure that seemed confusing to them, but, as in Coiro and Dobler's (2005) study, they were occasionally prompted with questions such as, "What is it that you're thinking about now as you look at that word?" or "Why did you pause and then restart?" These questions were asked in order to remind participants to verbalize their thoughts.

## Strategy Identification and Analysis

The data gleaned from the think-aloud protocols were analyzed in order to identify not only students' strategies, or the "…conscious and flexible plans that readers apply and adapt to particular texts and tasks" (Jiménez, Garcia, & Pearson, 1996, p. 98), but also to ascertain their "strategic reading purposes" or "…any overt purposeful effort or activity used on the part of the reader to make sense of the printed material with which he or she was interacting" (Jiménez, Garcia, & Pearson, 1996, p. 98). Specifically, we were interested in discovering students' thoughts and motivations regarding their strategy use; in other words, we wanted to know why the students used certain strategies (and not others) and what awareness or knowledge they had about the processes and procedures they deploy when they read online and printed texts.

In order to identify strategies, we used the three-step framework established by Van Someren et al. (1994), which consists of data transcription, data segmentation, and data coding. Data transcription consisted, first, of listening to each tape to make sure that all recordings were legible. Following this step, all tapes were transcribed, which included participants' comments not only about the reading task itself, but also their perceptions of themselves as readers, their general reading habits, and their attitudes toward reading.

Once transcripts were established, the first author segmented the data into individual strategic episodes. Where applicable, specific strategic episodes used while reading paper-based texts were identified using the inventory contained in the SORS instrument in order to 0examine the strategies ESL learners use while reading in virtual settings. The second author then analyzed the first author's strategic episodes, following which they discussed the results until they reached a consensus concerning the type and number of strategies observed in the data.

Following segmentation, individual strategies were coded using the three strategic subscales found in the SORS instrument: global, problem-solving, and support strategies. Global strategies are those which learners use to direct their reading, such as monitoring, previewing a text, and establishing a rationale for reading. Problem-solving strategies are those learners use to deal with difficulties while actually reading the texts, such as rereading difficult passages, guessing the meaning of unfamiliar vocabulary, and altering one's reading speed according to text difficulty. Support strategies are tools used to enhance comprehension, such as utilizing a bilingual dictionary and underlining keywords and phrases.

More specifically, each participant's strategies in both hard copy and online were put in the appropriate subscale. Following codification, we independently compared the strategies participants used while reading in print and online, repeatedly returning to the data in order to confirm our conclusion. After completing this step, we exchanged our findings and discovered that we agreed not only on the differences in print and online strategy use, but also on their similarities.

## Results

For ease of presentation, our results are organized thematically with examples of strategies used in context to support the emerging themes. An examination of the data obtained revealed three major themes that help us determine the reading strategies our 7 ESL students used when reading texts in traditional print and online formats. These themes included (i) reliance or dependency on a certain cluster of strategies when reading, (ii) deployment of multiple strategies when encountering a reading problem, and (iii) dependency on the use of a bilingual dictionary as a support mechanism. A discussion of each theme follows.

*Theme 1: Reliance or Dependency on a Specific Cluster of Strategies*

The first theme we extracted from the data available pertains to the participants' reliance or dependency on a cluster of reading strategies when reading texts in traditional print and online formats. As Table 14.2 shows, the 7 participants used a total of 13 strategies while reading both text types. These strategies can be characterized as global reading strategies (e.g., using prior knowledge), problem-solving strategies (e.g., pausing and thinking), and support reading strategies (e.g., using dictionaries).

Table 14.2 Reading Strategies (in Bold) Used by All participants When Reading Texts in Traditional Print and Online Formats

| *Global Reading Strategies* | *Problem-Solving Strategies* | *Support Reading Strategies* |
|---|---|---|
| • Setting purpose for reading<br>• **Using prior knowledge**<br>• Previewing text<br>• Checking how content fits purpose<br>• Noting text characteristics<br>• Determining what to read<br>• **Using text features (e.g., tables)**<br>• **Using context clues**<br>• Using textual aids (e.g., italics)<br>• **Critically evaluating reading**<br>• Checking understanding<br>• **Predicting text meaning**<br>• Confirming predictions | • Reading slowly and carefully<br>• Staying focused on reading<br>• Adjusting reading rate<br>• Paying attention to reading<br>• **Pausing and thinking**<br>• Visualizing information<br>• **Rereading**<br>• **Guessing word meanings** | • Taking notes<br>• Reading aloud<br>• Underlining or highlighting<br>• **Using dictionaries**<br>• **Paraphrasing**<br>• **Going back and forth in text**<br>• **Asking questions**<br>• **Translating**<br>• Thinking across languages |

An examination of the total number of times individual strategies were invoked across the two text types indicates that the majority of the strategies used were of a few individual strategy types, and most strategy types were used less than half a dozen times. As Table 14.3 shows, of the 163 instances of strategy use while reading text in traditional print, 75 of them concerned one strategy, namely "paraphrasing." Similarly, of the 128 instances of strategy use while reading online, more than half were of two types, namely "paraphrasing" and "critically evaluating what is read."

Table 14.3 Number of Instances Reading Strategies Were Used by Text Type

| | Print text | Online text | Total |
|---|---|---|---|
| **Global Reading Strategies** | | | |
| Setting purpose for reading | | | |
| **Using prior knowledge** | 07 | 10 | 17 |
| Previewing text | | | |
| Checking content fits purpose | | | |
| Noting text characteristics | | | |
| Determining what to read | | | |
| **Using text features (e.g., tables)** | 16 | 00 | 16 |
| **Using context clues** | 10 | 01 | 11 |
| Using textual aids (e.g., italics) | | | |
| **Critically evaluating reading** | 06 | 30 | 36 |
| Checking understanding | | | |
| **Predicting text meaning** | 03 | 03 | 06 |
| Confirming predictions | | | |
| | | | |
| **Problem-Solving Strategies** | | | |
| Reading slowly and carefully | | | |
| Staying focused on reading | | | |
| Adjusting reading rate | | | |
| Paying attention to reading | | | |
| **Pausing and thinking** | 02 | 00 | 02 |
| Visualizing information | | | |
| **Rereading** | 20 | 14 | 34 |
| **Guessing word meanings** | 12 | 01 | 13 |
| | | | |
| **Support Reading Strategies** | | | |
| Taking notes | | | |
| Reading aloud | | | |
| Underlining or highlighting | | | |
| **Using dictionaries** | 00 | 23 | 23 |
| **Paraphrasing** | 75 | 39 | 114 |
| **Going back and forth in text** | 03 | 01 | 04 |
| **Asking questions** | 03 | 01 | 04 |
| **Translating** | 06 | 05 | 11 |
| Thinking across languages | | | |
| | | | |
| **Total** | 163 | 128 | 291 |

When we analyzed strategy use in the two text types by individual participant, we found that while several of these strategies were used by most of the participants, each participant had a "preferred" set of strategies they depended on when reading the assigned texts. For instance, Table 14.3 shows that Clara used five strategies while reading text on paper, and she used six strategies while reading the text online; Manuel used four strategies while reading the text on paper and four while reading online; Pedro used eight strategies while reading on paper and eight while reading online; and Marwan used five strategies while reading on paper and five while reading online. Finally, when examining strategy use by text type, the data in Tables 14.3 and 14.4 show that three of the participants, namely, Anita, Danilo, and Selin, used almost twice as many strategies while reading text in traditional print format than they did while reading texts in online format.

*Theme 2: Simultaneous Deployment of Multiple Reading Strategies*

The second major theme or trend that emerged from the data pertains to the simultaneous deployment of a set of strategies by each of the participants when encountering problems while reading texts in print and online formats. In other words, in the midst of certain textual episodes, participants frequently used strategies in conjunction with one another, instead of in isolated and individual instances. There were several instances in which this trend was evident among all 7 participants when reading both types of text. We provide three examples to illustrate this interesting phenomenon.

In the following example, Anita invokes at least three strategies, namely, "pausing and thinking," "using of text features," and "asking questions," to construct an understanding of what she was reading. In one print text episode, she stops reading, looks at a photograph of Chief Red Cloud in order to help her understand why the article describes him as modern, and asks herself a question that she would like to have answered concerning his modernity:

> Anita: I'm going back to the picture here, I'm going to look at it again. They think it's modern because he's looking straight back at the camera? I don't know why that makes him modern.

In the transcript that follows, we noted the use of several strategies by one of the participants while reading the online text: "translating," "guessing word meanings," "using the dictionary," "rereading," and "asking questions." In this text episode, Clara reads the noun phrase "elected autocracy," verbally translates it into Spanish, her native language, speculates that it means basically the same in English, but then confirms her guess by searching for the definition of the words using the online dictionary:

> Clara: …elected autocracy, that's a new term that I'm learning; I'm going to look for that. It's very similar to Spanish…. I'm going to look it up in the dictionary.

In several textual episodes (both in print and online), we noted the

Table 14.4 Type of Strategies Used by Participants When Reading Texts in Traditional Print and Online Formats

| STRATEGIES | Clara Print | Clara Online | Manuel Print | Manuel Online | Anita Print | Anita Online | Danilo Print | Danilo Online | Selin Print | Selin Online | Pedro Print | Pedro Online | Marwan Print | Marwan Online |
|---|---|---|---|---|---|---|---|---|---|---|---|---|---|---|
| **Global Reading Strategies** | | | | | | | | | | | | | | |
| Setting purpose for reading | | | | | | | | | | | | | | |
| Using prior knowledge | | X | X | X | X | X | X | X | | | X | X | | |
| Previewing text | | | | | | | | | | | | | | |
| Checking content fits purpose | | | | | | | | | | | | | | |
| Noting text characteristics | | | | | | | | | | | | | | |
| Determining what to read | | | | | | | | | | | | | | |
| Using text features (e.g., tables) | X | | X | | X | | X | | | | X | | X | |
| Using context clues | X | | | X | X | | | | | | X | | | |
| Using textual aids (e.g., italics) | | | | | | | | | | | | | | |
| Critically evaluating reading | | X | | | X | X | | X | X | X | X | X | | X |
| Checking understanding | | | | | | | | | | | | | | |
| Predicting text meaning | | X | | | | | X | X | X | | X | X | | |
| Confirming predictions | | | | | | | | | | | | | | |
| **Problem-Solving Strategies** | | | | | | | | | | | | | | |
| Reading slowly and carefully | | | | | | | | | | | | | | |
| Staying focused on reading | | | | | | | | | | | | | | |
| Adjusting reading rate | | | | | | | | | | | | | | |
| Paying attention to reading | | | | | | | | | | | | | | |
| Pausing and thinking | | | | | | | X | | X | | | | | |
| Visualizing information | | | | | | | | | | | | | | |
| Rereading | | | | X | X | X | X | | X | X | X | X | X | X |
| Guessing word meanings | X | | | X | X | X | X | | X | | X | X | X | X |
| **Support Reading Strategies** | | | | | | | | | | | | | | |
| Taking notes | | | | | | | | | | | | | | |
| Reading aloud | | | | | | | | | | | | | | |
| Underlining or highlighting | | X | | | | | | | | X | | | | X |
| Using dictionaries | | X | | | | | | X | | | | | | X |
| Paraphrasing | X | X | | X | X | X | X | X | X | | X | X | X | X |
| Going back and forth in text | | | | | X | | | | X | | | X | X | |
| Asking questions | | | | | | | | | | | | X | | |
| Translating | X | X | | X | X | X | | | | | | | X | |
| Thinking across languages | | | | | | | | | | | | | | |

simultaneous deployment of several combinations of reading strategies, including "use of prior knowledge," "rereading," "guessing word meanings," and "paraphrasing." In the following textual episode, Pedro rereads a sentence that he has not understood and then paraphrases it:

> Pedro: As a kind of diplomatic gesture, Goodyear says, he agreed to have his picture taken. Okay, let's see. [silently rereads a text section] OK. Now it makes sense. He was very angry at the American but as a goodwill betrayal, goodwill action, goodwill gesture, he agreed to have his picture taken, so he would like compromise for him.

In the next episode, Pedro cannot comprehend the word "gaze," guesses its meaning, and then reads the sentence that contains it again:

> Pedro: Red Cloud fixes his gaze directly forward—a strikingly modern view, Goodyear says. I have always problem with this gaze because I have seen it many times, but I still can't remember it. Maybe what I understand is the way he poses [guesses word meaning]—Red Cloud fixes his gaze directly forward—a strikingly modern view, Goodyear says.... . [rereads sentence with difficult vocabulary word guessing its meaning]

*Theme 3: Reliance on the Use of the Bilingual Dictionary*

The third major trend that emerged from the data indicated the participants' apparent dependency on the use of a bilingual dictionary, especially when reading text online. Indeed, for 4 of the 7 participants, the use of a bilingual dictionary was a marked strategic difference between reading text in print and online formats. In fact, there were no instances of any type of dictionary use when students read text in print, although there were 23 instances of dictionary use while they were reading text online. Interestingly, when reading the paper-based text, most participants denied ever using the dictionary when reading text in print. For instance, here's how one participant felt about using the dictionary when reading:

> Selin: The thing I do when I'm reading the essays or the paragraphs, I just read without checking the dictionaries, without looking at the words or vocabulary, then I read from the beginning again, and I looked at the vocabulary I don't know.

On the contrary, when reading text online, Selin used an online dictionary nine times. In fact, while reading the paper-based text, she stated that she would have looked up the word "amicable" had an Internet dictionary been available, implying a general dislike for print dictionaries:

> Selin: I don't know the meaning of the word' amicable'. What's amicable? If I had a dictionary, I would look for it. Generally, for words I don't know, I use the Internet.

During the online readings, we noticed that some of the participants opened another window before beginning to read, and went to their preferred online bilingual dictionary, as Selin does below:

> Selin: Here is my dictionary, my Turkish dictionary. I want to connect to that Web site before I start to read the article. I got it. I found my famous dictionary on the Internet. Okay.

In other cases, when encountering unknown words, some participants had a tendency to open another window in order to search for the
definition and/or the translation of the word, as Clara does below using
the *Babel Fish Translation*, a well-known multilingual online dictionary, in
order to look up the meaning of the word "threshold":

> Clara: I'm going to look for a word that I don't know that is "threshold."
> I usually use *Babel Fish Translation*.

When looking up the meanings of unknown words or phrases, participants typically went about this in two ways. They would highlight
the unknown words, copy them, and then paste them into the appropriate space on the Web site; or, they would close the window with the text
on it, open the window with the dictionary on it, and type the word they
wanted translated, as Pedro does in the following example, in which he
searches for the word "lagged":

> Pedro: ...I think I don't understand this, lagged. Let's see. [Types into
> bilingual dictionary] Lagged is, lagged behind, quedar atras, okay, let's
> see, lagged. It's not very clear. This definition is not the best one. Let's
> see. I'm looking for the paragraph. Okay, the good news is that while
> democracy has lagged behind, the right to vote—lagged behind is to be
> behind—it is also on the rise.

While most dictionary users used an online bilingual dictionary, one
participant, Marwan, chose to use a monolingual English dictionary. In
the following example, he searches for the meaning of the word "legiti-
macy," and proceeds to read synonyms:

> Marwan: ...legitimacy, legitimacy, what is it? Let's see. Legitimacy
> means eminent domain, like government try to acquire right to prop-
> erty, okay...

Indeed, some participants in this study exhibited a sophisticated use
of the dictionary in that they only looked up words that they felt were
easily available, which may be one of the reasons that terms that were
technical, literary, germane to a specific academic or professional genre,
or very colloquial were generally deciphered using other strategies or
simply ignored. Pedro, for example, explains that specialized vocabulary
was one of the reasons why he did not utilize the dictionary while reading text in print format:

> Pedro: Okay, I'm done. I just want to add that sometimes when I read
> this stuff, I have problems with some words, because they are very spe-
> cific words. I think with this kind of literature, you find more difficult
> words than when you read a book or an article related to a very techni-
> cal part. It's more like an historical account. They're talking about this
> picture and how this chief was helping his tribe, but they are using some
> words I'm not familiar with and I think this kind of reading is some-
> times a little more difficult. Well, they sometimes choose words I'm not
> familiar with and sometimes this kind of article allows you to conclude
> certain things and sometimes they have open thoughts.

Unlike reading text online, most participants had a tendency to skip
rather than look up words in the dictionary when reading text in print

format, as illustrated in the following two examples. In the first example, Selin is reading a passage in which the word "clamored" appears. She acknowledges not understanding its meaning, but makes no effort to make sense out of it:

> Selin: In years to come, Red Cloud would journey from his home in Pine Ridge, South Dakota, to Washington eight more times and hobnob with officials from three other administrations, frequently on his own initiative. Photographers clamored to capture him on film—What's the meaning of clamored? Photographers clamored to capture him on film…

In the second example, Clara comes across the word "hobnob," acknowledges not understanding it, but just continues to read:

> Clara: In years to come, Red Cloud would journey from his home in Pine Ridge, South Dakota, to Washington eight more times and hobnob. I don't know what hobnob means—with officials from three other administrations, frequently on his own initiative.

## Discussion

In this qualitative case study, we examined the reading strategies 7 ESL college students used when reading texts in traditional print and online formats. The results revealed three major trends or themes that enabled us to capture unique patterns of strategy use among these readers. First, we found that the 7 participants had a tendency to rely on a certain cluster of strategies when reading regardless of whether they read text in traditional print or online formats. While the cluster of strategies differed slightly across print and online texts among the participants, each of them had a suite of reading strategies when reading texts in both formats.

Second, we found that the 7 participants had a tendency to deploy multiple reading strategies simultaneously when encountering a reading problem. Examples of reading strategies they used concurrently included "rereading," "translating," "guessing word meanings," and "paraphrasing." Again, while there were some differences in the cluster of strategies used by each participant during specific text episodes, the deployment of multiple strategies occurred when reading texts in print as well as online format.

Finally, we found that most of the participants depended a great deal on the use of a bilingual dictionary as a support mechanism, especially when reading text online. This tendency is understandable in light of the fact that these students are non-native speakers of English. However, we find somewhat intriguing this tendency to use the bilingual dictionary much more frequently when reading text online than when reading text in print. In fact, some of the students indicated that they enjoyed using online dictionaries while reading but were reluctant to use print dictionaries, which they thought was not only cumbersome, but also distracting and time consuming. One obvious reason for this variation is the availability and relative ease of access to the dictionaries in an online environment. This finding is consistent with prior research by Hulstijn (1993), who studied the use of a computer-based bilingual dictionary by adolescent Dutch ESL students. Among other things, he found that not only did participants frequently use the dictionary, but did so in sophisticated ways. More specifically, they looked up words that were important for comprehension and used other strategies to figure out words that were not essential for text comprehension. In addition, Lomicka (1998) studied the use of glossing in a beginning-level college French class and found that those students who had access to full glossing—as opposed to limited glossing or no glossing—made more causal inferences than the two other groups.

## Conclusion

The above findings have important implications for L1 and L2 reading research and instruction. First, given the importance of reading strategies when reading academic texts, we encourage teachers to learn about the ways in which students respond to reading in print and online. At the very least, they should determine their students' awareness and use of reading strategies when reading. Assessing students' awareness of reading strategies can be determined by administering instruments such as the SORS, while the actual use of reading strategies can be accomplished through informal interviews or focus group discussions, or by using verbal reports or think-aloud techniques, such as the one used in this study, if class time permits. Suggestions for conducting think-aloud protocols, which assist students in developing effective comprehension strategies when reading across different text types, can be found in an excellent book entitled *Improving Comprehension with Think-Aloud Strategies: Modeling what Good Readers Do?* (Wilhelm, 2001).

Second, teachers should use the results obtained from such measures to help students become more constructively responsive to their reading and thereby enhance their understanding of the text. To help students become constructively responsive to reading, teachers should consider creating classroom conditions in which students learn about and use effective reading strategies in the context of real reading. Reading strategies with documented effectiveness, such as setting a purpose for reading, using prior knowledge, monitoring one's comprehension, summarizing what one reads, paraphrasing, using context clues, and critically evaluating one's reading, can and should be taught to students through direct explanation, modeling, and guided practice.

Third, it is important to keep in mind that while many of the strategies effective readers use can be used across different text types (e.g., print vs. online), certain strategies (e.g., use of dictionaries), while evaded in print environments, can be very useful when reading online and should be encouraged, especially by those readers who may need vocabulary assistance. The use of a dictionary, which is easily accessible in online environments, has been found to be quite useful for understanding text (e.g., Hulstijn, 1993; Lomicka, 1998) and developing vocabulary skills, both of which are critical for efficient reading comprehension.

Finally, while it is important to determine whether students have an awareness of reading strategies when reading academic texts, and which types of strategies they actually use when they read, it is equally important to determine the conditions under which they use these strategies. Determining the conditions under which to invoke specific reading strategies cannot be answered through the data gathered for the present study. Consequently, we encourage further research in determining the extent to which the use of certain reading strategies varies as a function of text type, reading purpose, or reading ability. Answers to these questions, and others, can help a great deal in reaching a better understanding of how to help developing and struggling readers use the necessary strategies and skills for effective reading.

# 15 | Summary, Implications, and Future Directions

**Kouider Mokhtari**
*Miami University, Ohio*

**Ravi Sheorey**
*Oklahoma State University*

## Introduction

In the preceding chapters, we have provided an up-to-date examination of the metacognitive awareness and use of reading comprehension strategies by first- (L1) *and* second-language (L2) learners when reading texts in both conventional print and online formats. In these chapters, we addressed important theoretical, empirical, and pedagogical issues associated with various aspects of reading comprehension strategies, including the following:

- the distinction between reading skills and strategies
- the role of metacognitive awareness and use of reading strategies in reading academic materials by L1 and L2 readers
- the measurement of metacognitive awareness and use of reading strategies
- the differences that may exist between males and females with respect to their awareness and use of reading strategies when reading academic or school-related materials
- the role of reading ability and language proficiency (the latter in the case of L2 learners) in the awareness and use of reading strategies
- the distinctions between students' perceived and actual use of reading comprehension strategies when reading
- the activation and use of reading strategies across two or more languages and reading environments (namely, traditional vs. online reading)

In this chapter, we briefly summarize the research presented in the volume, discuss implications and applications of the findings for classroom practice, and offer recommendations for future directions for research that will help advance our understanding of how we can promote metacognitively competent reading among L1 and L2 readers.

We began our argument with the pedagogical assumption that one important cognitive ability that may have an impact on comprehension and academic achievement is the skill of reading, broadly defined as the ability to make a coherent representation of the text that matches the intended message of the writer (Snow, Burns, & Griffins, 1998). Research has shown that although there are many variables that contribute to reading skill, there are two attributes of skilled reading that are of particular interest in this project: metacognitive awareness and use of reading strategies while reading. We know, for instance, that skilled readers generate more inferences than less skilled readers because skilled readers are more strategic and have more aware of reading strategies (Kintsch, 1998; McNamara, 2004; Pressley, 2002). Skilled readers are more likely to monitor their comprehension and use active reading strategies, such as setting purpose for reading, previewing text, predicting, making inferences, using prior knowledge, summarizing, and evaluating their text understanding.

A number of L1 and L2 reading researchers have argued that the key difference between skilled and less skilled readers resides in the knowledge and the dispositions to use reading strategies in effective ways. As we have mentioned throughout this volume, Pressley and Afflerbach's (1995) work in examining a number of studies of verbal protocols of reading has shown a great deal of the complexity of skilled reading and what skilled readers know and do with the many different strategies they are aware of when responding to text. As they read, they occasionally take notes, they predict, paraphrase, and reread when confused, and deliberately monitor their reading comprehension processes. On the other hand, novice readers often focus on decoding single words, fail to adjust their reading for different texts or purposes, and seldom look ahead or back in text to monitor and improve comprehension.

Carrell (1998), after reviewing the research in L1 and L2 reading over a 25-year period, concurred and stated that young, unskilled readers do not use comprehension strategies often or effectively without help. These students often have difficulties understanding what they read, not because they are unable read, but because of how they read. Failure to use reading strategies effectively among young, unskilled readers can be marked by a lack of awareness of reading strategies, failure to monitor their comprehension, lack of knowledge of how information is organized in various texts, and a lack of disposition to use strategies when needed. According to Carrell (1998), such a failure in metacognitive awareness about reading and the nonuse of appropriate reading strategies may reflect a mixture of developmental inexperience, limited reading practice, lack of instruction, and motivational reluctance to use unfamiliar or effortful strategies.

Afflerbach, Pearson, and Paris (see chapter 2) clarified the distinction between skills and strategies and the relationship between the two concepts, a distinction that matters because both skills and strategies play an important role in reading instruction and because, the authors argued, reading instruction would suffer if the two constructs were not clear in the minds of researchers and practitioners. According to the authors, skills are automatic actions, while strategies are intentional efforts on the part of readers to make sense of the text. This distinction is consistent with that of other researchers, such as Carrell (1991), who defined reading strategies as the "actions that readers actively select and control to achieve desired goals or objectives" (p. 3). In her use of the term "strategies," Carrell aligns herself with Paris, Wasik, and Turner (1991), who argued that "skills" refer to information-processing procedures that are automatic and are applied to text reading nearly unconsciously, whether they refer to decoding words or summarizing a story. On the other hand, emerging skills can become strategies when they are used intentionally. Consequently, strategies are actions selected deliberately to achieve particular goals.

In chapter 3, Linda Baker discussed the role of metacognitive skills of reading, lists contributors to, and consequences of, metacognitive development, and examines experimental studies that evaluate the effects of enhancing metacognitive knowledge and strategies on reading comprehension. In her paper, she also addresses how instructional practices are changing to incorporate a stronger metacognitive focus, but she cautions that the ultimate goal of teaching conscious comprehension monitoring is to help students turn it into internalized self-regulation. Her insights are consistent with other researchers (e.g., Pressley, 2000; Pressley & Gaskins, 2006), who have argued that the ultimate goal of skilled reading is to enable the reader to become aware of the active nature of reading and the importance of employing effective problem-solving and troubleshooting routines to enhance understanding. Such self-awareness is a prerequisite for self-regulation, the ability to monitor and check one's own cognitive activities while reading.

In chapters 4 and 5, we addressed issues pertaining to the measurement of L1 and L2 readers' awareness of reading strategies when reading for academic or school-related purposes. In chapter 4, Mokhtari, Sheorey, and Reichard provided details about the development and psychometric characteristics of two instruments to identify the metacognitive awareness and reading strategy use of L1 and L2 readers, respectively: the Metacognitive Awareness of Reading Strategies Inventory (MARSI), and its "ESL adapted version," the Survey of Reading Strategies (SORS); we also provided information on how to administer and interpret the results of the instruments for classroom instructional purposes. In chapter 5, Mokhtari and Perry explored the use of Rasch analysis as a preliminary step in revising and updating MARSI as a measure of students' metacognitive awareness of reading strategies when applied to academic or school-related readings.

In chapters 6 and 7, we presented research findings from studies, carried out on various populations of native and non-native readers, which examined students' perceived and/or actual use of reading strategies while reading. In the one study, Mokhtari and Reichard (chapter 6), explored whether the type and frequency of reading strategies perceived to be used by students are impacted by two different purposes, namely, reading for school and reading for fun or enjoyment. The results of the study revealed that students do, indeed, modify their reading strategy use, depending on whether they were reading texts for academic purposes or for entertainment. In chapter 7, Mokhtari, Reichard, and Sheorey examined the differences between the strategies that high school native English speakers *say* they use versus the ones they *actually* do use when reading print materials for school-related purposes. The authors found that students did not report actually using as many reading strategies when reading two specific textbook chapters as they professed to use when thinking about reading for academic purposes in general. Chapter 8 provided a critical examination of the cognitive strategy instruction for bilingual and biliterate students. Jiménez, Handsfield, and Fisher took a critical look at theory, research, and cognitive strategy instruction in an effort to understand the comprehension processes of *bilingual* and *biliterate* readers. The authors critically examined how cognitive strategies have been taught in the classroom with multilingual students and argued that rather than viewing bilingual and biliterate students through the prism of mainstream monolinguality, reading teachers should try to utilize the potentially different ways of interacting with text when the reader is literate in more than one language.

In chapter 9, Sheorey and Mokhtari compared the metacognitive awareness or perceptions of the reading strategies of English as a second language (ESL) college students studying in the United States with those of native-English-speaking American college students. Among the findings the authors reported are that both groups showed a clear preference for problem-solving strategies, that non-native students reported using support strategies significantly more than native readers, and that in the U.S. group, the females show greater awareness of reading strategies. In chapter 10, Mokhtari presented a case study of the professed reading strategies of three triliterate readers versus their actual or real-time use to explore the potential impact of multiple literacies in languages (namely, Arabic, English, and French), which differ from one another in important ways. The author found that strategy transfer can occur even when reading in another language, such as Arabic, which is quite different from English or French in terms of direction, orthography, lexicon, and syntax. Overall, the results suggested that once a reader becomes aware of a set of strategies and their usefulness in one language, they are likely to use them when comprehending texts in another language.

Chapters 11 and 12 examined the reading strategies of two specific groups of students, studying in an environment where English is a *foreign* language (EFL). The two chapters dealt, respectively, with Hungarian and Japanese college students. Results of the Hungarian study revealed that Hungarian English majors appear to prefer strategies similar to those used by skilled readers (perhaps because of their high proficiency in the language); the results also showed a significant linear relationship between the time spent on reading (approximately 8 or more hours per week) and the perceived use of reading strategies. In the case of Japanese computer science students, unlike the results of the Hungarian study, a significant linear relationship was found between reported reading strategies and (self-rated) English proficiency. In neither group were there any significant differences between (self-rated) high- and low-reading-ability participants.

Chapters 13 and 14 briefly reviewed the new and exciting research field of online reading. Kymes (see chapter 13) made a case that because of the significant differences between print and electronic or online texts, we need to reconceptualize (print) reading strategies to fit the very different reading experience of online texts, and that we cannot assume that the reading skills and strategies used in conventional print material simply transfer to the online reading environment. Finally, in chapter 14, we presented findings of a pilot study aimed at exploring the reading strategies college ESL students report using when reading texts online and in print. In that chapter, Poole and Mokhtari reported that the 7 student participants in their qualitative study relied on a certain set of reading strategies regardless of whether they read the text in online or print format. One of the strategies used prominently in online reading was that of participants' reliance on an online bilingual dictionary, presumably because of the availability and relative ease of access to such dictionaries in an online environment.

In summary, the findings reported in the studies and reviews above emphasize the important role of students' metacognitive awareness and use of reading strategies when reading for academic or school-related purposes in a variety of L1 and L2 environments. This awareness, as we have argued throughout this volume, distinguishes skilled and less skilled readers, in that skilled readers are more likely to have the metacognitive knowledge and the dispositions to use reading comprehension strategies in effective ways than their less skilled counterparts. These findings have important implications for teaching and for future research.

## Implications for Instruction

The findings in the studies and reviews reported in this volume indicate that classroom teachers should take steps to determine their students' awareness of comprehension strategies when reading for various purposes. There are few instruments available for children, adolescent, and college readers aimed at assessing students' metacognitive awareness of reading strategies. Examples of such instruments include the *Index of Reading Awareness* (Jacobs & Paris, 1987), *Reading Strategy Use* (Pereira-Laird & Deane, 1997), a metacognitive reading awareness inventory (Miholic, 1994), and the *Metacognitive Strategy Index* (Schmitt, 1990). In this book, we included (see chapter 4) two relatively new instruments, namely, the MARSI, to measure native-English-speaking students' (sixth grade through college) awareness of reading strategies when reading academic materials, and the SORS, which was adapted for use with non-native speakers of English. The purpose of instruments such as the MARSI or SORS is to tap generalized perceptions of strategy use—not actual strategy use; when students complete either of these instruments, they are thinking about a broad range of reading tasks, and they report strategy use in a generalized sense, without referring to any specific use of any particular reading task.

We should caution that prior research in this important area of inquiry has shown that while generalized knowledge about reading processes and strategies may be necessary for skilled reading, it is not sufficient for metacognitively competent reading. For instance, Pressley and Afflerbach (1995) found that skilled readers not only know that there are different ways of reading, but that they also know how to monitor and regulate the use of such strategies. A plausible explanation was proposed by Hadwin, Winne, Stockley, Nesbit, and Woszczyna (2001), who maintained that students use strategies to a different extent in different contexts, even in academic reading, and that context-free measures do not accurately reflect strategy use for any of those contexts. An alterative explanation might be that people are generally poor at accurately estimating how able they are at specific cognitive tasks such as reading (see Kruger & Dunning, 1999; Schmeck, 2000, for an extensive discussion of this issue). It is conceivable that high-comprehending students may systematically underestimate, and low-comprehending students systematically overestimate their own use of the strategies on measures such as MARSI or SORS, and this observation needs to be taken into account when interpreting the results obtained. For those teachers interested in determining students' *actual* strategy use rather than perceived strategy use or awareness when reading specific texts, we recommend using concurrent measures that actually require students to enact strategies, such as think-aloud protocols, reaction times, error detection, and other such measures (for a more detailed review of multiple-method studies, see Veenman, 2005).

The findings reported in this volume also point to the need for teaching students to use reading strategies when they read diverse texts and for various purposes. Because young, novice readers may have misconceptions about the nature of reading and may lack awareness of the thinking processes involved in effective reading, or of the executive processes for monitoring and regulating comprehension, some researchers have called for fostering better metacognition and reading comprehension through direct instruction of reading comprehension strategies. The overall goal of the explicit and direct teaching of reading strategies was stated by Baker and Brown (1984) over two decades ago and has not changed much: "...to make the reader aware of the active nature of reading and the importance of employing problem-solving, troubleshooting routines to enhance understanding...Such self-awareness is a prerequisite for self-regulation, the ability to monitor and check one's own cognitive activities while reading..." (p. 376). Other researchers (e.g., Anderson, 1991; Carrell, 1991; Pressley, 2000) have argued that strategy awareness is a necessary, but not a sufficient, condition for metacognitively competent reading. In other words, readers should go beyond simply knowing what strategies to use; they must also know how to use the strategies successfully and know how to orchestrate their uses with other strategies when reading various texts for various purposes.

Pearson (2007) proposed that the teaching of reading comprehension should be integrated with the teaching of content areas, such as science, mathematics, or social studies. In doing so, he advises classroom teachers to have specific goals (e.g., students should be expert readers who are active, goal-oriented readers who read selectively and differentially, integrate their prior knowledge with materials read, and monitor their understanding), a supportive classroom context in which they are able to read, write, talk, and do things, and opportunity for real reading. He encourages teachers to provide opportunities for every child, in every classroom, and in every grade so their students spend a great deal of time actually reading a range of real texts, talking about text with teachers, and one another. As with decoding, he adds, all the explicit instruction in the world will not make strong readers unless accompanied by lots of experience applying their knowledge, skills, and strategies during actual reading.

In an attempt to raise students' awareness of reading strategies when reading different types of reading materials and for diverse purposes, we align ourselves with the many researchers and practitioners who advocate teaching students reading comprehension strategies through teacher modeling, guided practice, and independent practice. Research has shown that students become better readers when they learn to use reading strategies, such as setting purpose for reading, activating prior knowledge, asking questions when they read, using problem-solving strategies when they encounter a comprehension breakdown, and evaluating what they read to be sure they have accomplished their reading goals (e.g., Garner, 1987; Pressley, 2000). We also recommend that teachers consider following the lead of those classroom teachers who have successfully taught their students to become metacognitively competent, strategic readers. For instance, seventh-grade teacher Mari Beth Bennett (Bennett, 2003) and teacher educators Bishop, Reyes, and Pflaum (2006) and Fisk and Hurst (2003) have offered the following practical suggestions for classroom teachers:

1. *Practice what you teach.* One of the challenges often encountered by teachers when teaching their students to increase their metacognitive awareness and use of reading strategies is that they, themselves, are not strategy users. This observation is consistent with the implication that teachers do not always use comprehension strategies when they read (Keen & Zimmerman, 1997). Bennett (2003) recommends that teachers should tell their students about the strategies they themselves use when they read. In other words, teachers can easily model effective strategic reading by simply sharing with their students the processes they resort to when reading, the problems they encounter and how they solve them, and whether these strategies change based upon their reading purpose of type of reading. Bennett (2003) noted that often the strategies

that content-area teachers consider to be critical for their own reading may be at odds with the strategies their students are aware of and use when reading. Bennett (2003) pointed out that:

> ...the best way to encourage content-area teachers to learn reading strategies is to point out the discrepancy between what they teach and what they do. In this case, their own actions may become their guide for what to do. Recognizing the incongruity between the reading strategies students use might be the catalyst for the content-area teachers to learn about reading strategies so that they might teach what they practice. (p. 34)

2. *Informally investigate students' familiarity and knowledge of active reading.* Bennett (2003) recommends that teachers take time to find out whether their students are aware of the reading strategies used when reading by administering informal instruments, such as MARSI, to determine the extent to which students are "conscious of their own thinking and level of understanding during the process of reading" (p. 34). When looking through her student responses to the strategies in the MARSI instrument, Bennett noted that it is important to take time to assess students' awareness of reading strategies, and to help them become aware of their own thinking processes and to ultimately enable them to determine when and how to use them when reading.

3. *Teach students to read smarter, not harder.* Bishop, Reyes, and Pflaum (2006) noted that what sets strategic readers apart from those readers who can read but don't understand what they read is the understanding that they must read smarter and not harder. These educators maintain that many students are able to use support strategies, such as asking for help, using the dictionary, or re-reading, but many students find it difficult to use global reading strategies such as activating prior knowledge, making text predictions, using context clues, and textual structures and related features, in part because these strategies are challenging to teach. They recommend modeling global reading strategies in order to guide students through the thinking processes involved by actually telling them to "act out" or be more explicit with what they read. For instance, when teaching them to identify textual and visual clues, teachers can direct them to:

> Look at pictures and ask what meaning they might have in relation to the text. Direct students to read sidebars for key information that the authors emphasize. Model making predictions about the headings, subtopics, and italicized titles, and invite students to consider how those might influence their reading of the information. Are there any miscellaneous items, such as boxed information, italicized words, or graphs to attend to? Ask students to decide whether such information adds to or detracts from the meaning of the text. (Bishop, Reyes, & Pflaum, 2006, p. 68)

4. *Show students how to paraphrase for comprehension.* Fisk and Hurst

(2003) recommended that teachers should teach their students the strategy of "paraphrasing" in an attempt to help them better comprehend text. The authors argue that paraphrasing for comprehension is an excellent tool for reinforcing reading skills, such as identifying the main ideas, finding details, and identifying the authors' voice. The strategy of paraphrasing for comprehension works particularly well "because it integrates all modes of communication—reading, writing, listening, and speaking—which leads to a deeper understanding of text" (p. 182). When teaching students to paraphrase for comprehension, the authors recommend using the following four simple steps, which incorporate ways for students to interact with text. These steps include (i) initial reading of text followed by discussion, (ii) second reading of text with note taking, (iii) written paraphrasing, and (d) sharing of written paraphrases with peers. The strategy of paraphrasing for comprehension can be used in elementary, middle school, high school, and college classrooms as a way of promoting meaningful reading, writing, and learning.

5. *Use think alouds and think alongs to improve reading comprehension.* Roger Farr (2005) maintained that many struggling readers do not necessarily think while they are reading. Farr continued work on "using think alouds to improve reading." He developed a framework aimed at helping these readers develop comprehension involving the processes of "modeling, coached practice, and reflection." Robert Farr explains how this framework works as follows:

> **Modeling**—By modeling for students the types of behaviors good readers are engaged in as they read, we are providing them with the opportunity to become aware of the many strategies and monitoring behaviors that good readers use. When good readers are reading relatively simple texts (according to their own reading abilities), these strategic behaviors are fairly automatic. Typically, good readers only become aware of their strategy use when they recognize that they are failing to comprehend. Then, they are cognizant of the need to reevaluate their strategy use in order to remedy their failure to comprehend. Furthermore, good readers are more likely to fall back on appropriate strategies when the need to change strategies becomes apparent. For most poor readers, however, using a variety of strategies, using strategies appropriately, and monitoring strategies is not automatic. Therefore, modeling strategic behaviors for struggling readers by thinking aloud for them while we read (and hence, allowing students to think along) is the first step in raising their awareness of what it means to be a strategic reader.

> **Coached Practice**—By engaging poor readers in coached practice in the think-aloud method, we are providing them with the opportunity and guidance they need to choose useful, appropriate strategies to enhance reading comprehension. We are encouraging them to think about why and when to use certain strategies

and are providing them with the tools they need to successfully monitor their own comprehension. With enough modeling and coached practice, students will be on their way to becoming independent users of strategies. Eventually, they will become their own coaches. Ultimately, strategy use will become more automatic for them, so that the writing they were once doing in the boxes is happening automatically in their heads.

**Reflection**—By getting students to reflect on the process of thinking aloud as they read, we're encouraging them to recognize the difference between reading the words and comprehending the text. By talking about their own strategy use, students gain insights into the complexities of reading, and hence expand their understanding of what it means to be a good reader.

Additional guidelines for using the framework are available from Farr's Website at: http://www.indiana.edu/~crls/rogerfarr/mcr/usingta/usingta.html (retrieved March 29, 2007) or from his Web site at: http://www.rogerfarr.com/ (retrieved March 27, 2007).

When considering using any or all of the teaching strategies above, we caution teachers that skilled readers don't get that way overnight. They learn how to become metacognitively competent and strategic by engaging in reading over long periods of time, with lots of different texts, and with lots of opportunities to practice applying strategies, and monitoring their processes and evaluating the effectiveness of different strategies for themselves in different reading situations, with teachers explaining and modeling use of a wide variety of strategies, scaffolding student practice and application, providing explanations and additional modeling as necessary, and helping learners to experience reading strategies as personal cognitive and metacognitive tools for becoming metacognitively competent and "constructively responsive" to their reading. In teaching students to become metacognitively competent readers, teachers should also monitor whether or not their teaching is having an impact on their students' reading and then take steps to adjust instruction based on student needs.

## Future Directions for Research and Practice

The findings in the above studies and reviews certainly do not address the myriad of questions and issues that may be at work when examining students' awareness and use of reading strategies when reading. In fact, while the research presented has shed some light on this important topic, there is relatively little research concerning students'—and teachers'—knowledge and use of reading strategies, their impact on students' reading ability and academic performance as well as on teacher's performance, and how these factors relate to students' and teachers' knowledge of strategy use. The call for such research has been echoed in current and prior studies, which have indicated that teachers' levels of knowledge and use of strategic teaching options in reading and language are not often at desirable levels of performance (e.g., Hilden &

Pressley, 2007; Manzo & Manzo, 1998). Research is needed to ascertain not just how much students know and use reading strategies, but also how much teachers know about metacognitive reading strategies and reading instruction, and how frequently they use such strategies in their classrooms. Findings from such research can help us better understand the need for reading strategy interventions and how teachers can better meet the needs of their students.

Hilden and Pressley (2007) have recently documented the challenges and successes a group of five teachers encountered while participating in a 1-year-long professional development program designed to improve their reading comprehension instruction so as to increase their students' self-regulation successes and challenges. Their results indicated that while teachers reported positive changes in their own thinking with respect to reading comprehension instruction, as well as appreciable growth in their students' reading comprehension behaviors, teachers frequently faced obstacles related to texts, classroom management, instructional decisions, their students, time, and assessment issues. Using lessons learned over the course of more than a decade relative to teaching reading comprehension strategies, the authors offer the following recommendations, which we believe should be incorporated into future research studies aimed at promoting effective and productive teaching of reading strategies:

1. Teachers must become self-regulated strategy users themselves in order to effectively teach the strategies to their students. In doing so, they will have a firsthand appreciation of what it means to read strategically and ultimately feel better equipped to teach their students to develop an effective knowledge and use of reading strategies when reading.

2. Teachers should keep in mind that the effective, productive teaching of reading strategies takes time and effort. Consistent with prior research (e.g., Pressley et al., 1992), the effective teaching of reading comprehension strategies takes more than simple modeling, explanation, and practice. Becoming a comprehension strategies teacher is a long-term process, which gets easier with increased reading strategy knowledge and experience. It takes a few years for teachers to develop the ability to teach reading strategies well and for the effects of such teaching on student reading comprehension ability to endure.

3. Teachers should be mindful of the instructional language they use when explaining reading comprehension strategies to their students. Using descriptive labels when modeling and explaining reading comprehension strategies (e.g., setting purpose for reading, making predictions, or summarizing one's reading) and their uses enables students and teachers to communicate better about which strategies are important for which reading task, as well as when and how to use them when reading.

4. Teachers should consider teaching reading comprehension strategies

within the context of the whole school, not just at the level of one classroom or one individual student. In other words, the teaching of reading comprehension strategies should be integrated with the entire language arts curriculum. The authors noted that:

> only students who received several years of comprehension strat-
> egies instruction and practice used the strategies in a fully self-
> regulated way. Unfortunately, to date, no one has carefully studied
> the longitudinal development of comprehension strategies use in
> a school setting that offers years of teaching and encouragement
> of comprehension strategies. (Pressley et al., 1992, p. 73)

We suggest that future research consider developing instructional curricula aimed at teaching comprehension strategies and designing studies that examine the impact of comprehension strategy instruction on students' reading performance, learning, and motivation not just for individual students, but at the school levels. While such studies will certainly require substantial amounts of time, effort, and funding, they will be extremely helpful in increasing our understanding of the ways in which students and teachers become self-regulated learners and read-ers. In fact, with the high priority placed by the No Child Left Behind Act of 2001 legislation to address reading comprehension as an essen-tial element of effective reading instruction, we are aware of a handful of promising government-funded projects currently in various stages of development, which address various aspects of reading comprehension strategy instruction, both in traditional print and in online environments. A sampling of these projects includes the following:

*Metacognitively Competent Reading Comprehension Instruction at the Benchmark School*

An example of an organized effort to develop metacognitively com-petent readers within an entire school system is at the Benchmark School in Media, Pennsylvania. For decades, Michael Pressley and Irene Gaskins have collaborated on the development of a highly effective, Grades 1–8, across-the-curriculum comprehension strategies instruction program for struggling readers. In this school, metacognitive comprehension strate-gies instruction is infused across the curriculum over the long term for students to learn how to use the strategies flexibly and with a variety of texts. Throughout the program, "students learn where and when to use the strategies they are acquiring, how and when the strategies are helpful, and how learning and using strategies is part of general competence, not just at the school but in the larger world" (Pressley & Gaskins, 2006, p. 110).

*Improving Reading Comprehension for Struggling Readers*

Brigit Dalton, from the Center for Applied Special Technology (CAST), is collaborating with Patrick Proctor of Boston College and Catherine Snow of Harvard University on a study investigating the effect of Web-based hypertexts with interactive vocabulary and embedded strategy support on bilingual and monolingual students' reading achievement.

Their project, entitled "Improving Reading Comprehension for Struggling Readers: Understanding the Roles of Vocabulary Development, Guided Strategy Use, and Spanish Language Supports in a Digital Reading Environment," is designed to develop and test a technology-based instructional approach to improving reading comprehension among diverse fifth-grade struggling readers, including English-language learners. Over 3 years, the researchers are conducting three studies to develop and refine a digital reading environment, called a Universal Learning Edition (ULE), which has strong, embedded supports for reading strategies and active vocabulary learning. The results of this work will contribute to our understanding of how to design and implement digital reading environments that are customized to the needs of diverse readers.

*Web-Based Intelligent Tutoring System*

Researchers Kay Wijekumar and Bonnie J.F. Meyer (The Pennsylvania State University) have developed and piloted a Web-Based Intelligent Tutoring System for Structure Strategy (ITSS) model to provide fifth-through seventh-grade students instruction and tutoring in the structure strategy, an intervention aimed at improving expository text comprehension. The team reports several advantages of Web-based tutors, including consistent tutoring, modeling of good practice, scaffolding, immediate feedback, and motivation. More information on this project is available at: http://itss.br.psu.edu/ (retrieved April 20, 2007).

*New Literacies Research Team*

A team of researchers led by Donald Leu (University of Connecticut) and David Reinking (Clemson University) is currently working on expanding our understanding of reading comprehension to encompass what they call *new literacies*, emerging from the Internet and other information and communication technologies. Electronic texts, such as those found on the World Wide Web, they argue, introduce new supports as well as new challenges that can have a great impact on students' ability to navigate and makes sense of what they read (Coiro & Dobler, 2007; Leu et al., 2004). In addition, these researchers are engaged in developing a system of reciprocal teaching strategies for students who are at risk of dropping out of school (Leu & Reinking, 2005). These teaching strategies will allow teachers to focus on the new strategies for achieving comprehension and developing critical thinking and reading skills that are essential for online text reading. The team's Web site available at http://www.newliteracies.uconn.edu/iesproject/index.html (retrieved April 17, 2007), contains more details about these and other related projects.

## Conclusion

We believe researchers would do well to try to assemble converging evidence from multiple methods of investigating and analyzing students' metacognitive awareness of reading strategies and how teaching can help them become metacognitively competent readers. Single research methods tend to yield one-dimensional perspectives, which tend to be inadequate for a subject as complex as metacognition and reading comprehension (Garner, 1987). The studies examined in this volume used various methods of investigation focusing on a few basic research questions pertaining to students' awareness and use of comprehension strategies. These questions focused on (i) how reading skills and strategies are different, (ii) how metacognitive awareness and use of reading strategies are important for reading comprehension and learning in L1 and L2 reading, (iii) how to measure students' metacognitive awareness and use of reading strategies, (iv) whether males and females differ with respect to their awareness and use of reading strategies when reading academic or school-related materials, (v) whether reading ability and language proficiency play a role in metacognitively competent reading, (vi) whether students' perceived use of reading strategies is consistent with their actual use of reading strategies when reading, and (vii) whether students use similar reading strategies across languages and reading environments. We may not have provided authoritative answers to these questions, but the fact that many of our findings are consistent with previous research gives us a sense of our being at least on the right track.

# References

Achieve, Inc. (2005). *Rising to the challenge: Are high school graduates prepared for college and work?* Washington, DC: Author.

Afflerbach, P. (1990). The influence of prior knowledge of expert readers' main idea construction strategies. *Reading Research Quarterly, 25,* 31–46.

Afflerbach, P., & Cho, B. (In press; 2008). Identifying constructive reading comprehension processes. In S. Israel & G. Duffy (Eds.) *Handbook of Research on Reading Comprehension.* New York: Taylor & Francis.

Afflerbach, P., & Johnson, P. (1984). Research methodology on the use of verbal reports in reading research. *Journal of Reading Behavior, 16,* 307–321.

Afflerbach, P., & Meuwissen, K. (2005). Teaching and learning self-assessment strategies in middle school. In S. E. Israel, C. C. Block, K. L. Bauserman, & K Kinnucan-Welsch (Eds.), *Metacognition in literacy learning: Theory, assessment, instruction, and professional development* (pp. 141–164). Mahwah, NJ: Erlbaum.

Alderson, J. (1984). Reading in a foreign language: A reading problem or a language problem? In J. Alderson & A. Urquhart (Eds.), *Reading in a Foreign Language* (pp. 1–25). New York: Longman.

Alexander, P. A., & Jetton, T. L. (2000). Learning from text: a multidimensional and developmental perspective. In Kamil, M., Mosenthal, P., Pearson, P. D., Barr, R. (Eds.), *Handbook of Reading Research, Vol. 3* (pp. 285–310). Mahwah, NJ: Lawrence Erlbaum.

Alexander, P. A., Pate, E. P., Kulikowich, J. M., Farrell, D. M., & Wright, N.L. (1989). Domain-specific and strategic knowledge: Effects of training on students of differing ages or competence levels. *Learning and Individual Differences, 1,* 283–325.

Allington, R. (2000). *What really matters for struggling readers: Designing research-based programs.* New York: Longman.

Allington, R. L. (2005). *What really matters for struggling readers: Designing research-based programs (2nd edition).* New York: Longman.

Alvermann, D. E., & Guthrie, J. T. (1993). *Themes and directions of the National Reading Research Center: Perspectives in reading research, No. 1.* Athens, GA: University of Georgia and University of Maryland at College Park.

Alvermann, D., Phelps, S., & Ridgeway, V. (2007). *Content reading and literacy: Succeeding in today's classroom*. New York, NY: Allyn & Bacon.

Anderson, N. (1991). Individual differences in strategy use in second language reading and testing. *Modern Language Journal, 72*, 150–162.

Anderson, N. (1999). *Exploring second language reading: Issues and strategies*. Boston: Heinle & Heinle.

Anderson, N. (2003). Scrolling, clicking, and reading English: Online reading strategies in a second/foreign language. *The Reading Matrix, 3*, 1–33.

Anderson, R. C., & Pearson, P. D. (1984). A schema-theoretic view of basic processes in reading. In R. Barr, M. L. Kamil, P. Mosenthal, & P. D. Pearson (Eds.) *Handbook of reading research, Vol. 2* (pp. 255–292). White Plains, NY: Longman.

Anderson, R. C, & Pichert, J. (1978). Recall of previously unrecallable information following a   shift in perspective. *Journal of Verbal Learning and Verbal Behavior, 17*, 1–12.

Annevirta, T., & Vauras, M. (2001). Development of metacognitive knowledge in primary grades. *European Journal of Educational Psychology, 16*, 257–282.

Annevirta, T., & Vauras, M. (2006). Developmental changes of metacognitive skill in elementary school children. *The Journal of Experimental Education, 74*, 197–225.

Assor, A., & Connell, J. P. (1992). The validity of self-reports as measures of performance affecting self-appraisals. In D. H. Schunk & J. L. Meece (Eds.), *Student perceptions in the classroom* (pp. 25–50). Hillsdale, NJ: Erlbaum.

Atkinson, R., & Shiffrin, R. M. (1968). Human memory: A proposed system and its control processes. In K. W. Spence & J. T. Spence (Eds.), *The psychology of learning and motivation: Advance in research and theory Vol. 2* (pp. 89–195). New York: Academic Press.

Auerbach, E., & Paxton, D. (1997). "It's not the English thing": bringing reading research into the ESL classroom. *TESOL Quarterly 31*, 237–261.

August, D., & Hakuta, K. (1997). *Improving schooling for language-minority children: A research agenda*. Washington, D.C.: National Academy Press.

Baker, C. (2001). *Foundations of bilingual education and bilingualism (3rd edition)*. Philadelphia: Multilingual Matters.

Baker, L. (1985). How do we know when we don't understand? Standards for evaluating text comprehension. In D. L. Forrest-Pressley, G. E. MacKinnon & T. G. Waller (Eds.), *Metacognition, cognition, and human performance Vol. 1* (pp. 155–205). New York: Academic.

Baker, L. (1989). Metacognition, comprehension monitoring, and the adult reader. *Educational Psychology Review, 1*. 3–38.

Baker, L. (1994). Fostering metacognitive development. In H. Reese (Ed.), *Advances in child development and behavior Vol. 25* (pp. 201–239). San Diego: Academic Press.

Baker, L. (2002). Metacognition in comprehension instruction. In C. C. Block & M. Pressley (Eds.), *Comprehension instruction: Research based best practices* (pp. 77–95). New York: Guilford.

Baker, L. (2004). Reading comprehension and science inquiry: Metacognitive connections. In W. Saul (Ed.), *Crossing borders in literacy and science instruction: Perspectives on theory and practice* (pp. 239–257). Neward, DE: International Reading Association.

Baker, L. (2005). Developmental differences in metacognition: Implications for metacognitively-oriented reading instruction. In S. E. Israel, C. C. Block, K. L. Bauserman, & K. Kinnucan-Welsch (Eds.), *Metacognition in literacy learning: Theory, assessment, instruction, and professional development* (pp. 61–79). Mahwah, NJ: Erlbaum.

Baker, L. & Anderson, R. I. (1982). Effects of Inconsistent information on text processing: Evidence for comprehension monitoring. *Reading Research Quarterly, 17,* 281–294.

Baker, L. & Brown, A. L. (1984). Metacognitive skills and reading. In P. D. Pearson, R. Barr, M. L. Kamil, & P. Mosenthal (Eds.), *Handbook of research in reading* (pp. 353–394). White Plains, NY: Longman.

Baker, L., & Cerro, L. (2000). Assessing metacognition in children and adults. In G. Scrawl & J. Impara (Eds.), *Issues in the measurement of metacognition* (pp. 99–145). Lincoln, NE: Buros Institute of Mental Measurements, University of Nebraska.

Baker, L., & Cerro, L. C. (2000). Metacognitive skills and reading. In G. Schraw & J. C. Impara (Eds.), *Issues in the measurement of metacognition* (pp. 99–146). Lincoln, NE: Buros Institute of Mental Measurements, University of Nebraska.

Baker, L., Dreher, M. J., & Guthrie, J. T. (Eds.) (2000). *Engaging young readers: Promoting achievement and motivation.* New York: Guilford.

Barr, R., & Johnson, B. (1996). *Teaching Reading in Elementary Classrooms.* New York, NY: Pearson.

Barton, D., & Hamilton, M. (2000). Literacy practices. In D. Barton, M. Hamilton, & R. Ivani (Eds.), *Situated literacies: Reading and writing in context* (pp. 7–15). London: Routledge.

Bauserman, K. L. (2005). Metacognitive Processes Inventory: An informal instrument to assess a student's developmental level of metacognition. In S. E. Israel, C. C. Block, K. L. Bauserman, & K. Kinnucan-Welsch (Eds.), *Metacognition in literacy learning: Theory, assessment, instruction, and professional development* (pp. 165–180). Mahwah, NJ: Erlbaum.

Bennett, M. B. (2003). From practice to preaching: Helping content area teachers teach comprehension. *Voices from the Middle, 11,* 31–34.

Bernhardt, E. (2000). Second-language reading as a case study of reading scholarship in the 20th century. In M. Kamil, P. Mosenthal, P. Pearson, R. Barr (Eds.), *Handbook of reading research, Vol.3,* (pp. 791–811). Mahwah, NJ: Lawrence Erlbaum.

Bernhardt, E. (2003). Challenges to reading research from a multilingual world. *Reading Research Quarterly, 38,* 112–122.

Biancarosa, C., & Snow, C. E. (2006). *Reading next—A vision for action and research in middle and high school literacy: A report to Carnegie Corporation of New York (2nd Edition)*. Washington, DC: Alliance for Excellent Education.

Bishop, P., Reyes, C., & Pfluam, S. (2006). Read smarter, not harder: Global reading comprehension strategies. *The Reading Teacher, 60*, 66–69.

Bland, J. H. (1995). How adult readers navigate through expository text in a hypermedia environment to construct meaning (doctoral dissertation, University of North Texas, 1995). *Dissertation Abstracts International, 56*, 4710.

Block, E. (1986). The comprehension strategies of second language readers. *TESOL Quarterly, 20*, 463–494.

Block, E. (1992). See how they read: Comprehension monitoring of L1 and L2 readers. *TESOL Quarterly, 26*, 319–343.

Bodomo, A., Lam, M. L., & Lee, C. (2003). Some students still read books in the 21st century: A study of user preferences for print and electronic libraries. *The Reading Matrix, 3*(3), 34–49.

Bolter, J. D. (1998). Hypertext and the question of visual literacy. In D. Reinking, M. McKenna, L. D. Labbo, & R. D. Keifer (Eds.) *The handbook of literacy and technology: Transformations in a post-typographic world* (pp. 3–13). Mahwah, NJ: Lawrence Erlbaum Associates.

Bond, T. G., & Fox, C. M. (2001). *Applying the Rasch model: Fundamental measurement in the human sciences*. Hillsdale, NJ: Erlbaum.

Borkowski, J. G., Chan, L. K. S., & Muthukrishna, N. (2000). A process-oriented model of metacognition: Links between motivation and executive functioning. In G. Schraw & J. Impara (Eds.), *Issues in the measurement of metacognition* (pp. 1–42). Lincoln, NE: Buros Institute of Mental Measurements, University of Nebraska.

Bouchard, D. (1998). The distribution and interpretation of adjectives in French: A consequence of bare phrase structure. *Probus, 10*, 139–183.

Bourdieu, P. (1991). *Language and symbolic power*. Cambridge, MA: Harvard University Press.

Brandt, D. (2001). *Literacy in American lives*. New York: Cambridge.

Bråten, I., & Samuelstuen, M. S. (2004). Does the influence of reading purpose on reports of strategic text processing depend on students' topic knowledge? *Journal of Educational Psychology, 96*, 324–336.

Brenna, B. A. (1995). The metacognitive reading strategies of five early readers. *Journal of Research in Reading, 18*, 53–62.

Britt, M. A., & Gabrys, G. L. (2001). Teaching advanced literacy skills for the World Wide Web. In C. R. Wolfe (Ed.), *Learning and teaching on the World Wide Web* (pp. 73–90). San Diego: Academic Press.

Broache, A. (2005). Chief lobbyist. *Smithsonian, 36*, 21–22.

Brown, A. L. (1975). The development of memory: Knowing, knowing about knowing, and knowing how to know. In H. W. Reese (Ed.), *Advances in child development and behavior*, Vol. 10 (pp. 103–152). San Diego, CA: Academic Press.

Brown, A. L. (1980). Metacognitive development and reading. In R. J.

Spiro, B. C. Bruce, & W. F. Brewer (Eds.), *Theoretical issues in reading comprehension* (pp. 453–482). Hillsdale, NJ: Erlbaum.

Brown, A. L. (1985). Metacognition: The development of selective attention strategies for learning from texts. In H. Singer & R. B. Ruddell (Eds.), *Theoretical models and processes of reading* (pp. 501–526). Newark, DE: International Reading Association.

Brown, A.L., & Day, J. D. (1983). Macrorules for summarizing texts: The develo pment of expertise. *Journal of Verbal Learning and Verbal Behavior, 22,* 1–14.

Brown, R., Pressley, M., Van Meter, P., & Schuder, T. (1996). A quasi-experimental validation of transactional strategies instruction with low-achieving second grade readers. *Journal of Educational Psychology, 88,* 18–37.

Butterfield, E. C., Hacker, D. J., & Albertson, L. R. (1996). Environmental, cognitive, and metacognitive influences on text revision: Assessing the evidence. *Educational Psychology Review, 8,* 239–297.

Cain, K., Oakhill, J., & Bryant, P. (2004). Children's reading comprehension ability: Concurrent prediction by working memory, verbal ability, and component skills. *Journal of Educational Psychology, 96,* 31–42.

Calero-Breckheimer, A., & Goetz, E. T. (1993). Reading strategies of biliterate children for English and Spanish Texts. *Reading Psychology, 14,* 177–204.

Carrell, P. (1985). Facilitating ESL reading by teaching text structure: Classroom implications and applications. *TESOL Quarterly, 19,* 441–469.

Carrell, P. (1991). Second language reading: Reading ability or language proficiency. *Applied Linguistics, 12,* 159–179.

Carrell, P. (1998). Can reading strategies be successfully taught? *The Language Teacher.* Retrieved March 15, 2007, from http://www.jalt-publications.org/tlt/files/98/mar/carrell.htm

Carrell, P., & Eisterhold, J. (1983). Schema theory and ESL reading pedagogy. *TESOL Quarterly, 17,* 553–573.

Carrell, P., Pharis, B., & Liberto, J. (1989). Metacognitive strategy training for ESL reading. *TESOL Quarterly, 23,* 647–678.

Carson, J. G. (1992). Becoming biliterate: First language influences. *Journal of Second Language Writing, 1,* 37–60.

Center on Education Policy. (2004). Who's gaining, who's losing, and why. Report by Thomas W. Fagan and Nancy L. Kober, consultants to the Center on Education Policy.

Chambers, P., Izaute, M., & Marescaux, J. P. (2002). *Metacognition: Process, function, and use.* Dordrech: Kluwer Academic Publishers.

Chen, C., & Rada, R. (1996). Interacting with hypertext: A meta-analysis of experimental studies. *Human-Computer Interaction, 11,* 125–156.

Cheng, L. (1995). *What foreign learners do in their academic reading?* (ERIC Document Reproduction Service No. ED 386 041)

Chiesi, H. L., Spilich, G. J., & Voss, J. F. (1979). Acquisition of domain related information in relation to high and low domain knowledge. *Journal of Verbal Learning and Verbal Behavior, 18,* 257–274.

Chomsky, N. (1959). Review of Skinner's "Verbal Behavior." *Language, 35,* 26–58.

Chomsky, N. (1965). *Aspects of the theory of syntax.* Cambridge, MA: MIT Press.

Christensen, T. (1990). *Teaching reading to high school graduates in Japan.* Hokusei Junior College Bulletin. (ERIC Document Reproduction Service No. ED 342 213)

Ciborowski, J. (1999). *Textbooks and the students who can't read them: A guide for teaching of content.* Cambridge, MA: Brookline Books.

Clarke, M. (1979). Reading in Spanish and English. *Language Learning 29,* 121–215.

Clarke, M. (1980). The short circuit hypothesis of ESL reading—or when language competence interferes with reading performance. *Modern Language Journal, 64,* 203–209.

Clarke, M., & Silberstein, S. (1977). Toward a realization of psycholinguistic principles for the ESL reading class. *Language Learning 27,* 134–154.

Clay, M. M. (1998). *By different paths to common outcomes.* York, ME: Stenhouse.

Coady, J. (1979). A psycholinguistic model of the ESL reader. In R. Mackay, B. Barkman, & R. Jordan (Eds.), *Reading in a second language* (pp. 5–12) Rowley, MA: Newbury House.

Coiro, J. (2003). Reading comprehension on the Internet: Expanding our understanding of reading comprehension to encompass new literacies. *The Reading Teacher, 56,* 458–464.

Coiro, J., & Dobler, B. (2005). Reading comprehension on the internet: Exploring the comprehension strategies used by sixth-grade skilled readers as they search for and locate information on the Internet. Retrieved April 19, 2007, from http://ctell1.uconn.edu/coiro/research.html

Coiro, J., & Dobler, E. (2007). Exploring the online reading comprehension strategies used by sixth grade skilled readers to search for and locate information on the Internet. *Reading Research Quarterly, 42,* 214–257.

Collins, A., Brown, J. S., & Larkin, K. M. (1980). Inference in text understanding. In R. J. Spiro, B. C. Bruce, & W. F. Brewer (Eds.), *Theoretical issues in reading comprehension* (pp. 385–410). Hillsdale, NJ: Lawrence Erlbaum.

Collins, J., & Blott, R. K. (2003). *Literacy and literacies.* New York: Cambridge.

Cook, D. (2002). A new kind of reading and writing space: The online course site. *The Reading Matrix, 2*(3). Retrieved April 15, 2007, from http://www.readingmatrix.com/articles/cook/article.pdf

Cope, B., & Kalantzis, M. (Eds.). (2000). *Multiliteracies.* New York: Routledge.

Crawford, J. (1995). *Bilingual education: History, politics, theory and practice.* Los Angeles: Bilingual Educational Services, Inc.

Crocker, L., & Algina, J. (1986). *Introduction to classical and modern test theory*. New York: Harcourt.

Csizér, K., & Dörnyei, Z. (2005). Language learners' motivational profiles and their motivated learning behavior. *Language Learning, 55,* 613–659.

Cunningham, P., & Allington, R. (2006). *Classrooms that work: They can all read and write (4th ed.).* Boston: Allyn & Bacon.

Cziko, G. (1978). Differences in first and second language reading: The use of syntactic, semantic, and discourse constraints. *Canadian Modern Language Review, 34,* 473–489.

Dadour, E. S., & Robbins, J. (1996). University-level studies using strategy instruction to improve speaking ability in Egypt and Japan. In R. L. Oxford (Ed.), *Language learning strategies around the world: Cross-cultural perspectives* (pp. 157–166). Honolulu: University of Hawaii, Second Language Teaching & Curriculum Center.

Dail, J. S. (2004). Reading in an online hypertext environment: A case study of tenth-grade English students (doctoral dissertation, Florida State University, 2004). *Dissertation Abstracts International, 65,* 25–49.

Daud, N. M., & Husin, Z. (2004). Developing critical thinking skills in computer-assisted extended reading classes. *British Journal of Educational Technology, 35,* 477–487.

Davis, F. B. (1944). Fundamental factors of comprehension of reading. *Psychometrika, 9,* 185–197.

De Jager, B., Jansen, M., & Reezigt, G. (2005). The development of metacognition in primary school learning environments. *School Effectiveness and School Improvement, 16,* 179–196.

De la Peña, A., & Soler, L. (2001). Cognitive strategies for academic reading and listening in EFL. *Journal of College Reading and Learning, 31,* 217–232.

Deleuze, G., & Guattari, F. (1987). *A thousand plateaus: Capitalism and schizophrenia.* Minneapolis, MN: University of Minnesota Press.

De Sousa, I., & Oakhill, J. (1996). Do levels of interest have an effect on children's comprehension monitoring performance? *British Journal of Educational Psychology, 66,* 471–482.

Devine, J. (1993). The role of metacognition in second language reading and writing. In J. Carson & I. Leki (Eds.), *Reading in the composition classroom: Second language perspectives* (pp. 105–27). Boston: Heinle and Heinle.

Dole, J. A., Duffy, G. G., Roehler, L. R., & Pearson, D. P. (1991). Moving from the old to the new: Research on reading comprehension instruction. *Review of Educational Research, 61*(2), 239–264.

Dressman, M., Wilder, P., & Connor, J. J. (2005). Theories of failure and the failure of theories: A cognitive/sociocultural/macrostructural study of eight struggling students. *Research in the Teaching of English, 40,* 8–61.

Duke, N., & Pearson, P. D. (2002). Effective practices for developing reading comprehension. In A. Farstrup, S. J. Samuels, & J. Samuels, (Eds.), *What research has to say about reading instruction (3rd ed.)* (pp. 205–242).

Newark, DE: International Reading Association.

Elshair, H. M. (2002). The strategies used by students to read educational websites and their relation to website usability and text design (doctoral dissertation, University of Pittsburg, 2002). *Dissertation Abstracts International, 63,* 1687.

Ericsson, K. A., & Simon, H. A. (1984). *Protocol analysis: Verbal reports as data.* Cambridge, MA: MIT Press.

Ericsson, K. A., & Simon, H. A. (1993). *Protocol analysis: Verbal reports as data.* Cambridge, MA: MIT Press.

Fairbanks, C. M., & Ariail, M. (2006). The role of cultural resources in literacy and schooling: Three contrasting case studies. *Research in the Teaching of English, 40,* 310–354.

Farese, L., Kimbrell, G., & Woloszyk, C. (1997). *Marketing essentials* (pp. 44–55 & 86–99). Mission Hills, CA: McGraw-Hill School Publishing Company.

Farr, R. (2005). *Modeling, coached practice, and reflection.* Handouts retrieved on February 25, 2005 from http://www.rogerfarr.com/

Feng, X., & Mokhtari, K. (1998). Strategy use by native speakers of Chinese reading easy and difficult texts in English and Chinese. *Asian Journal of English Language Teaching, 8,* 19–40.

Fernandez-Duque, D., Baird, J. A., & Posner, M. I. (2000). Executive attention and metacognitive regulation. *Consciousness and Cognition, 9,* 288–307.

Field, M. L., & Aebersold, J. A. (1990). Cultural attitudes toward reading: Implications for teachers of ESL/bilingual readers. *Journal of Reading, 33,* 406–410.

Fisk, C., & Hurst, B. (2003). Paraphrasing for comprehension. *The Reading Teacher, 57,* 182–185.

Flavell, J. H. (1979). Metacognition and cognitive monitoring: A new area of cognitive-development inquiry. *American Psychologist, 34,* 906–911.

Flavell, J. H., & Wellman, H. M. (1977). Metamemory. In R. V. Kail & J. W. Hagen (Eds.), *Perspectives on the development of memory and cognition.* Hillsdale, NJ: Erlbaum.

Foltz, P. (1996). Comprehension, coherence, and strategies in hypertext and linear text. In J. Rouet, J. L. Levonen, A. Dillon, & R. J. Spiro (Eds.) *Hypertext and cognition.* (pp. 109–136). Mahwah, NJ: Erlbaum.

Fountas, I. C., & Pinnell, G. S. (2001). *Guiding readers and writers grades 3–6: Teaching comprehension, genre, and content literacy.* Portsmouth, NH: Heinemann.

García, E. (2000). Bilingual children's reading. In M. L. Kamil, P. B. Mosenthal, P. D. Pearson, & R. Barr (Eds.), *Handbook of reading research* Vol. 3 (pp. 813–834). Mahwah, NJ: Erlbaum.

García, E. (2005). *Teaching and learning in two languages.* New York: Teachers College Press.

Garcia, G. E., Jiménez, R.T., & Pearson, P.D. (1998). Metacognition, childhood bilingualism, and reading. In D. Hacker, J. Dunlowsky, & A.

Graesser, (Eds.), *Metacognition in educational theory and practice* (pp. 193–219). Mahwah, NJ: Erlbaum.

Garner, R. (1987). Metacognition and reading comprehension. Norwood, NJ: Ablex.

Garner, R., & Alexander, P. (1989). Metacognition: Answered and unanswered questions. *Educational Psychologist, 24,* 143–158.

Garner, R., & Reis, R. (1981). Monitoring and resolving comprehension obstacles: An investigation of spontaneous lookback among upper-grade good and poor comprehenders. *Reading Research Quarterly, 16,* 569–582.

Gaskins, I., & Elliot, T. (1991). *Implementing cognitive strategy instruction across the school.* Media, PA: Brookline Books.

Gillingham, M. G. (1996). Comprehending electronic text. In H. van Oostendorp & S. de Mul (Eds.), *Cognitive aspects of electronic text processing* (pp. 77–98). Norwood, NJ: Ablex.

Glaubman, R., Glaubman, H., & Ofir, L. (1997). Effects of self-directed learning, story comprehension, and self-questioning in kindergarten. *Journal of Educational Research, 90,* 361–374.

Goldman, S. (1996). Reading, writing, and learning in hypermedia environments. In H. van Oostendorp & S. de Mul (Eds.), *Cognitive aspects of electronic text processing* (pp. 7–42). Norwood, NJ: Ablex.

González, N., Moll, L. C., & Amanti, C. (Eds.), (2005). *Funds of knowledge: Theorizing practice in households, communities, and classrooms.* Mahwah, NJ: Erlbaum.

Goodman, K. (1967). Reading: A psycholinguistic guessing game. *Journal of the Reading Specialist, 6,* 126–135.

Goodman, K. (1975). Acquiring literacy is natural: Who skilled Cock Robin? In F. Gollasch (Ed.), *Language & literacy: The selected writings of Kenneth S. Goodman* Volume 2 (pp. 243–249). London: Routledge & Kegan Paul.

Grabe, W. (1991). Current developments in second language reading research. *TESOL Quarterly, 25,* 375–406.

Grabe, W., & Stoller, F. (2002). *Teaching and researching reading.* New York: Pearson Education.

Green, J., & Oxford, R. (1995). A closer look at learning strategies, L2 proficiency, and gender. *TESOL Quarterly, 29,* 261–297.

Grigg, W. S., Daane, M. C., Jin, Y., & Campbell, J. R. (2003). *The nation's report card: Reading 2002.* Washington, DC: National Center for Education Statistics.

Hacker, D. J. (1997). Comprehension monitoring of written discourse across early-to-middle adolescence. *Reading and Writing, 9,* 207–240.

Hacker, D. J. (1998). Self-regulated comprehension during normal reading. In D. J. Hacker, J. Dunlosky, & A. C. Grosser (Eds.) *Metacognition in educational theory and practice* (pp. 165–192). Mahwah, NJ: Erlbaum.

Hacker, D. J., Dunlosky, J., & Graesser, A. C. (Eds.) (1998). *Metacognition in educational theory and practice.* Mahwah, NJ: Erlbaum.

Hadwin, A., Winne, P., Stockley, D., Nesbit, J., & Woszczyna, C. (2001). Context moderates students' self-reports about how they study. *Journal of Educational Psychology, 93*, 477–487.

Haller, E. P., Child, D. A., & Walberg, H. J. (1988). Can comprehension be taught? A quantitative synthesis of "metacognitive" studies. *Educational Researcher, 17*, 5–8.

Hanten, G., Bartha, M., & Levin, H. S. (2000). Metacognition following pediatric traumatic brain injury: A preliminary study. *Developmental Neuropsychology, 18*, 383–398.

Harlen, W. (2004). Can teachers learn through enquiry on-line? Studying professional development in science delivered on-line and on-campus. *International Journal of Science Education, 26*, 1247–1267.

Harrington, M. (1987). Processing transfer: Language-specific processing strategies as a source of interlanguage variation. *Applied Psycholinguistics, 8*, 351–377.

Hartley, K., & Bendixen, L. D. (2001). Educational research in the Internet age: Examining the role of individual characteristics. *Educational Researcher, 30*, 22–26.

Harvey, S., & Goudvis, A. (2000). *Strategies that work: Teaching comprehension to enhance understanding*. York, ME: Stenhouse Publishers.

Heath, S. B. (1982). Questioning at home and at school: A comparative study. In G. Spindler (Ed.), *Doing the ethnography of schooling* (pp. 102–131). New York: Holt, Rinehart and Winston.

Heath, S. B. (1983). *Ways with words: Language, life, and work in communities and classrooms*. New York: Cambridge University Press.

Heffner, M., & Cohen, S. H. (2005). Evaluating student use of Web-based course material. *Journal of Instructional Psychology, 32*, 74–81.

Henk, W. A., & Melnick, S. A. (1995). The Reader Self-Perception Scale (RSPS): A new tool for measuring how children feel about themselves as readers. *The Reading Teacher, 48*, 470–482.

Hilden, K. & Pressley, M. (2007). Self-regulation through transactional strategies instruction. *Reading and Writing, 23*, 51–75.

Hill, J. R., & Hannafin, M. J. (1997). Cognitive strategies and learning from the World Wide Web. *Educational Technology Research and Development, 45*, 37–64.

Holland, D., Lachicotte, W., Skinner, D., & Cain, C. (1998). *Identity and agency in cultural worlds*. Cambridge, MA: Harvard University Press.

Huey, E. (1908). *The psychology and pedagogy of reading*. Cambridge, MA: MIT Press.

Hulstijn, J. (1993). When do foreign-language readers look up the meaning of unfamiliar words? The influences of task and learner variables. *The Modern Language Journal, 77*, 139–147.

Israel, S. E., Block, C. C., Bauserman, K. L., & Kinnucan-Welsch, K. (Eds.). (2005). *Metacognition in literacy learning: Theory, assessment, instruction, and professional development*. Mahwa, NJ: Lawrence Erlbaum Associates.

Jacobs, J. E., & Paris, S. G. (1987). Children's metacognition about reading: Issues in definition, measurement, and instruction. *Educational Psychologist, 22,* 255–278.

Jiménez, R., Garcia, G., & Pearson, P. (1995). Three children, two languages, and strategic reading: Case studies in bilingual/monolingual reading. *American Educational Research Journal, 32,* 67–97.

Jiménez, R. T., García, G. E., & Pearson, P. D. (1996). The reading strategies of bilingual Latina/o students who are successful English readers: Opportunities and obstacles. *Reading Research Quarterly, 31,* 90–112.

Jiménez, R. T. (1997). The strategic reading abilities and potential of five low-literacy Latina/o readers in middle school. *Reading Research Quarterly, 32,* 224–243.

Juliebo, M., Malicky, G. V., & Norman, C. (1998). Metacognition of young readers in an early intervention programme. *Journal of Research in Reading, 21,* 24–35.

Kamhi-Stein, L. (1998). Profiles of underprepared second-language readers. *Journal of Adolescent & Adult Literacy, 41,* 610–619.

Kamil, M. L., Intrator, S. M., & Kim, H. S. (2000). The effects of other technologies on literacy and literacy learning. In M. L. Kamil, P. Mosenthal, P. D. Pearson, & R. Barr (Eds.), *Handbook of reading research,* Vol. 3 (pp. 771–788). Mahwah, NJ: Erlbaum.

Kamil, M. L., & Lane, D. M. (1998). Researching the relation between technology and literacy: An agenda for the 21st century. In D. Reinking, M. McKenna, L. D. Labbo, & R. D. Keifer (Eds.) *The handbook of literacy and technology: Transformations in a post-typographic world* (pp. 323–341). Mahwah, NJ: Erlbaum.

Karchmer, R. A., Mallette, M. H., Kara-Soteriou, J., & Leu, D. J. (2005). *Innovative approaches to literacy education: Using the Internet to support new literacies.* Newark, DE: International Reading Association.

Kaylani, C. (1996). The influence of gender and motivation on EFL learning strategy use in Jordan. In R. Oxford (Ed.), *Language learning strategies around the world: Cross-cultural perspectives* (pp. 75–88.) Honolulu, HI: University of Hawaii Press.

Keene, E., & Zimmermann, S. (1997). *Mosaic of thought: Teaching comprehension in a reader's workshop.* Portsmouth, NH: Heinemann.

Kern, R. (1989). Second language reading strategy instruction: Its effects on comprehension and word inference ability. *Modern Language Journal, 73,* 135–146.

Kinnunen, R., Vauras, M., & Niemi, P. (1998). Comprehension monitoring in beginning readers. *Scientific Studies of Reading, 2,* 353–375.

Kintsch, W. (1998). *Comprehension: A paradigm for cognition.* Cambridge, MA: Oxford University Press.

Kitano, K. (1994). *Getting students to read actively.* Doshisha Studies in English. (ERIC Document Reproduction Service No. ED 379 991)

Kletzien, S. (1991). Strategy use by good and poor comprehenders reading expository text of differing levels. *Reading Research Quarterly, 25,* 67–86.

Knight, S., Padron, Y., & Waxman, H. (1985). The cognitive reading strategies of ESL students. *TESOL Quarterly, 19*, 789–792.

Koda, K. (1993). Transferred L1 strategies and L2 syntactic structure in L2 sentence comprehension. *Modern Language Journal, 77*, 490–500.

Konishi, M. (2003). Strategies for reading hypertext by Japanese ESL learners. *The Reading Matrix, 3*(3). Retrieved December 19, 2006, from http://www.readingmatrix.com/articles/konishi/article.pdf.

Korbin, J., & Young, J. (2003). The cognitive equivalence of reading comprehension test items via computerized and paper and pencil administration. *Applied Measurement in Education, 16*, 115–140.

Krashen, S. (1993). *The power of reading*. Portsmouth, NH: Heinemann.

Kress, G. (2003). *Literacy in the new media age*. London, UK: Routledge.

Kreutzer, M. A., Leonard, C., Flavell, J. H., & Hagen, J. W. (1975) An interview study of children's knowledge about memory. *Monographs of the Society for Research in Child Development, 40*, 1–60.

Kruger, J., & Dunning, D. (1999). Unskilled and unaware of it: Difficulties in recognizing one's own incompetence lead to inflated self-assessments. *Journal of Personality and Social Psychology, 77*, 1121–1134.

Kvale, S. (1996). *Interviews: An introduction to qualitative research interviewing*. Thousand Oaks, CA: Sage.

Lange, K. (2004, November). A vote for democracy. *National Geographic, 206*, 3.

Le Fevre, D. M., Moore, D. W., & Wilkinson, I. A. G. (2003). Tape-assisted reciprocal teaching: Cognitive bootstrapping for poor decoders. *British Journal of Educational Psychology, 73*, 37–52.

Lemke, J. L. (1995). *Textual politics: Discourse and social dynamics*. Bristol, PA: Taylor and Francis.

Lenski, S. D., & Nierstheimer, S. L. (2004). *Becoming a teacher of reading: A developmental approach*. Upper Saddle River, NJ: Pearson Merrill Prentice Hall.

Leu, D. J., Jr. (2000). Literacy and technology: Deictic consequences for literacy education in an information age. In M. L. Kamil, P. Mosenthal, P. D. Pearson, & R. Barr (Eds.), *Handbook of reading research*, Vol. 3 (pp. 743-770). Mahwah, NJ: Erlbaum.

Leu, D. J., Jr., Kinzer, C. K., Coiro, J. L., & Cammack, D. W. (2004). Toward a theory of new literacies emerging from the Internet and other information and communication technologies. In R. B. Ruddell & N. J. Unrau (Eds.), *Theoretical models and processes of reading*, 5th ed. (pp. 1570–1613). Newark, DE: International Reading Association.

Leu, D. J., Jr., & Reinking, D. (1996). Bringing insights from reading research to research on electronic learning environments. In H. van Oostendorp & S. Mul (Eds.), *Cognitive aspects of electronic text processing*. (pp. 43–75). Norwood, NJ: Ablex Publishing.

Leu, D. J., & Reinking, D. (2005). *Developing Internet Comprehension Strategies among Adolescent Students at Risk to Become Dropouts*. U. S. Department of Education, Institute of Education Sciences Research Grant. Retrieved June 20, 2006, from http://www.newliteracies.uconn.edu/ies.html

Levine, A., & Reves, T. (1998). Data-collecting on reading-writing strategies: A comparison of instruments: A case study. *TESL-EJ, 3*(3), A-1. Retrived December 19, 2006, from http://writing.berkeley.edu/tesl-ej/ej11/a1.html

Li, S., & Munby, H. (1996). Metacognitive strategies in second-language academic reading: A qualitative investigation. *English for Specific Purposes, 15,* 199–216.

Linacre, J. M. (2006). WINSTEPS Rasch measurement computer program (Version 3.61). Chicago: Winsteps.com.

Liou, H. C. (2000). The electronic bilingual dictionary as a reading aid to EFL learners: Research findings and implications. *Computer Assisted Language Learning, 13,* 467–476.

Lomicka, L. (1998). "To gloss or not to gloss": An investigation of reading comprehension online. *Language Learning & Technology, 1,* 41–50.

Lorch, R. F., Lorch, E. P., & Klusewitz, M. A. (1993). College students' conditional knowledge about reading. *Journal of Educational Psychology, 85,* 239–252.

Luke, A. (1992). The body literate: Discourse and inscription in early literacy training. *Linguistics and Education, 4,* 107–129.

Luke, A., & Freebody, P. (1997). Shaping the social practices of reading. In S. Muspratt, A. Luke, & P. Freebody (Eds.), *Constructing critical literacies: Teaching and learning textual practice* (pp. 185–225). Cresskill, NJ: Hampton Press.

Macedo, S. (2000). *Diversity and distrust: Civic education in a multicultural democracy.* Cambridge, MA: Harvard University Press.

Manzo, A., & Manzo, U. (1998). *Content area reading: A heuristic approach.* Columbus, OH: Merrill Publishing Company.

Manzo, A.V., Manzo, U. C., & Estes, T. H. (2001). *Content area literacy: Interactive teaching for active learning.* New York: Wiley.

Markman, E. (1977). Realizing that you don't understand: A preliminary investigation. *Child Development, 48,* 986–992.

Mayer, R. E. (1997). Multimedia learning: Are we asking the right questions? *Educational Psychologist, 32,* 1–19.

Mayer, R. E., & Moreno, R. (1998). A split-attention effect in multimedia learning: Evidence for dual processing systems in working memory. *Journal of Educational Psychology, 90,* 312–320.

McClain, K. V. M., Gridley, B. E., & McIntosh, D. (1991). Value of a scale used to measure metacognitive reading processes. *Journal of Educational Research, 85,* 81–87.

McEneaney, J. E. (2003). Does hypertext disadvantage less able readers? *Journal of Educational Computing Research, 29,* 1–12.

McKnight, C. (1996). What makes a good hypertext? In H. van Oostendorp & S. de Mul (Eds.), *Cognitive aspects of electronic text processing.* Norwood, NJ: Ablex.

McNamara, D. S. (2004). SERT: Self-explanation reading training. *Discourse Processes, 38,* 1–30.

McVee, M., Dunsmore, K. L., Gavelek, J. (2005). Revisiting schema theory.

*Review of Educational Research, 75*(4), 531–566.

Meier, S. T., & Schmeck, R. R. (1984). The burned-out college student: A descriptive profile. *Journal of College Student Personnel, 42,* 63–69.

Meier, S. T., McCarthy, P. R., & Schmeck, R. R. (1984). Validity of self-efficacy as a predictor of writing performance. *Cognitive Therapy and Research , 8,* 107–120.

Merriam, S. B. (1998). *Qualitative research and case study applications in education.* San Francisco: Jossey-Bass.

Michaels, S. (1981). "Sharing time": Children's narrative styles and differential access to literacy. *Language in Society, 10,* 423–442.

Miholic, V. (1994). An inventory to pique students' metacognitive awareness of reading strategies. *Journal of Reading, 38,* 84–86.

Mokhtari, K., & Reichard, C. A. (2002). Assessing students' metacognitive awareness of reading strategies. *Journal of Educational Psychology, 94,* 249–259.

Mokhtari, K., & Reichard, C. (2004). Investigating the strategic reading processes of first- and second-language readers in two different cultural contexts. *System: An International Journal of Educational Technology and Applied Linguistics, 32,* 379–394.

Mokhtari, K., & Sheorey, R. (2002). Measuring ESL students' awareness of reading strategies. *Journal of Developmental Education, 25,* 2–10.

Moll, L. C., Estrada, E., Díaz, E., & Lopes, L. M. (1980). The organization of bilingual lessons: Implications for schooling. *The Quarterly Newsletter of the Laboratory of Comparative Human Cognition, 2,* 53–58.

Monos, K. (2005). A study of the English reading strategies of university students in Debrecen with implications for reading instruction in an academic context. In J. Kiss-Gulyas & I. Furkone Banka (Eds), *Studies in English language learning and teaching* (pp. 53–68). Debrecen: University of Debrecen Institute of English and American Studies.

Myers, M., & Paris, S. (1978). Children's metacognitive knowledge about reading. *Journal of Educational Psychology, 70,* 680–690.

Narvaez, D., van der Broek, P., & Ruiz, A. B. (1999). The influence of reading purpose on inference generation and comprehension in reading. *Journal of Educational Psychology, 91,* 488–496.

National Center for Education Statistics. (2003). *The Nation's Report Card: Reading Highlights 2003,* NCES 2004–452, by P. L. Donahue, M. C. Daane, and W. S. Grigg. Washington, DC:. U.S. Department of Education. Institute of Education Sciences.

National Institute of Child Health and Human Development. (2000). *The report of the National Reading Panel: Teaching children to read: An evidence-based assessment of the scientific research literature on reading and its implications for reading instruction.* Washington, DC: U.S. Government Printing Office.

National Reading Panel (NRP). (2000). *Teaching children to read: An evidence-based assessment of the scientific research literature on reading and its implications for reading instruction: Reports of the subgroups.* Bethesda, MD: NICHD.

New London Group. (2000). A pedagogy of multiliteracies. In B. Cope & M. Kalantzis (Eds.), *Multiliteracies* (pp. 9–37). New York: Routledge.

Nichols, J. (1992). Students as educational theorists. In D. H. Schunk & J. L. Meece (Eds.), *Student perceptions in the classroom* (pp. 267–86). Hillsdale, NJ: Erlbaum.

Nikolov, M. (2002). *Issues in English language education.* Bern: Peter Lang AG.

Oakhill, J., Hartt, J., & Samols, D. (2005). Levels of comprehension monitoring and working memory in good and poor comprehenders. *Reading and Writing, 18,* 657–686.

Oxford, R. (1990). *Language learning strategies: What every teacher should know.* Boston: Heinle and Heinle.

Oxford, R. (1993). *La difference continue . . .* gender differences in second/foreign language learning styles and strategies. In J. Sutherland (Ed.), *Exploring gender* (pp. 140–147). Englewood Cliffs, NJ: Prentice Hall.

Oxford, R., & Burry-Stock, J. (1995). Assessing the use of language learning strategies worldwide with the ESL/EFL version of the strategy inventory for language learning SILL. *System, 23,* 1–23.

Oxford, R., Ehrman, M., & Nyikos, M. (1988). *Vive la difference?* Reflections on sex differences in use of language learning strategies. *Foreign Language Annals, 21,* 321–329.

Oxford, R., & Nyikos, M. (1989). Variables affecting choice of language learning strategies by university students. *Modern Language Journal, 73,* 291–300.

Palincsar, A. S., & Brown, A. (1984). Reciprocal teaching of comprehension-fostering and comprehension-monitoring activities. *Cognition and Instruction, 1,* 117–175.

Padron, Y. N., Knight, S. L., & Waxman, H. C. (1986). Analyzing bilingual and monolingual students' perceptions of their reading strategies. *The Reading Teacher, 39,* 430–433.

Paris, S. G. (2002). *Linking reading assessment and instruction in elementary grades.* In C. Roller (Ed.), Comprehensive reading instruction across the grade levels (pp. 55–69). Newark, DE: International Reading Association.

Paris, S. G., Cross, D. R., & Lipson, M. Y. (1984). Informed strategies for learning: A program to improve children's reading awareness and comprehension. *Journal of Educational Psychology, 76,* 1239–1252.

Paris, S. G., & Flukes, J. (2005). Assessing children's metacognition about strategic reading. In S. E. Israel, C. C. Block, K. L. Bauserman, & K. Kinnucan-Welsch (Eds.), *Metacognition in literacy learning: Theory, assessment, instruction, and professional development* (pp. 121–139). Mahwah, NJ: Erlbaum.

Paris, S., & Jacobs, J. (1984). The benefits of informed instruction for children's reading awareness and comprehension skills. *Child Development, 55,* 2083–2093.

Paris, S. G., Jacobs, J. E., & Cross, D. R. (1987). Toward an individualistic psychology of exceptional children. In J. D. Day & J. G. Borkowski

(Eds.), *Intelligence and exceptionality: New directions for theory assessment, and instructional practices* (pp. 215–248)  Norwood, NJ: Ablex.

Paris, S. G., Lipson, M. Y., & Wixon, K. K. (1983). Becoming a strategic reader. *Contemporary Educational Psychology, 8,* 293–216.

Paris, S. G., Lipson, M. Y.,& Wixon, K. K. (1994). Becoming a strategic reader. In R. B. Ruddell, M. R. Ruddell, & H. Singer (Eds.), *Theoretical models and processes of reading (4th ed.).* Newark, DE: International Reading Association.

Paris, S. G., & Myers, M. (1981). Comprehension monitoring, memory, and study strategies of good and poor readers. *Journal of Reading Behavior, 13,* 5–22.

Paris, S. G., Newman, R. S.,& McVey, K. A. (1982). Learning the functional significance of mnemonic actions: A microgenic study of strategy acquisition. *Journal of Experimental Child Psychology, 34,* 490–509.

Paris, S. G., Wasik, B. A., & Turner, J. C. (1991). The development of strategic readers. In R. Barr, M. Kamil, P. Mosenthal, & P. D. Pearson (Eds.), *Handbook of reading research,* Vol. 2 (pp. 609–640). New York: Longman.

Paris, S., & Winograd, P. (1990). How metacognition can promote academic learning and instruction. In B. Jones & L. Idol (Eds.*), Dimensions of thinking and cognitive instruction* (pp. 15–54). Hillsdale, NJ: Erlbaum.

Parry, K. J. (1987). Reading in a second culture.  In Devine, J., Carrell, P. L. and Eskey, D. E. (Eds). *Research in reading in English as a second language.* Washington D.C.: TESOL.

Parry, K. J. (1996). Culture, literacy, and L2 reading. *TESOL Quarterly, 30,* 665-692.

Parry, K., J. (1993). The social construction of reading strategies: New directions for research. *Journal of research in reading, 16,* 148-158.

Pearson, P. D. (2004). The reading wars: The politics of reading research and policy—1988 through 2003. *Educational Policy, 18,* 216–252.

Pearson, P. D. (2007). *Facilitating comprehension.* Retrieved April 19, 2007, from http://www.scienceandliteracy.org/

Pearson, P. D., & Duke, N. K. (2002). Comprehension instruction in the primary grades. In C. C. Block & M. Pressley (Eds.), *Comprehension instruction: Research-based best practices* (pp. 247–258). New York: Guilford.

Pearson P. D., & Fielding, L. (1991). Comprehension Instruction. In R. Barr, M. L. Kamil, P. Mosenthal, & P.D. Pearson (Eds.), *Handbook of reading research,* Vol. 2  (pp. 815–860). New York:  Longman.

Pennycook, A. (2001). *Critical applied linguistics.* Mahwah, NJ: Erlbaum.

Pereira-Laird, J. S., & Deane, F. P. (1997). Development and validation of a self-report measure of reading strategy use. *Reading Psychology: An International Journal, 18,* 185–235.

Petzold, R., & Berns, M. (2000). Catching up with Europe: Speakers and functions of English in Hungary. *World Englishes, 19,* 113–124.

Phiffer, S. J., & Glover, J.  A. (1982). Don't take students' word for what they do while reading. *Bulletin of the Psychonomic Society, 19,* 194–196.

Pintrich, P. (2000). Multiple goals, multiple pathways: The role of goal orientation in learning and achievement. *Journal of Educational Psychology, 92*, 544–555.

Pintrich, P., & De Groot, E. (1990). Motivational and self-regulated learning components of classroom academic performance. *Journal of Educational Psychology, 82*, 33–40.

Pintrich, P. R., & Zusho, A. (2002). The development of academic self-regulation: The role of cognitive and motivational factors. In A. Wigfield & J. S. Eccles (Eds.), *Development of achievement motivation* (pp. 249–284). San Diego: Academic Press.

Pressley, M. (2000). What should comprehension instruction be the instruction of? In M. L. Kamil, P. B. Mosenthal, P. D. Pearson, & R. Barr (Eds.), *Handbook of reading research*, Vol. 3 (pp. 545–561). Mahwah NJ: Erlbaum.

Pressley, M. (2002). Metacognition and self-regulated comprehension. In A. E. Farstrup & S. Samuels (Eds.), *What research has to say about reading instruction* (pp. 291–309). Newark, DE: International Reading Association.

Pressley, M., & Afflerbach, P. (1995). *Verbal protocols of reading: The nature of constructively responsive reading.* Hillsdale, NJ: Erlbaum.

Pressley, M., Almasi, J., Schuder, T., Bergman, J., & Kurita, J. A. (1994). Transactional instruction of comprehension strategies: The Montgomery County Maryland SAIL program. *Reading and Writing Quarterly: Overcoming Learning Difficulties, 10*, 5–19.

Pressley, M., Beard El-Dinary, P., & Brown, R. (1992). Skilled and not-so-skilled reading: Good information processing or not-so-good processing. In M. Pressley, K. Harris, & J. Guthrie (Eds.), *Promoting Academic Competence and Literacy in School* (pp. 91–127). San Diego, CA: Academic Press.

Pressley, M., & Block, C. C. (2002). Summing up: What comprehension instruction could be. In C. C. Block & M. Pressley (Eds.), *Comprehension instruction: Research based best practices* (pp. 383–392). New York: Guilford.

Pressley, M., El-Dinary, P. B., Gaskins, I. W., Schuder, T., Bergman, J., Almasi, L., & Brown, R. (1992). Beyond direct explanation: Transactional instruction of reading comprehension strategies. *Elementary School Journal, 92*, 511–554.

Pressley, M., & Gaskins, I. (2006). Metacognitively competent reading is constructively responsive reading comprehension: How can such reading be developed in students? *Metacognition and Learning, 1*, 99–113.

Pritchard, R. (1990). The effects of cultural schemata on reading process strategies. *Reading Research Quarterly 25*, 273–295.

Raphael, T. E. (1982). Question-answering strategies for children. *The Reading Teacher*, November, 36, 186–190.

Raphael, T. E., & Pearson, P. D. (1985). Increasing students' awareness of sources of information for answering questions. *American Educational Research Journal, 22*, 217–235.

Reardon, S. F., & Galindo, C. (2002, April 1–5). *Do high stakes tests affect students' decision to drop out of school? Evidence from NELS.* Paper presented at the annual meeting of the American Educational Research Association, New Orleans, LA.

Reid, J. (1987). The learning style preferences of ESL students. *TESOL Quarterly 21,* 87–111.

Reinking, D., Hayes, D. A., & McEneaney, J. E. (1988). Good and poor readers' use of explicitly cued graphic aids. *Journal of Reading Behavior, 22,* 229–247.

Reinking, D., & Rickman, S. (1990). The effects of computer-mediated texts on the vocabulary learning and comprehension of intermediate-grade readers. *Journal of Reading Behavior, 22,* 395–411.

Reinking, D., & Schreiner, R. (1985). The effects of computer-mediated text on measures of reading comprehension and reading behavior. *Reading Research Quarterly, 20,* 536–551.

Reynolds, R. E., Taylor, M. A., Steffenson, M. S., Shirey, L. L., & Anderson, R. C. (1982). Cultural schemata and reading comprehension. *Reading Research Quarterly, 17,* 353–366.

Rigg, P. (1977). Reading in ESL. In J. Fanslow & R. Crymes (Eds.), *On TESOL '76* (pp. 345–355). Washington, DC: TESOL.

Roeschl-Heils, A., Schneider, W., & van Kraayenoord, C. E. (2003). Reading, metacognition, and motivation: A follow-up study of German students 7 and 8. *European Journal of Psychology of Education, 18,* 75–86.

Romano, L. (2005, December 25). Literacy of college graduates is on decline. *Washington Post,* A12. Retrieved February 9, 2006, from www.washingtonpost.com

Rosenblatt, L. M. (1978). *The reader: The text: The poem.* Carbondale, IL: Southern Illinois University.

Rosenblatt, L. (1985). The transactional theory of the literary work: Implications for research. In C. R. Cooper (Ed.), *Researching response to literature and the teaching of literature: Points of departure* (pp. 33–53). Norwood, NJ: Ablex.

Rosenshine, B., & Meister, C. (1994). Reciprocal teaching: A review of the research. *Review of Educational Research, 64,* 479–530.

Rouet, J. F., Lenoven, J. J., Dillon, A., & Spiro, R. J. (1996). *Hypertext and Cognition.* Mahwah, NJ: Erlbaum.

Rowe, D. W., & Rayford, L. (1987). Activating background knowledge in reading comprehension assessment. *Reading Research Quarterly, 22,* 160–176.

Rumelhart, D. E. (1980). Schemata: The building blocks of cognition. In R. J. Spiro, B. C. Bruce, & W. F. Brewer (Eds.), *Theoretical issues in reading comprehension* (pp. 38–58). Hillsdale, NJ: Erlbaum.

Ryan, J. (2005). Young people choose: Adolescents' text pleasures. *Australian Journal of Language and Literacy, 28,* 38–47.

Samuels, S. J., Willcutt, J. & Palumbo, T. (2006). Reading Fluency and Metacognition. In C. Block and S. Israel (Editors), *Unlocking the Power of Metacognition.* Newark, DE: International Reading Association.

Sarig, G. (1987). High-level reading in the first and the foreign language: Some comparative data. In J. Devine, P. Carrell, & D. Eskey (Eds.), *Research in reading English as a second language* (pp. 105–120). Washington, DC: TESOL.

Sawaki, Y. (2001). Comparability of conventional and computerized tests of reading in a second language. *Language Learning & Technology, 5,* 38–59.

Sax, G. (1997). *Principles of educational and psychological measurement and evaluation.* Belmont, CA: Wadsworth.

Schmar-Dobler, E. (2003). Reading on the Internet: The link between literacy and technology. *Journal of Adolescent and Adult Literacy, 47,* 80–85.

Schmeck, R. (2000). Thoughtful learners: Students who engage in deep and elaborative processing. In R. J. Riding & S. G. Rayner (Eds.). *International perspectives on individual differences,* Vol. 1 (pp. 79–96). Stamford, CT: Ablex.

Schmitt, M. C. (1990). A questionnaire to measure children's awareness of strategic reading processes. *The Reading Teacher, 43,* 454–461.

Schoonen, R., Hulstijin, J., & Bossers, B. (1998). Metacognitive and language-specific knowledge in native and foreign language reading comprehension: An empirical study among Dutch students in grades 6, 8, and 10. *Language Learning, 48,* 71–106.

Schraw, G. (1998). On the development of adult metacognition. In M. C. Smith & T. Pourchot (Eds.), *Adult learning and development: Perspectives from educational psychology* (pp. 89–106). Mahwah, NJ: Erlbaum.

Schraw, G., & Impara, J. C. (2000) *Issues in the measurement of metacognition.* Lincoln, NE: University of Nebraska Press

Schunk, D. H. (1992). Theory and research on student perceptions in the classroom. In D. H. Schunk & J. L. Meece (Eds.), *Student perceptions in the classroom.* Hillsdale, NJ: Erlbaum.

Schunk, D. H., & Meece, L. L. (1992). *Student perceptions in the classroom.* Hillsdale, NJ: Erlbaum.

Selber, S. A. (2004). Reimagining the functional side of computer literacy. *College Composition and Communication, 55,* 470–503.

Shapiro, A. M., & Niederhauser, D. S. (2003). Learning from hypertext: Research issues and findings. In D. Jonassen (Ed.), *Handbook of research for educational communications and technology* (pp. 605–620). Mahwah, NJ: Erlbaum.

Sheorey, R. (1999). An examination of language learning strategy use in the setting of an indigenized variety of English. *System: An International Journal of Educational Technology and Applied Linguistics, 27,* 173–190.

Sheorey, R. (2006). *Learning and teaching of English in India.* New Delhi: Sage Publications.

Sheorey, R., Mahar, M., & Miller, S. (2001, March 1). *Reading strategies of American and ESL college students.* Paper presented at the 34th Annual

Convention of Teachers of English to Speakers of Other Languages, St. Louis, MO.

Sheorey, R., & Mokhtari, K. (2001). Coping with academic materials: Differences in the reading strategies of native and non-native readers. *System: An International Journal of Educational Technology and Applied Linguistics, 29,* 431–449.

Shimamura, A. P. (2000). Toward a cognitive neuroscience of metacognition. *Consciousness and Cognition, 9, 313–323.*

Simpson, M., & Nist, S. (2002). Encouraging active reading at the college level. In C. C. Block & M. Pressley (Eds.), *Comprehension instruction: Research-based best practices* (pp. 365–378). New York: Guildford.

Singhal, M. (1998). *Reading comprehension in the second language classroom: A hands-on approach to teaching and learning reading strategies.* (ERIC Document Reproduction Service No. 424 748).

Skarakis-Doyle, E. (2002). Young children's detection of violations in familiar stories and emerging comprehension monitoring. *Discourse Processes, 33,* 175–197.

Smith, F. (1979). *Reading without nonsense.* New York: Teachers College Press.

Smith, F. (1982). *Understanding Reading.* New York: Holt, Rinehart, and Winston.

Smith, N. B. (1965). *American reading instruction.* Newark, DE: International Reading Association.

Smolkin, L. B., & Donovan, C. A. (2002). "Oh excellent, excellent question!" Developmental differences and comprehension instruction. In C. C. Block & M. Pressley (Eds.), *Comprehension instruction: Research-based best practices* (pp. 140–157). New York: Guilford.

Snow, C. (2001). *Reading for understanding: Toward and R & D program in reading comprehension.* Report prepared by the RAND Reading Study Group for the Office of Education Research and Improvement. Arlington, VA: Rand Education.

Snow, C. (2002). *Reading for understanding: Toward an R&D program in reading comprehension.* Washington, DC: RAND.

Snow, C. E., Burns, M. S., & Griffin, P. (Eds.). (1998). *Preventing reading difficulties in young children.* Washington, DC: National Academy Press.

Snow, K., & Sweet, A. P. (Eds.). (2003). Reading for comprehension. *Rethinking reading comprehension* (pp. 1–11). New York: Guilford.

Song, M. (1998). Teaching reading strategies in an ongoing EFL university reading classroom. *Asian Journal of English Language Teaching, 8,* 41–54.

Sowell, E. R., Thompson, P. M., Holmes, C. J., Jernigan, T. L., & Toga, A. W. (1999). *In vivo* evidence for post-adolescent brain maturation in frontal and striatal regions. *Nature Neuroscience, 2,* 859–886.

Sperling, R. A., Howard, B. C., Miller, L. A., & Murphy, C. (2002). Measures of children's knowledge and regulation of cognition. *Contemporary Educational Psychology, 27,* 51–79.

Spires, H., & Estes, T. H. (2002) Reading in Web-based learning environments. In C. Block & M. Pressley (Eds.), *Comprehension instruction: research-based best practices* (pp. 115–125). New York: Guilford.

Spiro, R. (1980). Constructive process in prose comprehension and recall. In R. Spiro, B. C. Bruce, & W. F. Brewer (Eds.), *Theoretical issues in reading comprehension* (pp. 245–278). Hillsdale, NJ: Erlbaum.

Steffensen, M. S., Joag-Dev, C., & Anderson, R. C. (1979). A cross-cultural perspective on reading comprehension. *Reading Research Quarterly, 15,* 10–29.

Steffensen, M., & Joag-Dev, C. (1984). Cultural knowledge and reading. In C. Alderson & X. Urquhart (Eds.), *Reading in a foreign language* (pp. 48–61). New York: Longman.

Stimson, M. J. (1998). *Learning from hypertext depends on metacognition.* Unpublished doctoral dissertation, University of Georgia.

Sun, Y. C. (2003). Extensive reading online: An overview and evaluation. *Journal of Computer Assisted Learning, 19,* 438–446.

Templeton, S. (1991). *Teaching the integrated language arts.* Boston: Houghton Mifflin.

Thorndike, E. (1917). Reading as reasoning: A study of mistakes in paragraph reading. *Journal of Educational Research, 8,* 323–332.

Tompkins, G. E. (2006). *Literacy for the 21st century: A balanced approach (4th ed.).* Upper Saddle River, NJ: Pearson Merrill Prentice Hall.

Trabasso, T., & Bouchard, E. (2002). Teaching readers how to comprehend text strategically. In C. C. Block & M. Pressley (Eds.), *Comprehension instruction: Research based best practices* (pp. 176–200). New York: Guilford.

Vacca, R. T., & Vacca, J. L. (1999). *Content area reading: Literacy and learning across the curriculum.* New York: Longman.

Van Dijk, T. A., & Kintsch, W. (1983). *Strategies of discourse comprehension.* Orlando, FL: Academic Press.

Van Kraayenoord, C. E., & Schneider, W. E. (1999). Reading achievement, metacognition, reading self-concept, and interest: A study of German students in Grades 3 and 4. *European Journal of Psychology of Education, 14,* 305–324.

Van Leuvan, P., & Wang, M. C. (1997) An analysis of students' self-monitoring in first- and second-grade classrooms. *The journal of Educational Research, 97,* 132–144.

Van Someren, M. W., Barnard, Y. F., & Sandberg, J. A. C. (1994). *The think aloud method: A practical guide to modeling cognitive processes.* New York: Academic Press.

Veenman, M. V. J. (2005). *The assessment of metacognitive skills: What can be learned from multi-method designs?* In B. Moschner & C. Artelt (Eds), *Lernstrategien und Metakognition: Implikationen für Forschung und Praxis* (pp. 75–97). Berlin: Waxmann.

Veenman, M. V. J., Elshout, J. J., & Groen, M. G. M. (1993). Thinking aloud: Does it affect regulatory processes in learning? *Tijdschrift voor Onderwijsresearch, 18,* 322–330.

Vellutino, F. R. (2003). Individual differences as sources of variability in reading comprehension in elementary school children. In A. P. Sweet & K. Snow (Eds.), *Rethinking reading comprehension* (pp. 1–11). New York: Guilford.

Von Eckerdt, B. (1995). *What is cognitive science?* Cambridge, MA: MIT Press.

Vye, N. J., Schwartz, D. L., Bransford, J. D., Barron, B. J., & Zech, L. (1998). Smart environments that support monitoring, reflection, and revision. In D. J. Hacker, J. Dunlosky, & A. C. Grosser (Eds.), *Metacognition in educational theory and practice* (pp. 305–346). Mahwah, NJ: Erlbaum.

Vygotsky, L. S. (1978). *Mind in society: The development of higher psychological processes.* Cambridge, MA: Harvard University Press.

Wagner, D. (1993). *Literacy, culture, and development: Becoming literate in Morocco.* Boston: Cambridge University Press.

Wagner, R. K., & Sternberg, R. J. (1987). Executive control in reading comprehension. In B. K. Britton & S. M. Glyn (Eds.), *Executive control processes in reading* (pp. 1–21). Hillsdale, NJ: Erlbaum.

Walczyk, J. J., Marsiglia, C. S., Johns, A. K., & Bryan, K. S. (2004). Children's compensations for poorly automated reading skills. *Discourse Processes, 37,* 47–66.

Weber, R., (1991). Linguistic diversity and reading in American society. In R. Barr (Ed.), *Handbook of reading research,* Vol. 2 (pp. 97–119). New York: Longman.

Wilhelm, J. D. (2001). *Improving comprehension with think-aloud strategies: Modeling what good readers do.* New York: Scholastic.

Woodson, J. (2001). *The other side.* New York: Putnam Juvenile.

Yorio, C. (1971). Some sources of reading problems in foreign language learners. *Language Learning, 21,* 107–115.

Zhicheng, Z. (1992). *The effects of teaching reading strategies on improving reading comprehension for ESL learners.* Knoxville, TN: Annual Meeting of the Mid-South Educational Research Association. (ERIC Document Reproduction Service No. ED 356 643).

Zimmerman, B. J., & Martinez-Ponz, M. (1992). Perceptions of efficacy and strategy use in the self-regulation of learning. In D. H. Schunk & J. L. Meece (Eds.), *Student perceptions in the classroom* (pp. 185–207). Hillsdale, NJ: Erlbaum.

# Index

# About the Editors

**Kouider Mokhtari** (Ph.D., Ohio University) is a Professor of Reading Education in the Department of Teacher Education at Miami University, Ohio, where he teaches undergraduate and graduate courses in literacy education. Prior to joining Miami University in August 2004, he spent 13 years on the faculty of Oklahoma State University in the Department of Curriculum and Instruction, where he conducted research, taught graduate and undergraduate reading courses, and coordinated the college reading program. His research has focused on the acquisition of language and literacy by first- and second-language learners, with a particular focus on the metacognitive awareness and use of reading strategies and the role of language awareness in literacy development. His research work has been published in various journals, including the *Journal of Research in Reading, Canadian Modern Language Review, Reading Research and Instruction, Journal of Educational Psychology,* and *System: International Journal of Applied Linguistics and Technology.* Professor Mokhtari currently serves as Coeditor of the *Balanced Reading Instruction,* a journal of the Balanced Reading Instruction Special Interest Group of the International Reading Association. He also serves on the Editorial Review Boards of *The Reading Teacher, Journal of Adolescent and Adult Literacy,* and *System.*

**Ravi Sheorey** (Ph.D., University of Texas—Austin) is Professor of English at Oklahoma State University, where he teaches courses in applied linguistics and teaching English as a second language. His research has focused on the learning and teaching of English as a second or foreign language, especially the learning and reading strategies of second-language learners. His papers (including several coauthored with Kouider Mokhtari) have appeared in a variety of international journals, including *Canadian Modern Language Review, ELT Journal, Indian Journal of Applied Linguistics, Journal of Research in Reading, TESOL Matters, TESOL Quarterly,* and *System.* His book, *Learning and Teaching English in India* (Sage, 2006), has been dubbed by a reviewer as "an invaluable resource of research findings about students and teachers engaged in the pursuit of English education in India." In the Spring Semester 2004, he was awarded a Fulbright Professorship and taught courses in TEFL and Applied Linguistics and conducted research at the University of Veszprém in Hungary. In 2005, Professor Sheorey was the recipient of OKTESOL's "ESL Professional of the Year" award. He currently serves as Coeditor of the *Balanced Reading Instruction,* a journal of the Balanced Reading Instruction Special Interest Group of the International Reading Association.

Both Professors Mokhtari and Sheorey have been recipients of Oklahoma State University's "Regents Distinguished Teaching" award.